Global Justice Reform

Global Justice Reform

A Comparative Methodology

Hiram E. Chodosh

NEW YORK UNIVERSITY PRESS

New York and London

NEW YORK UNIVERSITY PRESS
New York and London
www.nyupress.org

Library of Congress Cataloging-in-Publication Data
Chodosh, Hiram.
Global justice reform : a comparative methodology /
Hiram E. Chodosh.
p. cm.
Includes bibliographical references and index.
ISBN 0–8147–1635–0 (cloth : alk. paper)
1. Justice, Administration of—Cross- cultural studies.
2. Judicial power—Cross-cultural studies.
3. Justice and politics—Cross-cultural studies.   I. Title.
K2100.C52 2004   2004014400

New York University Press books are printed on acid-free paper, and
their binding materials are chosen for strength and durability.

Manufactured in the United States of America
10 9 8 7 6 5 4 3 2 1

For my parents

Contents

Contents

Preface

Two nightmares (one imagined, the other all too real) inspired this project.

At the conclusion of the spring 1996 semester, I gave an oral examination to my class in comparisons of law. The night before the exam, I imagined that my students examined me. The students posed the following question: "Prove the nonexistence of the comparative method in two words or less." Aware of the philosophical problem, I responded: "What method?!?" I thought I had performed well, but the students gave me a grade of B.

When I protested that the grade was too low, they justified it. The students had two criticisms. First, they explained that my answer expressed no explicit justification for my position. Second, notwithstanding the accurate, albeit conclusory, nature of my response, they concluded that I did not add any constructive suggestions for addressing the problem. Because I had demanded of them that they endeavor to go beyond the parameters of limited questions to rebuild whatever they chose to tear down, I could hardly disagree with their evaluation and resigned myself to the disappointing grade.

Research for this book began as an effort to account for this first point of failure. (Regrettably, I relaxed the two-word restriction.) The modest steps advanced in these pages to account for the second criticism, I fear, will require much more effort than what is reflected here. Thus, the journey from this first nightmare is still in an early phase of exploration.

A more practically oriented struggle ran parallel to my mind's battle with the elusive nature of comparison. For the past decade, I have studied the harsh realities of badly neglected judicial systems (mainly in the Middle East and Asia, where I have been involved in various judicial reform initiatives). These collaborative projects focused on issues explored in the second part of the book: political interference with judicial impartiality, backlog and delay, and corruption. Throughout this work, I have felt deeply frustrated by the limits in our comparative understanding of both the nature of these problems and responsive remedies designed to resolve them. The questions perplex and the answers discourage me. Can an Indonesian citizen expect the judiciary to stand up to a government that controls judges' terms of employment, or can he trust judges to eradicate corruption within their own ranks? Does an Indian national have any hope of collecting compensation for a legally cognizable injury within a ten- or even fifteen-year period? If not, do the current reform initiatives in these and similar countries have a strong likelihood of success? The answer to each of these questions is, sadly, no.

Just as the first half of the book (the search for comparative methodology) is a response to my first nightmare, the second half of the book (the search for global justice reform) is a response to this harsh conclusion about the prospects of improving critical aspects of judicial performance. Here again, my students would admonish me that frank appraisals are necessary but insufficient. We cannot afford to rest on negative assessments of a desperate situation but need to press on creatively in response to the challenge. Thus, with a deep sense of my own limitations, I have attempted to breathe some fresh ideas into a depressing set of conditions.

Beyond these dreams, I have no delusions that the abstract nature of a comparative methodology or any of the strategies I have articulated will solve these pressing problems. The questions raised are many, and the answers will require much more committed study and collective action; however, I hope to demonstrate in these pages that greater attention to the nature of comparison might contribute to our understanding of the complex nature of these problems. Only through such inquiries might we expand the narrow path to alternatively responsive solutions. In sum, comparative methodology alone will not improve justice systems; yet, deeper thinking about the questions it raises may help to inform the choice of alternative, and ultimately more effective, reform approaches.

This book submits, synthesizes, and builds upon contributions from many prior publications. An earlier version of chapters 2 and 3 first appeared in an article published in the *Iowa Law Review* in 1999. Chapters 4, 5, and 6 draw on a series of special presentations and symposium essays (through opportunities at Stanford, DePaul, Texas, and Ohio State). Research on Indonesia derives from an essay prepared for an Association of American Law Schools' panel for the Comparative Law Section

(2003), an encyclopedia chapter I completed in 2001, four trips to Indonesia I took between 1999 and 2001, an exchange in the United States I hosted for the Indonesian Supreme Court in November 2002, and ongoing consulting work I've done for the International Monetary Fund's Legal Department since 1999, with a particular focus on Indonesian judicial reform. Research on India is drawn from a national study performed under the auspices of the Indian Supreme Court, published in 1999 by NYU, my recent Fulbright trip as a Senior Scholar at the Indian Law Institute in New Delhi (spring 2003), and a book published there based on three regional workshops I conducted on mediation in India and one national conference with the Law Commission of India. Finally, many of the ideas in these pages were first presented to my wonderful students: in my first-year Global Perspectives course, comparative law, and a new course I taught in the fall of 2002 in comparative judicial systems as a lab in reform.

Because this book reflects more than a decade of comparative teaching, research, and reform experience in upward of a dozen foreign legal systems, I am particularly indebted to those who made these experiences possible, including in particular my fellow traveler and dear friend Stephen A. Mayo, executive director of the Institute for the Study and Development of Legal Systems. I also wish to thank and acknowledge many colleagues for their comments, support, and guidance: Dean Gerald Korngold; former Associate Dean Andrew P. Morriss; Professors Sidney I. Picker, Jr., and Jane Picker, co-directors of the St. Petersburg Summer Law Institute; Professor Ronald J. Coffey, who initiated my interest and guided my preliminary inquiry into the distinction between method and methodology, Professors Peter M. Gerhart, Robert P. Lawry, Edward A. Mearns, Jr., Michael P. Scharf, and Calvin W. Sharpe, all of Case; Professor Melissa A. Waters (Washington and Lee); Professor Michael Heise (Cornell); Professor Raj K. Bhala (George Washington); Professor David D. Caron (Berkeley); Professor David S. Clark (Tulsa); Professor Owen D. Jones (Arizona State); Dean Harold H. Koh (Yale); Professor Chibli Mallat (University Saint Joseph, Lebanon); Professor Peter H. Schuck (Yale); Professor Paul M. Schwartz (Brooklyn); Professor Gregory C. Shaffer (Wisconsin); Professor Shimon Shetreet (Hebrew University); and Professor Adrien K. Wing (Iowa); as well as Sean Hagan, deputy general counsel at the International Monetary Fund; Ceda Ogada (senior counsel at the Fund); and Martin A. Sabelli, who practices criminal law in San Francisco. In particular, my study is largely derivative of a decade of interactions and friendships with leading reformers throughout the world. This is particularly true in the Indonesian and Indian contexts, where I would like to express my deepest appreciation to Chief Justice A. M. Ahmadi and incoming Chief Justice R. C. Lahoti (2004) of the Indian Supreme Court; Chairman M. J. Rao (retired justice from the Supreme Court); Member-Secretary T. K. Viswanathan of the Law Commission; Abhishek Singvhi; Firdosh Kassam (the new director of the Bombay High Court ADR unit); Chief Justice Thakkar (the country's leading expert in civil procedure); Justice Dananjay Chandrachud of the Bombay High Court; and my close friend Niranjan Bhatt, director of the Ahmedabad Mediation Center; as well as Chief Justice Bagir Manan, Deputy Chief Justice Paulus Lotulung, Deputy Justice Marianna Sutadi, and Justice Abdulrahman of the Indonesian Supreme Court; and Sebastiaan Pompe, Mardjono Reksodiputro, Gregory Churchill, and Rifqi Assegaf, all from Jakarta. The contributions advanced here are largely theirs—the mistakes my own.

Finally, I would like to thank our international specialist in the library, Andy Dorchak; my former assistant, Nancy Pratt Kantor; my current assistant Cynthia Hill-Graham; and many fine students who helped me gather voluminous research materials over the past few years: Tiffany Buxton, Erin Connor, Steven Emery, Seema Kella, Julie Lady, Joshua Levy, Wendy Marantz, Todd Morth, Scott Nadeau, Chris Rassi, Donovan Steltzner, and Ted Theofrastous.

Most of all, I am deeply indebted to my wife, Preeti, and children, Saja and Caleb, for all of the love, joy, and inspiration they have given me throughout these many journeys.

In Search of Comparative Methodology

There is no such thing as The Scientific Method—as the scientific method, that is the point: there is no one rounded art or system of rules. . . . The face-saving formula is that although there is indeed a Scientific Method, scientists observe its rules unconsciously and do not understand it in the sense of being able to put it clearly into words.[1]

The key to comparative studies is the comparison of comparisons.[2]

The methodology of a science is its rationale for accepting or rejecting its theories or hypotheses.[3]

1

Introduction

A. *The Promise and Limits of the Comparative Method*

In the dawn of a new millennium, most national legal systems have made sweeping commitments to three areas of substantive political and economic reform. First, traditionally authoritarian political systems have sought to achieve democracy through popular elections,[4] more accountable and transparent public service, and the effectuation of domestic human rights protections.[5] Second, governments have loosened their grips on economic systems,[6] embraced a freer marketplace, and recognized a broader range of real and intellectual property rights.[7] Third, the international community has embarked on a nearly uncontrollable and irreversible process of globalization. Unprecedented daily flows of capital,[8] technology,[9] goods,[10] services,[11] information,[12] and people[13] currently permeate national borders.

As democracy, markets, and globalization spread, intensify,[14] and even collide,[15] decision-makers and commentators increasingly compare conflicting, interacting, and transforming laws[16] and institutions of national legal systems.[17] These comparisons serve critical and overlapping purposes. First, they enhance an appreciation of similarities and differences among competing laws and institutions. Second, they inform law reform initiatives designed to advance these increasingly widespread policy commitments. Finally, comparisons inform the creation of private[18] and public international law and supranational institutions.[19] Accordingly, contemporary comparative law scholars champion the comparative method as an indispensable tool of legal science, law reform, and international conflict resolution and unification.[20]

Repeated cheers for the comparative method, however, beg a provocative question: What exactly is *the* method? Specifically, which objectives do comparisons serve? Which phenomena should be compared? How should they be contrasted and differentiated? As Dean Pound aptly wrote nearly seventy years ago, "[M]uch if not all depends on . . . what is compared and how it is compared."[21]

If comparisons are indispensable, one may justifiably wonder how well legal comparisons meet these contemporary needs. If the putative utility of the tool is dependent on the quality of its performance,[22] comparative and international legal scholars might be expected to provide a method for evaluating the effectiveness of different comparisons. This would entail a theory or a methodology of comparison capable of explaining how comparisons are or should be made in light of their underlying purposes. Do they shed light on the similarities and differences of national legal systems for purposes of cross-national understanding, reform, or unification? This book takes a critical (and potentially reconstructive)[23] look at explications of comparative methodology with this pressing question in mind.[24]

The search renders (and explains) a series of disappointing findings.[25] The critique reveals that the discipline of comparative legal studies currently offers little explanatory insight or practical guidance about the nature of comparison.[26] Compared to methodological and theoretical debate in other related disciplines, including anthropology,[27] political science,[28] linguistics,[29] history,[30] sociology,[31] economics,[32] accounting,[33] and philosophy of science,[34] a theory or methodology[35] of legal comparison appears to be significantly underdeveloped[36] in three critical respects.

First, comparative legal scholarship has not explained adequately what the comparative method is or should be. Second, the discipline appears to lack a conceptual framework for doing what may be the key to its success:[37] that is, the ability to compare comparisons (which might be termed metacomparison).[38] Third, without this metacomparative ability, comparative law has not yet formalized justifications for distinguishing superior from inferior comparisons.[39] In sum, the comparative method fails to exhibit what Peter Medawar called a "rounded art or system of rules,"[40] a framework for Alasdair MacIntyre's notion of "comparing comparisons,"[41] or Mark Blaug's emphasis on a "rationale for accepting or rejecting"[42] legal comparisons.[43]

B. *The Importance of Comparative Method in Justice Reform*

Twenty-first-century global commitments bring new practical importance to these philosophical concerns. Democracy, human rights, and free markets (and the substantive law made in the wake of these commitments) presume a strong role for impartial and effective adjudication systems (or some functional equivalent). Accordingly, the courts and supporting public and private institutions are a critical component of widely championed global objectives. The desired features of judicial institutions (themselves derived from comparative understanding),[44] however, appear increasingly elusive to obtain in practice. Underfunded, undersupported, undertrained, and underprotected, the courts in many countries function as the *most neglected* branch of government. Political and economic interference with impartiality and substantial delays in the judicial process undermine core values of judicial performance.

The judicial systems of Indonesia and India provide rich and important examples of severe problems and the underlying factors that contribute to them. In Indonesia, weak terms of judicial employment, vague ethical norms and weak disciplinary systems, and opaque procedures have produced conditions conducive to political and economic interference with impartial judicial decision making. In India, ineffective court management systems, fragmented and discontinuous proceedings, and unattractive alternatives to trial lead to vicious cycles of backlog and delay. Attempted reform interventions (e.g., a judicial commission for Indonesia and court mediation for India) appear to be weak remedies for a profoundly systemic array of problems. In these countries and elsewhere, institutional justice reform efforts (to combat political interference, corruption, or backlog and delay) often presuppose financial and political support that is sadly lacking.

Reforms also rely in part on shaky comparative theories about which features of a judicial system cause or alleviate these problems. Comparative theories fall into two frequently overlapping categories. Latitudinal (cross-national) theories rely on cross-national comparisons of a reforming system and another arguably well-functioning one. Longitudinal (intranational) theories rely on comparisons of the current features in the status quo with anticipated alterations and their expected impacts. Indeed, even if they are not motivated or guided in any way by cross-national comparisons, reform proposals necessarily rely on the second type of comparison.

For example, efforts to enhance judicial independence, combat corruption, or reduce backlog and delay are profoundly comparative in nature. The terms in which the aims are expressed, the models advocated (whether foreign or future), and the methods of distinguishing successful (or failing) systems require a series of comparisons. The *right degree* of independence and accountability presupposes an agreed value or aim (among alternatives, e.g., impartiality or responsiveness to the will of society); the correct selection of which features in the system to alter (e.g., terms of employment); and a threshold for distinguishing sufficient from insufficient gradients of independence. The successful reduction of backlog and delay requires the assignment of different weights to time well or poorly spent, the alteration of purportedly inefficient components or processes, and a normative determination of how long various legal matters should take to resolve or decide in light of the judicial product or private settlement derived from the process.

Successful justice reform may be at least in part dependent on the quality of the particular cross- or intranational comparisons that serve to justify specific proposals. These embedded comparisons, however, are frequently unclear in purpose, skewed in their choice of content, or imprecise as a basis of reform design or determination. Shaky comparisons may further weaken needed reforms.

To illustrate these points from a broad array of examples, with particular attention paid to contemporary reforms in Indonesia and India, this book critically observes the distressing condition of contemporary justice systems, the deep impediments to reform, focusing on weaknesses in comparative understanding that tend to undermine reform determinations, and the resulting perplexing dilemmas faced by reformers. In response to these problems, the book also sketches some novel approaches to *thinking* about reform by drawing on the metaphor of emergent systems (e.g., slime mold, computer software, urban neighborhoods) and articulating multiple strategies to overcome a series of common design, method, and social dilemmas. The critical attention to questions of comparative methodology in reform thus attempts to illuminate more promising paths for justice systems to emerge from their seemingly insuperable predicaments.

C. A Road Map

To initiate critical attention to the underdevelopment of comparative methodology,[45] chapter 2 explains why the question of comparison is significant, evaluates the inadequacy of current explanations, and explores why so little appears to have been achieved. Part A emphasizes the importance of comparison in general and of legal comparison in both domestic and global contexts. Part B critically illustrates the common tendency to avoid detailed explications of the comparative method. Part C explores alternative explanations for this inadequacy and argues that comparisons are neither too uniform, heterogeneous, nor incomparable to justify satisfaction with the current condition of methodological underdevelopment. Part C concludes that the complex nature of comparison best explains the inattention to significant methodological concerns.

Building upon an extensive critique of the scholarly literature, chapter 3 sketches a preliminary conceptual framework for identifying and addressing critical issues in the why, what, and how of comparison. Part A identifies the general purposes served by comparison and notes problems of inconsistency among a variety of explicit and implicit objectives. Part B raises questions about the content of comparison and exposes weaknesses in the deployment of classification, prototypes, and micro- and macrodistinctions. Part C identifies and critiques alternative modes of differentiation employed in comparison and draws attention to the strengths and weaknesses of conceptual categorical relationships, including dichotomy, overlap, relativity, interdependence, equivalence, and indeterminacy. Part C continues by advancing an alternative mode of differentiation that draws on the strengths and mitigates the weaknesses of conventional methods. In sum, chapter 3 articulates preliminary methodological rationales upon which to base the acceptance or rejection of comparisons.

The second half of this book explores the underdevelopment of comparative methodology in key, illustrative areas of global justice reform and offers some targeted responses that draw heavily on the tools developed in chapter 3. To begin the search for justice reform, with particular attention to national efforts in Indonesia and India, chapter 4 critically observes the major trends in global justice reform and the gap between the high expectations and weak performance of judicial institutions. Part A observes major legal trends and identifies the major institutional challenges they pose. Part B describes the poor performance of judicial systems in pursuit of common aims. Part C illustrates these observations through two national examples: interference with impartiality in Indonesia and backlog and delay in India.

Chapter 5 explains why responsive reforms appear so elusive. Part A identifies several common sources of comparative misunderstanding: rash judgments, the role of powerful interests in preserving the status quo, limited self-awareness, myopic views of complex problems, inexplicit aims, poor design choices, weak theories of institutional change, the underestimation of collective action problems, and inattention to resource deficiencies. Part B outlines three major types of predicaments encountered in justice-reform efforts. These include questions of design (independence or accountability, justice or settlement), method (incremental or systemic, top-down or bottom-up, external or internal interventions, research or reform), and the competing, if not always divergent, interests of the individual and the collective (including subcollectives). With much established cause for pessimism, chapter 6 then searches for (conceptual) sources of hope. Part A advances a novel analogy between legal and *emergent* systems, a concept drawn from many unrelated disciplines outside the law (e.g., biology, computer science, and urban planning). Part B sketches a series of original antidilemma strategies in an attempt to advance constructive methodological suggestions that might help national communities overcome the overwhelming reform challenges they currently face.

Because many problems of a methodological nature elude simple remedy, the conclusion cautions against the risks of hastily crystallizing any particular approach or methodology in either general or specific justice-reform contexts. Before understanding more about the nature of comparison (and how to compare one comparison or strategy to another), prematurely determined methodological rationales may do more harm than good. Nonetheless, lessons taken from the exposition need not be drowned by an overabundance of caution. The urgent need for justice reform is simply too pressing to be stalled by the pretenses of scientific formulae on specific remedies. Therefore, even with these considerable risks, the book concludes that weighty global concerns merit greater intellectual investment in the nature, limits, and vehicles of comparative methodology in justice reform.

2

The Comparative Method

Which Method?!?

This chapter draws critical attention to the inadequacy of currently available explanations of the comparative method. Part A stresses the significance of comparison in the development of human intelligence and judgment in nonlegal and legal decision making within domestic and global contexts. Part B demonstrates that the study of comparative law has dedicated inadequate attention to explaining how comparisons are (or should be) made. Part C evaluates alternative justifications for the relative inadequacy of these explanations.

A. *The Significance of Comparison*

Comparison pervades all forms of human decision making. Thus, from the minutiae of daily decisions (e.g., preferences of music[1] or computer software[2]), potentially life-altering personal choices (e.g., where to go to law school,[3] or whom to appoint as a child's guardian[4]) to issues of great social importance (e.g., whether to go to war[5]), comparisons provide guidance and justification.[6]

Comparison also appears to be indispensable to the development of human intelligence and judgment.[7] Comprehension, criticism, and decision all rest on a profound comparative dimension.[8] The unfamiliar becomes understood in relation to the familiar.[9] Evaluation distinguishes between the is and the ought.[10] Decision requires a comparison of imperfect alternatives.[11] Distinctions between the known and unknown,[12] the real and ideal, and the status quo and change all involve a process of comparison.[13]

Legal historians have long noted the importance of comparison.[14] Likewise, legal commentators increasingly realize that comparisons are embedded in a variety of legal determinations. For example, the choice of a particular law,[15] the design of a legal process,[16] the essential features of a legal system,[17] the conception and design of an independent judiciary,[18] or the allocation of decision-making power to a variety of public and private institutions, including the courts, each require various and important comparisons.[19] Such comparisons are thus crucial to the ultimate structure and course of the legal process.

Beyond purely domestic concerns, increases in cross-border activity and the resulting collision of communities defined in large part by political borders intensify the need for comparisons of different national, transnational, and international legal provisions, processes, and institutions.[20] These comparisons thus serve the primary aims of comparative understanding, law reform, and international unification.

Specifically, the interaction of disparate national or cultural communities raises troubling questions about which differences to protect or eliminate.[21] Scholars debate questions of national convergence and divergence.[22] Experts on court systems consider whether judiciaries should become institutionally more independent,[23] procedurally less passive,[24] or more open to consensual alternatives to litigation.[25] Furthermore, international experts and decision makers debate applications of international law in domestic courts.[26] They explore alternative condominiums of power allocated to national, regional, and international institutions.[27] Finally, they search for explanations of whether,[28] how,[29] and why nations behave in compliance with international law.[30] In sum, each view of the increasingly penetrating role of an international law, institution, or process in a traditionally national ambit of authority relies on a comparison.

Recognizing the importance of comparison in these varied scenarios imposes a heavy burden to explain, evaluate, and if necessary, improve upon comparative legal thinking. Which circumstances should or should not prompt governments to intervene in private decision making?[31] Which features and measurements define a sufficiently independent judiciary?[32] Which provisions counsel support for the creation of permanent international tribunals?[33] Under which circumstances should the international community engage or isolate "rogue" states?[34] These decisions are based in part on a comparative understanding of alternative choices. As a result, decision makers should be concerned that the underlying comparisons are sufficiently explicit in purpose, comprehensive and justified in choice of content, precise in their contrasts, and sound in their determinations of comparative harms and risks.

The recognized role of comparison in these varied contexts implicates a need for, and an exposition of, significant inquiry into the process of comparison. Insight into the obstacles and vehicles of comparative thinking would provide guidance to decision makers and commentators on the soundness of their explicit or implicit comparative views. Such explications would justify the selection of viewpoints. Moreover, explication of the comparative underpinnings of justifications would make decision makers more accountable for their positions.[35] Thus, with the benefit of sufficient insight into the process, the putative utility of the comparative method could be reasonably and easily questioned in the event that it failed to provide greater guidance, stronger justifications, or an increase in accountability.

Given the potential value of greater comparative understanding, it is reasonable to expect that the great works of comparative legal studies would candidly address underlying methodological difficulties and, short of definitive solutions, offer some helpful suggestions to those interested in the general role of legal comparison in identifying critical differences and similarities.[36] Frequently cited writings, however, often fall short of providing sufficient explanation of comparative methodological tools.[37]

B. *Inadequate Explanations of the Comparative Method*

Frequently equated with "the comparative method,"[38] comparative law is the only legal discipline to carry an explicit denotation of comparison in its nomenclature.[39] One might expect to find in comparative legal studies an approach to fundamental questions about the purposes, content, and differentiating modes of comparison, given the common reiteration of the discipline's objectives.[40] Indeed, the claim that well-established theoretical ground rules for application of the comparative method exist[41] heightens these expectations.[42] Subject to a few exceptions,[43] however, this field of study fails to deliver substantial insight on the basic issues involved in a study of comparative methodology.[44]

Invocations of the comparative method offer no explanation of what the method entails, and, thus, leave open the question of which method ought to be deployed.[45] Implicit in this general question is a set of more specific inquiries. Is the comparative method anything more than mere comparison?[46] What purposes are served by legal comparisons? What exactly is chosen for comparison, and from which perspective?[47] By which techniques are comparisons of specific variables differentiated?[48] Why choose a particular variable or standard of differentiation? How might comparisons be evaluated and on what basis or rationale? How do these questions and the responses they generate relate to one another, and will these inquiries yield satisfactory answers?

Whereas the comparative method is often equated with comparison itself, many scholars disagree about its purpose and content.[49] Moreover, only a few scholars address the relationship between the questions of why and what one should compare,[50] and still fewer ask how comparisons are or should be made.[51] Even when the concept of comparative method is deemed a "point of departure,"[52] comparatists appear reluctant to "consider the problems associated with defining that concept."[53]

Surprisingly, the contemporary comparative legal literature fails to conduct a fruitful discussion about the role of comparison. The student of comparative law in search of strategies to address problems of purpose identification, variable selection, modes of differentiation, and their interrelationships will find little more than warnings about potential research obstacles and tentatively recommended tips designed to overcome these impediments.

The most prominent comparatists and internationalists of recent decades reflect general reluctance to explicate the comparative method. Some scholars fall back on questionable generalities, thus avoiding the specifics of the methodological contours they describe. Others justify their avoidance of methodological inquiry by arguing that the role of comparison itself is merely incidental to comparative legal scholarship.[54] Finally, the few who address methodological issues proceed reluctantly.

1. General Avoidance

Many scholars tend to avoid general methodological questions. Both Lawson and Watson stressed that comparative law "can scarcely be systematic."[55] Even ostensible attempts to treat problems of comparison generally avoid fundamental questions.

For example, in his book *Comparative Law* Gutteridge dedicates an entire chapter to the process of comparison.[56] Gutteridge thoughtfully addresses significant obstacles to useful comparisons (for example, the identification of sources and materials) and suggests strategies for overcoming them.[57] Notwithstanding the explicit chapter heading, however, he does not describe comparison as a process. Instead, Gutteridge makes reference only to the need to compare "like" with "like"[58] in systems at the "same stage of legal, political, and economic development."[59] He neglects to discuss how one establishes "likeness" or "sameness" as a starting point or to propose a method for finding differences, however small, among "like" phenomena. Furthermore, he does not consider whether alternative purposes might be served by examining or comparing strikingly dissimilar systems. His failure to relate the choice of comparatives to the purpose to be served leaves unanswered the basic question of why like-system comparisons are superior to different-system comparisons.

Schlesinger, Baade, Herzog, and Wise dedicate the introduction of their popular casebook to the topic of comparative method.[60] These authors define comparative law as a "method, a way of looking at legal problems, legal institutions, and entire legal systems, . . . [which can be used for] a wide variety of practical or scholarly purposes."[61] Most of this discussion attempts to illustrate through cases and extensive notes the many uses of comparative method. The authors explain that valuable use of comparisons may be made in the application of a foreign solution as a model in a rule of decision[62] or a piece of legislation,[63] to demonstrate perspective[64] by way of a contrast in the resolution of cross-border disputes through unification or harmonization,[65] or in legal science, including empirical social science and jurisprudence.[66] Despite the acknowledgement of the potential significance of this tool, the method of comparison is nowhere described, and methodological questions are left largely unexplored.

The approach taken by the authors described above is not unique. Instead, many works of comparative legal scholarship contain limited reference to a particular method of comparison. Even when choices of purpose and content are clearly articulated, prominent comparatists do not explain how to compare and contrast the phenomena they study. For example, Merryman's *The Civil Law Tradition*,[67] David and Brierley's *Grands Systèmes de Droit Contemporains*,[68] Cappelletti's *The Judicial Process in Comparative Perspective*,[69] and Damaska's *The Faces of Justice and State Authority*[70] explain the purpose of their work. Merryman seeks to describe what is common to a foreign tradition. David and Brierley aim to catalogue the world's systems. Cappelletti endeavors to solve socially significant problems. Damaska aspires to reconcile diverse legal cultures. They also identify and explain the specific content they compare. Merryman identifies deep-seated belief systems and related systemic attributes of a legal tradition. David and Brierley define legal families according to ideology and sources of law.[71] Cappelletti focuses on observable phenomena of judicial process.[72] Damaska takes a bifocal view of the structure of authority and function of government.[73] Yet, they pay little attention to the actual measures they articulate and employ to differentiate these traditions, families, processes, and structures.[74] The general avoidance of such questions makes it difficult to evaluate the implicit methodological choices of leading contributions to comparative law.

2. Specific Avoidance

Many scholars venture further to raise central methodological questions but stop short of generating specific answers. In an article written more than fifty years ago, Myres McDougal calls for "a clear and realistic notion of what is being compared . . . an understanding of an interest in the purposes of the comparison sufficient to guide and sustain it," and "techniques of comparison adequate to yield knowledge relevant to and sufficiently precise for the purposes established."[75] McDougal, however, ultimately offers only "a few preliminary and tentative observations."[76] He seeks to develop the "democratic values in a peaceful world"[77] (the purpose), through a comprehensive focus on "decisions"[78] (the variable), with a "comprehensive guiding theory"[79] and "adequate" "techniques"[80] (the method). Because McDougal does not attempt[81] to describe these techniques in any detail, he fails to provide instruction on how to conduct comparisons of complex phenomena in pursuit of these ambitious purposes.

Eric Stein, too, discusses problems of uses, nonuses, and misuses, without detailing the comparative methods employed in sorting out these problems. For example, he writes that the "debate on the relative ease of transplants . . . [makes] little sense without a tacit assumption that a law maker does in fact use the method and considers foreign law models."[82] Instead of describing a method for comparison, he simply raises the question of whether legal decision makers actually conduct comparisons of foreign models. Later he notes the absence of any "broadening of interest in the systematic use of the comparative method."[83]

Glendon, Gordon, and Osakwe raise methodological questions and draw on the accomplishments of Rabel and Rheinstein, who concentrate on function and context.[84] They describe comparison as a basic form of the scientific method (i.e., forming hypotheses, testing them).[85] As in other fields, an emphasis on scientific method raises as many questions as it answers. Controversies in the philosophy of science over the scientific method should cause the reader to pause before embracing this formulation as theoretically well settled and consistently followed in practice.[86] Scientists and philosophers of science have not resolved (and may never resolve) questions concerning the prescriptive standards for scientific methodology, the compliance or noncompliance with requisite standards in practice, or the desirability of the methodological rules themselves.[87] Furthermore, comparisons of scientific with comparative methods[88] tend to avoid addressing several key issues including the potentially varying objectives of different areas of scientific inquiry, the limitations of non-laboratory settings, or the impact of these factors on the methods of comparison employed.[89] Additionally, stating that the comparative method is the equivalent of the scientific method does not explain in detail the comparative dimensions of formulating and testing hypotheses that are integral to data interpretation.[90] Despite the proclaimed equivalence of the comparative with the scientific method,[91] this treatment fails to explicate either a "rounded art or system of rules"[92] or "a rationale for accepting or rejecting"[93] legal comparisons.

3. Justified Avoidance

Other scholars, including Merryman, Clark, and Haley, express more modest expectations for the role of comparison in comparative law. This approach serves as a partial justification for the general absence of explicitly comparative research in their work. To these authors, comparative law is "only incidentally comparative. True comparative law does exist, but it is relatively rare."[94] The three comparatists explain that "the titles of many commonly taught courses, such as French law, Latin American law, or European Union law, more accurately indicate their primarily descriptive, rather than comparative nature. Some comparison does go on in such courses, but it usually has a descriptive purpose."[95]

The foregoing passage describes a relatively modest role for comparison in the discipline that is labeled by the comparative function. Yet, the modestly circumscribed role for comparison contrasts sharply with the objectives identified by the authors. The authors list a number of comparative purposes: "to deprovincialize students, broaden their perspectives, and show them that other people can do things differently,"[96] "to confront foreign problems,"[97] "to examine a source of ideas, of examples of different ways of defining and dealing with common social problems,"[98] to unify private law "through description and evaluation of different private law systems,"[99] or to conduct "comparative studies" in "the relations between law and society."[100] Usage of the term "different" implies a comparison has already taken place and that comparison may actually be at the very core, rather than the incidental periphery, of deprovincialization, problem solving, unification, and alternative aims.

The problems associated with these comparisons will remain largely unexplored as long as one accepts the view that comparison is merely "incidental" to comparative law itself. The incidental view also conflicts with the shared view that comparative law is more method than law.[101] Merryman and his colleagues correctly point out that contrasts of law may serve a variety of purposes. Without describing what should be done following the initial contrast, however, efforts to justify the use of the comparative method remain incomplete.[102]

4. Partial Avoidance

Other comparatists have attempted, albeit partially, to define and address methodological problems encountered in legal comparisons. For example, in order to ensure objectivity, Zweigert and Kötz contemplate as a first step to comparison a full reporting on each system without evaluation or bias.[103] This advice underestimates the importance of the questions motivating the study. Without clarity of purpose, it is difficult to determine the content of what to report. Without specific attention to the choice of content, comparisons are vulnerable to bias and inaccuracy. Without developed techniques of contrast and differentiation, the goal of objectivity is elusive.

Zweigert and Kötz acknowledge only that rare problems require the material to emerge from a comparison itself (e.g., judicial development of the law in a country where there are no statutory or doctrinal rules).[104] Frequently, however, the mere recitation of available rules is not likely to be of much assistance in comparing the practical operation of legal systems. Accordingly, Zweigert and Kötz argue that "it is precisely the more taxing legal questions which justify comparative treatment."[105] They recognize that the process of comparison "is the most difficult part of any work in comparative law."[106] Due to the peculiarities of each problem, they claim that "it is impossible to lay down any firm rules about it."[107]

Despite their partial avoidance of methodological concerns, Zweigert and Kötz state some basic points about legal comparisons. For example, they claim that because explanations of legal systems are often stated in terms internally unique to each system, one must "free" these explanations "from the context of [each] system."[108] Arguably, they support creating an abstract heuristic conceptual framework within which contrasts of chosen variables can be understood. As a second step, Zweigert and Kötz stress that function[109] is "the start-point and basis of all comparative law . . . [because] different legal systems can be compared only if they solve the same factual problem."[110] It would be misleading to compare only parts of a solution. Instead, one must "build a system . . . [with a] special syntax and vocabulary."[111] Here Zweigert and Kötz recognize the importance of shifting back and forth between micro- and macroanalysis. As a third step, a comparative system must be flexible enough to grasp a wide variety of "heterogeneous institutions which are functionally comparable."[112] Comparability involves finding a "higher concept,"[113] a greater abstraction of generality upon which specific differences may be cast.[114] The abstraction is derived from an observed phenomenon and then used to differentiate between comparative analogues and phenomena. Finally, the comparison ought to produce an evaluation;[115] otherwise, comparative legal studies amounts to little more than "piling up blocks of stone that no one will build with."[116] Accordingly, the comparatist must keep the original purpose in mind. Comparisons without purpose cannot provide the foundation necessary to support understanding, reform, or international conflict resolution and unification.

Anthropologists and political scientists interested in legal issues have paid more attention to problems of comparison than have legal scholars.[117] Typically, both anthropologists and political scientists have struggled with questions of purpose identification, variable selection, and mode of differentiation. These problems include what language to use in characterizing similarity and difference, as well as what to compare, and to what end. Numerous studies tend to concentrate on disagreement about purpose and selection and interrelationships of variables.[118] Scholars in these other fields do not appear adequately interested in exploring weaknesses in alternative modes of differentiation. Consequently, more attention to comparative methodology in the social sciences is needed.[119]

For example, Sally Falk Moore argues that "the greatest disagreements and difficulties concerning comparisons do not lie at the comparative stage of study."[120] Rather, she contends, "It is the other stages that have the biggest hazards, the formulation of the problem and the choice of the criteria of relevance on the basis of which data are selected and classified for study."[121] Moore thus narrowly defines the comparative stage of the study as the last stage of comparing selected variables. The initial formulation of the problem, however, has an equally significant comparative foundation because the very concepts used to pose the questions are comparative in nature. Many of the terms she uses, such as "law,"[122] "dispute,"[123] "court,"[124] "judge,"[125] and "mediation"[126] are comparative terms.

Moore explains the classical debate between Gluckman and Bohannan over the correct language for comparison as a discourse not only on "units" of comparison but, rather, on the broader "subject" of study.[127] On questions of differentiation, however, her exposition is not as abundantly helpful. Moore notes that "obviously, all of these various classifications are coping with a series, either by setting up a graduated progression from one pole to the other or by characterizing the two poles themselves."[128] Yet, she does not proceed to justify the mode of classification, the variable chosen in support of posited taxonomies, the method of opposition, the establishment of a series between the established poles, or the problems solved by the specific articulation of such schema.

Comparative political science is another related discipline worthy of greater critical attention. Like anthropologists, political scientists interested in law have developed comparative frameworks for cross-national legal research.[129] Some scholars focus on the courts in order to integrate the comparative research in judicial institutions into the broader study of politics.[130] They cope not only with problems of "the equivalence of language" but with "concepts, operationalizations, and measurements."[131] Tate, for example, compared and assessed several comparative conceptual frameworks[132] for their "utility in cross-national courts research, . . . [and] especially, the ease or difficulty of the operationalization and measurement of the concepts, and the apparent breadth of their applicability to the universe of the world's court systems."[133]

His evaluation is based on the utility of the concepts, the relevance of the chosen indicia to operationalize the dimension, and the ability to measure the indicia empirically.[134] Tate's framework reflects, without expressly raising several critical problems in comparative political science, the use of idealized, multifactor prototypes and relativity as a mode of differentiation.[135] Many questions of values embedded in the chosen concepts, the alternative choice of variables as indicia of these concepts, and problems of comparative differentiation remain insufficiently explored in these inquiries.

5. Conclusion

A review of the literature reveals that the assessment of Merryman and his colleagues is the most accurate. Comparative law focuses on foreign law and only incidentally on comparison.[136] Even where comparisons appear to be central, potentially useful explanations are insufficient. Notwithstanding this view's descriptive accuracy, it presents an unsatisfactory condition of the discipline because a fundamental question remains unanswered: Can comparative law as a cross-border discipline realize its primary aspirations without justifying the comparisons it makes?

Decision makers and scholars cannot be expected to understand the foreign without comparison to the familiar. Likewise, if aspects of foreign law are to shed light on domestic law, comparison is a primary and necessary tool. Foreign legal successes can inspire domestic reform only through a comparative process. The notion of unification of national law presupposes a comparative determination that reveals which national differences must be eliminated. Therefore, the successful end to each pursuit depends in part on the quality of the means of comparison.

Notwithstanding their accomplishments, scholars of comparative law have only begun to address the many issues that arise from attempts to understand, evaluate, and if necessary, improve legal comparisons. Without greater methodological development, it is difficult to justify acceptance or rejection of legal comparisons. As a result, comparisons are likely to remain subject to criticism for carrying a hidden agenda, selectively narrowing variables, or skewing standards of differentiation in ways that prefigure their conclusions. The question of how comparisons are or should be made thus requires a greater investment of critical attention and creative energy.

Although this critique illuminates a deficiency in methodological development, this underdevelopment may reflect an understandable stage in the evolution of comparative legal studies. Knowledge of what is foreign implies a comparison with what is familiar; yet, it is also true that comparisons assume knowledge of what is being compared. Therefore, it is necessary to know foreign law before comparing it. Given the widely recognized risk of "getting the foreign law wrong,"[137] attempts to accumulate knowledge of what is foreign prior to any explicit comparison are justified. Nonetheless, implicit comparisons may filter the accumulation of this knowledge. Thus, the claim that comparison should only follow rather than also coincide with the knowledge of foreign law is untenable.

The gap between the significance of comparison and the relative underdevelopment of comparative methodology is not cause for despair. Drawing attention to what is absent may create a preliminary basis for further inquiry. Moreover, assessing this gap is antecedent to the development and application of theoretically constructive proposals. Vexing questions and the critical assessment generated in response provide a preliminary framework for comparing (and distinguishing) comparisons in the short term and developing a methodology of comparison (as justification for the acceptance and rejection of alternative comparisons) in the long run. Before proceeding to raise issues of comparison in purpose identification, variable selection, and mode of differentiation, however, it would be useful to explore alternative explanations for the methodological underdevelopment of comparative law.

C. Explaining the Inadequacy

The inadequacy of methodological explanations of comparison may be explained in at least four alternative ways. First, the comparative method is innately uniform. Thus, regardless of what is being compared, each process of comparison is indistinguishable from any another. Under this view, the method can be named but not defined as anything more or less than comparison itself. Second, the comparative method is a necessary eclecticism of heterogeneous methods, defiant of methodological generalization. Because of their diversity, comparisons may not be intelligibly compared and contrasted, and as a result, not even minor improvements can be made. Third, there is no method. All comparisons are subject to the apples/oranges objection: comparisons are actually incomparable. Fourth, comparison is extremely complex and thus difficult to grasp. Because the obstacles to understanding the complexity of comparison are seemingly insurmountable, there is an insufficient willingness to raise and address the conceptual and practical limitations of comparative knowledge. Recognition of overwhelming complexity may produce at least two distinctive reactions. Some may view this realization as professionally devastating to comparative legal scholars. Others, however, may argue that inattention to these questions is advised: if the complexities of comparison cannot be easily grasped, any attempt to do so carries a significant risk of inaccuracy and distortion.

The following discussion evaluates these four alternative explanations. This inquiry concludes that comparisons are neither too uniform to prevent differentiation, too heterogeneous to defy generalization, nor too incomparable to justify methodological resignation. Instead, the unavoidable complexity of comparison (combined with a fear of methodological vulnerability) best explains the general unwillingness to pose and address vexing methodological questions.

1. The Uniformity of Comparisons

According to the first view, the comparative method is so well settled and consistent that there is only one way to do it (connoted by the choice of the article "the"). In fact, this position maintains that the comparative method is so fundamental that no theory is required to explain how it is done.[138] Moreover, if the method were unassailable, there would be no need to develop a way of distinguishing good from bad comparisons.

The identification and emphasis on the uniformity of comparison is partially correct. First, comparison itself appears to be fundamental to the acquisition of knowledge. The unknown is seen in terms of the known in a constant process of identifying both similarity and difference.[139] From this perspective, the process is generic,[140] innate, biological, and to a certain degree beyond either rejection or refinement.[141]

This explanation is less persuasive when one considers both the vast knowledge of and disagreements among contemporary scholars engaged in serious comparative endeavors.[142] Both the achievements and difficulties encountered by these scholars should cause one to pause before passing over the methodological challenges and opportunities of comparative legal knowledge. As to the first view, intelligible disagreements should raise doubts that the comparative method is innately uniform and incapable of contrasts. Therefore, this view, though convenient, is not persuasive.

2. The Heterogeneity of Comparisons

In contrast to the first explanation of the comparative method as innately uniform, a second view describes the comparative method as "a variety of methods for looking at law."[143] This explanation warns against reliance on "a singular methodological and theoretical framework, . . .

[or a] single basis or a set of approaches that are structured in hierarchical order."[144] Though justifiably cautious, this view provides no practical guidance for making comparisons. Even if one rejects the proposal for a singular comparative framework, it does not follow that all comparative frameworks are equally useful. Attempts to build on this explanation tend to propose only a broader scope of variables (coined as context) for comparison.[145] Generally, such attempts do not, however, explain how to be more systematic. Despite these criticisms, the heterogeneity of comparisons as an explanation of methodological underdevelopment is partially correct. The methods employed by comparative legal scholars are justifiably and widely heterogeneous. To a significant degree, heterogeneity results from the variety of purposes and problems that motivate and command scholarly attention. The divergence of goals, subject matter, and techniques in part justifies reluctance to derive any generalities in the comparative method.[146]

The knowledge of so many accomplished and thoughtful scholars might make one particularly wary of a resignation to the conclusion that comparatists should remain appropriately eclectic. This is arguably, however, an accurate assessment of the current state of much comparative scholarship. It is also intellectually dissatisfying. Permitting an eclectic approach to comparative thought may avoid the risk of rigid and doctrinaire methodological criteria, but it also underestimates, and thereby discourages the potential for evaluating and improving upon readily available comparative techniques. Indeed, the world's use of more than four thousand languages, "each a complex system of many parts," has not prevented linguists from developing "substantive universals."[147] The methodological development of legal comparisons is not likely to advance from an overly negative view of methodology.

3. The Incomparability of Comparisons

If legal phenomena were incomparable, there would be no need to explain the basis upon which they would be compared. The comparative method would actually be equivalent to no method whatsoever.[148] Moreover, if comparisons were incomparable, a comparative methodology would be fundamentally untenable and comparisons could not be qualitatively distinguished. Therefore, the discussion now turns to the professed incomparability of both legal phenomena (even putative incomparables)[149] and legal comparisons.

It is common to encounter resistance to a posited comparison, which is often expressed with the reaction "that is [like comparing] apples and oranges!"[150] This response implies, first, that apples and oranges are incomparable, and, second, that the incomparability of apples and oranges is itself comparable to the incomparability of the two objects in the primary comparison.[151] The reasoning implicit in the apples and oranges objection is weak in three critical respects. First, the "apples and oranges" objection is paradoxical. Second, it relies on two inconsistent propositions. Third, the objection is false.

First, the reaction is paradoxical because the conclusion that two objects are incomparable is itself based on a comparison. This comparison concludes that the differences so outweigh the similarities that the identification of similarities is not useful.[152]

Second, the comment is also internally inconsistent. Instead of resting on a comparison of two fruits (or two legal phenomena), the "apples and oranges" objection remarkably analogizes two comparisons, and, thus, implicitly judges the incomparability of two legal phenomena to be comparable to the incomparability of two fruits. The contestable implication here is that the two comparisons are more comparable in their common degree of extreme incomparability than are either two legal phenomena or apples and oranges.[153]

Finally, the implied incomparability of the two fruits is false. The putative incomparability of apples and oranges is easily contradicted by many comparisons of the two phenomena. Possible comparisons of apples and oranges select from a variety of criteria, such as origin; appearance, including size, shape, and color; texture; nutritional content (e.g., sugars, acids); economics (e.g., market price, costs of cultivation, production, distribution); symbolic value (e.g., the expression, "as American as apple pie"); or convenience of consumption (i.e., edibility or ability to extract peel; or the insulation of pits in the core).

The paradoxical, inconsistent, and false nature of the "apples and oranges" objection thus requires further consideration of alternative explanations for methodological inattention.

4. The Complexity of Comparisons

The fourth explanation does not rely on pretensions of an authoritative orthodoxy of comparative method or presumptions of an extreme heterogeneity that defies commonality. Instead, the last view recognizes the difficulty in grasping the complexity of comparison. Based on this recognition, the absence of explicit and tested comparative methodologies renders the comparison of comparisons extremely perilous. It is easier to compare than to justify a comparison in light of competing alternatives.

For example, a consumer may feel confident about her choice of an automobile until she is asked about how she reached the decision. She might encounter confusion and doubt when questioned about her primary purposes in owning a car (transportation from A to B, comfort, speed, safety, panache, cargo capacity, fuel efficiency). She might find it difficult to justify her choice of comparative variables (value retention, safety record, design and color, moon roof, seat covering, trunk size, miles per gallon). Finally, she might have trouble articulating the measures and weights she applies to the variables (how fast, how comfortable, how safe, how cool, how big, how conserving). In other words, her decision will be easier to make than to justify in methodological terms. The challenge posed to the consumer is overwhelming, and few will take the time to pose and answer these questions. Therefore, the complexity of comparing and of justifying comparisons may best explain the consumer's relative inattention to methodological concerns.

Complexity may be not only the most persuasive explanation but also the most constructive. At one extreme, the view of uniformity is arrogant in its projection that comparisons cannot be critically contrasted. At the other extreme, the view of heterogeneity is defeatist in its implication that no generalities apply to the method of comparison. And yet neither explanation is likely to generate theoretically coherent or practically applicable models of comparative methodology. Finally, the incomparability objection leads to intellectual paralysis because it contends that comparisons are necessarily incoherent.

The explanation that emphasizes complexity as a primary cause of methodological underdevelopment draws upon, but ultimately rejects, explanations based on presupposed uniformity, heterogeneity, or incomparability. This position suggests that insufficient explanations of the comparative method derive from an inadequate search for methodology. The recognition of comparison's complexity is cautiously hopeful that scholars can develop a comparative methodology that is at once universally applicable and adaptable to specific means and ends.[154] The inadequacy of prior efforts reflects the difficulties of explicating what seems simultaneously to be implicitly innate on the one hand, and yet defiant of generalization on the other. Finally, this view also recognizes that because the underlying purposes of comparison differ, it is difficult to justify appropriate kinds and degrees of incomparability.

Furthermore, this explanation creates skepticism toward the view that the lack of attention to these issues is a sign of either the discipline's youth (based on the view that it has not had time to develop) or its strength (based on the view that only "weak sciences" are questioned by their own members).[155] This skepticism derives from the dual conviction that no discipline is too young to be questioned and that self-questioning signifies strength, not weakness. For these reasons, it may be more fruitful to view comparisons as more varied than purely uniform, more uniform than purely heterogeneous, more comparable than incomparable, and more complex and in need of explanation than is currently understood.

5. Conclusion

How, then, should one cope with this complexity in the search for methodological explanations? One might begin with basic questions about the motivations underlying comparisons, the content chosen for comparative purposes, and the modes of differentiation. Do comparisons change depending on the purpose one has in making them? How does the purpose affect the choice of the content to be compared? By what standard of differentiation is the contrast to be measured? Are differentiation standards also affected by the underlying motivation? Through these questions and the answers they generate, the ability to compare (and distinguish) comparisons might emerge; and as comparisons are distinguished, methodological rationales for accepting or rejecting a comparison might be developed.

It is true that the mere juxtaposition of two phenomena constrains the comparison but does not by itself predetermine the purpose, choice of variable, or test of differentiation. Criticism of a well-articulated, thoughtful, and self-described postmodern perspective illustrates this point. Andrew Huxley argued that "while a comparison of chalk with cheese must necessarily highlight the question of edibility, a comparison of chalk with marker pens will focus on legibility."[156] Further reflection will demonstrate that these comparisons may constrain but do not necessarily dictate the discovery of any specific contrast or similarity. The choice of comparative feature and test for differentiation depends upon the context and the motivations of the person making the comparison.

For example, a two-year-old might reasonably prefer to draw on the kitchen table with cheese rather than chalk. The child might focus on legibility (instead of edibility) based on her justifiable view that cheese is more legible than chalk on the table's surface. In another context, a parent concerned about ink poisoning might prefer to put a piece of chalk, rather than a marking pen, in the hands of a two-year-old who is prone to taste inedible objects. In this case, the parent's focus, with good reason, is on (in)edibility rather than legibility and leads the parent to the conclusion that the chalk is less inedible than the ink pen.[157]

As in these comparisons of cheese and chalk or chalk and ink pens, many varied purposes may motivate different comparisons. Inconsistent comparative content may reflect inconsistent comparative motivations.[158] In comparing apples and oranges, for example, the farmer may be interested in the climate conducive to cultivating apples and oranges, the greengrocer may be concerned with shelf life, the botanist with origins, or the baker with water/solid ratios.[159]

Moreover, even when the comparatist has identified purpose and chosen variables in pursuit of her purpose, she must still apply the differentiating criteria to the phenomena under comparative consideration. These criteria are applicable either in absolute or relative terms. Absolute differentiations characterize the comparison in terms of complete difference (dichotomy) or similarity (equivalence). The distinction between two sides of a coin provides an illustrative example of a nonrelative demarcation: heads or tails is a matter of kind, not degree. In contrast, relative distinctions express degrees of similarity and difference. The measurement of degree is based on an either explicit or implicit test or standard, a threshold that rests somewhere along a continuum between two extremes. The identification of this threshold itself represents a comparative choice, which, like the selection of content, will depend on comparison's purpose.[160]

Each of these considerations—purpose, content, and mode of differentiation—plays a significant role in many comparisons. Insufficient consideration of the complex interaction of these three features of comparison is likely to render poor results. In order to distinguish comparisons qualitatively, a framework for comparison is required. Chapter 3 takes a first step in that direction.

D. Conclusion

Through the foregoing evaluation of the comparative method, this chapter emphasizes four major points. First, comparison is a significant intellectual underpinning of legal decision making and commentary. Second, literature on the comparative method provides inadequate explanations of comparison itself. Third, the complexity of comparison best explains the relative inattention to methodological development. Finally, embracing that complexity by posing and addressing questions about motivating purposes, choices of variable content, and the employed mode of differentiation might provide a preliminary framework for comparing (and distinguishing) comparisons in search of a comparative methodology. With this objective in mind, chapter 3 explores the more specific problems of comparative choice in comparative legal scholarship.

3

Comparing Comparisons

The conclusion to chapter 2 identifies three general choices in the process of comparison: purpose, content, and mode of differentiation. This chapter raises more specific issues about each of these choices and provides a preliminary basis for comparing (and developing rationales for the acceptance or rejection of) legal comparisons. It also identifies and evaluates the choice of comparative purpose. Part A addresses the tension between the three major purposes of comparative law—understanding, reform, and unification—and the underlying purpose of developing an autonomous discipline. Moreover, it emphasizes the need for specificity in the identification of purpose. Part B addresses issues encountered in the choice of comparative variables. It scrutinizes the potentially distorting effects of classification based on limited criteria and the embedded deployment of crude measures of differentiation. It also discusses the use of prototypes and choice of comparative variables at the macro- and microlevels of legal systems. Part C confronts problems in the choice of comparative measures of differentiation. In particular, it demonstrates the ineffectiveness of categorical relationships on the one hand, and promising techniques of threshold differentiation on the other.

An exploration of comparative choices in purpose, variables, modes of differentiation, and their interrelationships suggests that many agreements and disagreements over comparisons may be attributed to differences in methodological choices. The conclusions of parts A, B, and C identify and briefly explore different contexts in which the disagreements might be better understood, if not reconciled.

A. Comparative Purposes

The three most frequently cited purposes of comparative law are understanding, reform, and international unification. Each of these purposes is widely accepted as an important justification for cross-national comparisons. In order to compare underlying purposes, it may be helpful to do so with even greater specificity. Divergent views about the role of comparison in meeting general objectives may be reconciled in part by drawing attention to the wide variety of purposes underlying each of the three general rubrics. If what should be compared is a function of underlying motivations, greater specificity may shed light on disagreements over the content of comparative legal studies. Furthermore, it is equally important to ask whether the delimitation of comparative law as an autonomous discipline serves or frustrates the field's explicit objectives.

1. Purposes in General

Notwithstanding disagreements[1] on points of emphasis, most[2] scholars claim that comparative legal studies serves three major purposes: understanding, reform, and unification.[3] Understanding[4] encompasses explanation,[5] knowledge,[6] legal history,[7] jurisprudence,[8] and legal science.[9] Reform covers comparative judicial decision making[10] and comparative legislation.[11] International unification extends to cross-border conflict resolution through private and public international law and international organizations.[12]

Understanding is one of comparative law's main purposes. Pursuant to this purpose, the comparative method attempts to understand the nature of law and legal change in both foreign and (by reverse projection) domestic environments.[13] As Pierre Lepaulle once wrote: "To see things in their true light, we must see them from a certain distance, as strangers, which is impossible when we study any phenomena of our own country."[14] More recently, scholars have drawn a direct relationship between the starkness of the contrast with foreign legal culture and the light shed on one's own legal cosmology.[15] Beyond the search for differences, some scholars attempt to draw universal evolutionary lessons from comparative understanding.[16]

Reform is another of the fundamental aims of comparative law.[17] Reform engenders attempts to improve a legal regime[18] based on foreign borrowing.[19] Reform may draw not only on foreign or historical experience but also on projections of comparative advantages generated by contrasts of different systems.

A third major purpose of comparative legal studies is international legal dispute resolution, harmonization, and unification. David and

Brierley noted that comparative law assists "in the creation of a healthy context for the development of international relations."[20] Stein emphasized the role of comparative legal studies in making lawyers more persuasive in transnational settings.[21] The "unification"[22] of law may be achieved in different ways. Reform efforts may produce national laws that are more uniform. Viewed from a comparative and international perspective, conflict of law principles supply the sources of private international law.[23] Comparative law also serves the objectives of public international law. This body of law includes specifically the identification of "custom" or "general principles" as a source of international law under Article 38 of the Statute for the International Court of Justice.[24] Findings of customary law (general practice accepted as law) or general principles require comparative research into the practices, laws, and principles of the disputing nations and the community of nations to which they belong.[25] Finally, supranational forms of legal process and institutions built on national models provide another area where one may harvest the fruits of comparative legal scholarship.[26]

2. Specific Purposes

Assuming that understanding, reform, and unification are valid objectives of comparative legal studies, their identification raises as many questions as it answers. What exactly should be understood, reformed, and/or unified?

A. UNDERSTANDING

Scholars disagree about the comparative understanding they strive to glean from their projects. For example, arguments spawn from topics such as whether one should focus on what the law is, the decisions reached in specific cases, the interaction between multiple laws in producing "formants,"[27] the functions law serves, the practical operation of the legal process,[28] the practical limits of formal rule making,[29] or the underlying philosophy of law or legal cultures.[30] These arguments are derived from competing motivations of comparative legal scholars.[31] Disagreements over what should be compared are in part a function of divergent theoretical and practical objectives.[32] Reconciliation of these disagreements requires a greater specification of purpose and critical attention to related choices of variable selection and measurement.

B. REFORM

Scholars also disagree on the substance of meaningful legal reform. The divergent motivations of the reformer or the commentator on reform have an impact on the role of comparison. Some commentators choose to focus on the substantive law of codes and constitutions; others concentrate on institutions and legal process.[33] It is still common to view reform primarily in terms of legislation.[34] These reform projects are comparative, but their comparative dimensions are relatively crude, superficial, and limited in scope.[35] They largely ignore Dean Pound's admonishment that "a fruitful comparative law . . . has to do much more than set side by side sections of codes or general legislation."[36]

Based in part on their specific objectives and views about the proper relationship between law and society, scholars disagree about the degree to which transplantation and transferability of legal rules from one legal system to another is possible, and the variables selected for comparison. Eric Stein reconciled the conflicting views of Otto Kahn-Freund and Alan Watson on borrowed law reforms by illustrating the problem of linking purpose to differentiating criteria.[37]

Kahn-Freund employed Montesquieu's view and found that when the law is more closely tied to its local habitat, a foreign rule is less transplantable.[38] In distinguishing rules that are immediately transferable from those that can be tailored only to the host, Kahn-Freund applied environmental and political factors, and stressed the increased importance of the latter.[39] Thus, according to Kahn-Freund, the most important factor in the transplantability of foreign models is the congruence between the comparative power structure of the transplantee and transplantor countries.[40] Failure to take this factor into account will cause the transplantee country to "reject" the foreign institution or rule and, thus, if law reform is to be achieved, the political context must not be ignored.[41]

Watson argues persuasively that Kahn-Freund badly underestimated the transplantability of legal rules.[42] He takes the position that "many legal rules make little impact on individuals, and that very often . . . it is important that there be a rule; but what rule actually is adopted is of restricted significance for general human happiness."[43]

Stein reconciles these opposing views by suggesting that Kahn-Freund and Watson are simply talking past each other.[44] Watson, the historian, is concerned with a macroview of legal change;[45] Kahn-Freund, the sociologist, assumes a microview.[46] According to Stein, "An historian sees a wealth of receptions and his vista across centuries is bound to blur the detail and soften the difficulties."[47] Conversely, a lawyer-sociologist "is close to the contemporary scene," "views the law in its operational context," and "is likely to disagree with the historian on what is or is not 'socially easy.'"[48] Thus, when dealing with legal reforms, historical and contemporary perspectives disagree about what is to be compared.[49]

The disagreement between Kahn-Freund and Watson may also be explained by their divergent views about the purpose of meaningful legal reform. Whereas Kahn-Freund cares more about the impact of a legal rule, Watson appears indifferent to its social impact.[50] Their divergent attitudes about the success or failure of a reform derive from two distinct views of law. Kahn-Freund tended to project a view of law as socially integrated—as one of many organs within a larger social organism.[51] Watson, however, views law as an appendage that can be borrowed at will.[52] For Kahn-Freund, comparison would be essential to ensuring that the host organism does not reject the transplanted organ.[53] To Watson, comparison is hardly necessary; comparison is important only in deciding whether or not to borrow.[54] In Watson's view, even these decisions are either imposed from without or made by a small elite from within.[55] Even though Watson compiles a daunting body of evidence to explain how transplants have been made historically, Kahn-Freund appears more concerned with how they should be approached prospectively.[56] These differences in temporal perspective, orientation, and purpose help to explain the divergent views of the requisite factors and standards for successfully transplanted reforms.

C. UNIFICATION

Beyond understanding and national reform, comparative legal scholarship may serve the general objective of international unification. Most scholars speak in general terms of harmonization,[57] international legal process,[58] or unification.[59] The claim that comparative law plays a significant role in international decision making, however, requires much greater specification. An analytical exposition of common patterns will help to explain the distinctive roles of comparison in international legal decision making.

Consider a typical pattern of cross-border activity, illustrated in the table below.

States	A	B
Parties	P/D	
Conduct		*
Law	X	Y

This pattern produces a conflict of law X and law Y (where they are different) between State A and State B, where P (plaintiff) and D (defendant) have a permanent connection (e.g., citizenship, domicile) with State A but conduct themselves in State B. In order to address the conflict from either a structural or doctrinal point of view several comparisons must be made.

To address the conflict, the jurisdiction of A may pursue a number of competing strategies.[60] First, A may choose to attempt to stop future cross-border activity between A and B.[61] Second, A may decide to allow the activity but develop and apply choice of law principles in order to decide whether X law should apply.[62] To make this doctrinal determination, A must compare the pattern components and give priority to one or more factors. These include (in isolation or combination) the identity;[63] relationship;[64] comparative interests or harms[65] of state A (the forum)[66] and state B; the legal personality of the parties (from A);[67] the location of the critical conduct at issue (state B);[68] or the nature of the law in conflict.[69] Third, A may decide that either X or Y law should be altered in order to reduce or eliminate future conflicts through national law reform (X changes to Y, or Y changes to X).[70] Fourth, these conflicts may be eliminated or reduced through the creation and imposition of a uniform international law (imposing, favoring, or compromising X or Y law).[71] Fifth, A and B may decide to unify their jurisdictional personalities in part or in whole in one supranational form of political and legal organization.[72]

Each of these strategy choices necessitates comparison. First, one must decide whether or not to discourage or prevent cross-border activity.[73] Generally, one must compare the costs of the conflict and the benefits of the cross-border activity with the opportunity costs of preventing the activity and the benefits of eliminating the conflict. Second, the selection and emphasis of legal principles or fact-pattern elements also involves many comparisons. These comparisons include but are not limited to the importance of the interstate relationship, the significance of the parties' relationship to the state, the comparative harm of the conduct, and the public policy importance of the law itself.[74] Third, both reform and uniformity approaches require comparisons between the status quo and the newly recommended law. Fourth, the creation of international institutions necessitates a comparison between different allocations of authority and power to national and international forms of human organization.[75] Fifth, the choice of any one particular strategy, whether used exclusively or in combination, requires a comparison with other competing strategies.

By outlining these options, the potentially useful role of comparison in the subdisciplines of comparative and international law may be better appreciated. The utility of comparative law thus expands beyond the potentially static comparisons of different national legal systems. Comparative law becomes a subtopic of private international law (or choice of law), public international law, and international organizations. Further, by recognizing the role comparison may play in advancing alternative strategies of cross-border conflict resolution, the potential inconsistency of comparative purposes and the comparisons they motivate is revealed.[76]

The pursuit of understanding, reform, and international unification may lead to different fields of inquiry, which are not always compatible. Each focus may lead to a variation in emphasis on similarities and differences. For example, attempts at taxonomy, as an expression of comparative understanding, may stress differences between systems.[77] Reform initiatives may emphasize functional similarities.[78] The reformer may encounter difficulties when seeking to borrow from a different category of systems.[79] Also, many reforms seek to improve the domestic systems without regard to international pressures, whereas international attempts at uniformity or unification may seek primarily to reduce conflicts between systems.[80] These distinctive goals may conflict and affect the choice of variable and standard of differentiation to be applied.

3. Implicit Purposes

The foregoing discussion focuses on the explicit purposes of comparative law. This discussion shifts the examination to the discipline's implicit goal: to preserve or increase its status as an autonomous discipline. The question of autonomy usually focuses on whether or not comparative law should be taught as an independent discipline or integrated into other parts of the curriculum.[81] This debate is similar to arguments about whether to teach legal ethics,[82] or law and economics[83] separately or pervasively, and focuses on the sequence and concentration with which comparative law should be taught. Embedded in these issues are deeper questions about the scope and focus of comparative law. Specifically, should the discipline be identified primarily by the subject matter it investigates (i.e., what it compares) or by reference to the specific intellectual process of comparison in the law (i.e., how it compares)?

The definition of comparative law by subject matter as "the comparison of the different legal systems of the world"[84] may be both too broad and too narrow. First, with a broad focus on cross-national comparisons,[85] comparative legal studies is limited to a set of legal comparisons that carry the greatest methodological obstacles.[86] Because of the varied purposes, multiple variables, and significant contrasts of cross-national comparisons, this approach is likely to cause this field to fall short of its aims. Those who seek to achieve understanding, reform, and/or unification may justifiably hesitate before basing their efforts on potentially methodologically unsound cross-national comparisons.

Second, in addition to its role in international settings, comparative legal studies could play a more significant role in purely domestic contexts. In this respect, the cross-border delimitation of the discipline may be unfortunately underinclusive of other potentially fruitful purposes. Comparatists assert their autonomy by claiming that comparativism is something more than "what lawyers naturally do"[87] when they "constantly have to juxtapose and harmonize the rules of their own system."[88] This cross-national delineation has the unintended effect of marginalizing the discipline and stunting the discipline's reach into comparative functions in domestic legislation, adjudication, and legal practice. Legislators compare policy objectives, allocations of power and responsibility to the public and private sectors, and competing bills proposed for legislation. Judges compare management schedules, fact patterns, holdings, interpretations,[89] and alternative justifications for their decisions. Lawyers compare arguments, strategies, risks in transactional settings, and venues in which to settle disputes. Therefore, the ability to compare, evaluate, and improve comparisons is also important within national legal systems.[90]

This nearly exclusive focus of comparative law on foreign law and cross-national comparisons may explain why the importance of the comparative method has been realized in legal history (as a form of diachronic comparison)[91] but has been much less successful in other fields. It may also explain, in part, the complaints of United States–based comparatists that domestic audiences are not generally responsive to comparative law.[92]

In an assessment of the status of comparative law in the United States, Langbein complained about the lack of American interest in comparative legal studies, particularly in areas of procedure.[93] Short of offering a solution to the problem, Langbein explored several factors that explain this widespread apathy. For example, he identified some combination of pragmatic and ideological parochialism in the United States as worthy of blame. Langbein wrote, "American legal dialogue starts from the premise that no relevant insights are to be found beyond water's edge."[94] Langbein argues that American jurists "operate on the assumption that the foreigners have nothing to teach."[95]

At best, this complaint identifies only one side of the problem. A more self-critical approach that focuses on what, exactly, comparative law has to offer the target audience may complement this critique. Indeed, without explicitly doing so, Langbein explored the preliminary basis for a more modest evaluation of comparative procedure itself.[96] Tellingly, he addressed the complex functional and systemic relationship of what is being compared among national legal systems. He catalogued the interconnectedness of legal procedure, actors, and institutions.[97] Based on his view that a "legal procedure bears the most intimate relation to the institutions that operate the procedures,"[98] Langbein conceded that it is difficult to reform Anglo-American procedure on the basis of Continental European models because "the different procedures presuppose different institutions."[99] Furthermore, he acknowledged the importance of the human factor: legal professionals apply the rules. Thus, he noted that "most borrowings would affect . . . the legal professionals,"[100] who may object to the required changes. Langbein concluded that this interconnectedness makes the borrowing of procedural models a complicated task.[101]

Given this complexity of comparison in the cross-national context, the practical insight to be gained from one system's view of another cannot be left for the audience to derive on its own. Instead, the comparatist must be able to demonstrate and persuade the audience of the lessons it should take from the contrast. For instance, if comparative law were directed toward domestic reform, and if one were to assume that reforms tend to proceed in small steps, then comparisons with foreign law would almost always be self-defeating.[102] Langbein, himself, conceded, "[A]cross the divide between the Anglo-American and Continental procedure, there is really no such thing as a small reform."[103]

Defining the scope of comparative law to include only comparisons with foreign law reflects the impulse to distinguish comparative law from other legal disciplines. Delimiting comparative law by the law to be compared rather than by the function of comparison, however, limits the potential impact of insights to be gained from the field. By choosing comparisons that are arguably the most difficult to make, comparative law is ill prepared to draw potentially valuable lessons from legal comparisons that are easier to make and justify. In this way, the assertion of autonomy (i.e., comparative law as something more than what lawyers do in a typical domestic practice) may actually serve to undermine the stature of the discipline.[104] Therefore, cross-national delineation of the discipline may be a root cause of complaints that comparative law has a marginal place in U.S. legal education.

Theoretical and practical attention to the process of comparison may provide guidance in domestic legal contexts, where a greater number of variables can be controlled and differentiating standards can be derived with a greater degree of consensus than in cross-national comparisons.[105] If comparative legal studies could serve to shed light, evaluate, or improve the manner in which legal comparisons of all types are made, its stature as an autonomous discipline would likely increase.

4. Conclusion

By identifying, specifying, and discussing the purposes important to the mission of comparative legal studies, this chapter explores the choice of purpose as one potential rationale for the acceptance or rejection of a proposed comparison, whether in domestic[106] or cross-national legal contexts.[107] Whether Germany has an advantage over the United States in civil procedure is in part a question of comparing one set of perceived advantages or values (e.g., efficiency, privacy) with another (e.g., fairness, access).[108] Whether litigation or alternative dispute resolution is preferable is in part a question of the primary aim of the legal process (e.g., justice through social control or peace through settlement).[109] Whether or not nations behave is in part a question of how strongly one believes they should or should not comply with particular norms or principles of international law.[110]

An accurate comparative understanding, helpful reform, and successful international approaches (based in part on comparison with domestic settings) in these particular settings will be significantly more likely with an explicit comparison of purposes, goals, or values.[111] Thus, comparisons may be compared and differentiated[112] in part by identifying the potentially contrasting purposes and valuations that motivate them.[113]

Understanding the role of purpose in comparison necessitates a differentiation (and evaluative comparison) of such purposes.

Beyond the articulation and comparison of purposes, the choices of variable selection (part B) and modes of differentiation (part C) made pursuant to these aims provide two additional bases for comparing comparisons as well as grounds of justification for their acceptance or rejection.

B. Comparative Variables

Even assuming agreement on purpose, the choice of what to compare provides a second major methodological concern. Many disagreements can emerge from the choice of an informational basis for the comparison.[114] Any two or more phenomena may have a multiplicity of potentially comparable attributes.[115] It may be neither desirable nor practical to compare all of these attributes simultaneously, if at all.[116] Therefore, it is reasonable that comparisons are commonly more selective than configurative.[117] Comparisons tend to focus on a particular subset of variables, while ignoring others. Notwithstanding their significance, these comparative variable choices are infrequently explained or justified.[118] How then are variables chosen, and what are some common problems in their selection?

In further pursuit of methodological explanations, this part identifies three common mechanisms that profoundly affect the choice of variables: classification, prototypes, and micro- and macrodistinctions. The following discussion demonstrates that the choice of variables provides a second general rationale for the acceptance or rejection of comparisons.

1. Classification

Classification, or the differentiation of phenomena into categorical schemes or taxonomies, is a common tool of comparative legal studies.[119] The following discussion identifies four fundamental flaws in such use. First, many classifications are a starting point for comparison rather than a conclusion based on preceding comparative study. Second, many scholars seek to justify classifications by reference to a limited number of comparative variables. Third, differentiating criteria are often poorly or inconsistently applied. Fourth, even the scholarship of persons who object to specific classifications or to classification in general suffers from the same weaknesses they identify in the work of others.[120]

A. *A PRIORI* CLASSIFICATION

First, classification gives rise to a significant problem prior to comparison. Most comparative legal scholars work with preexisting categories of classification (e.g., common and civil law) as a starting point instead of developing a set of classifications from independent study.[121] The categories with which most lawyers begin their comparative legal studies are crudely conceived and passively accepted. Frequently, rather than question the given classification, one attempts to justify a classification by finding the most persuasive demarcation.

For example, the common versus civil law dichotomy provides a basic example of this tendency. Dichotomies attempt to explain the "essential" difference between presumably different models of law. Writings alternatively stress the significance of recognized legal sources,[122] including judicial precedent[123] or legislative code;[124] legal process distinctions between adversarial and inquisitorial process;[125] or ideals of institutional authority, distinguishing coordinate and hierarchical ideals.[126] Because the common/civil law comparison was traditionally cast in dichotomous terms, many scholars have searched for the single feature capable of explaining the preexisting category. Ehrmann's claim that "[a]ll comparison proceeds from classification"[127] reflects this common tendency. Thus, comparisons tend to follow rather than generate the classifications.

B. LIMITED-FEATURE CLASSIFICATION

Closely related to the search for essential differences, conventional taxonomies tend to focus on a limited number of comparative variables.[128] From David and Brierley[129] to Zweigert and Kötz,[130] scholarly efforts have focused on explaining alternative classifications of legal systems (e.g., common, civil, or socialist law) according to one or two factors. Purported attempts to increase the number of differentiating factors frequently collapse into the identification of one composite factor.[131] Efforts to revise the classifications also focus on a very limited number of comparative features.[132]

Limited-feature theories—in support of the taxonomies—have differed widely in their choice of differentiating criteria.[133] The most frequently chosen criteria focus on the varied ways in which societies recognize law, including rules governing sources of law or rules of recognition.[134] Another basis of differentiation is whether the legal process is adversarial or inquisitorial.[135] More insightful examination has focused on institutional structure and the ideals of authority at its root. This is exemplified by Damaska's distinction between hierarchical and coordinate systems.[136] Others have drawn attention to the explanatory value of contextual societal factors,[137] like the political[138] or economic[139] system in which the legal system functions.[140] The Soviet comparatist Tumanov, for example, argued that typologies of legal systems should not be based on "legal criteria (for example, the nature of sources of law)" but rather on "[d]ifferences in social-economic system."[141] Focusing on the former deemphasized the importance of Soviet law as an expression of a civil law system; concentration on the latter set the Soviet system apart in its own category.[142] This consequence largely explains Tumanov's reason for differentiating legal systems through selection of the latter criterion. Some jurisprudentially oriented scholars argue that the discipline should focus on the philosophical underpinnings of broad principles of law.[143] Others combine two or more of these features in a bifocal view of comparative legal processes.[144] A few acknowledge the breadth of criteria but still apply only one or two factors to reach the conclusions with which they began.[145] A final group cites weaknesses in the limited scope of a comparison and attributes these deficiencies to the comparative method itself.[146] Finally, some identify broader abstractions that attempt to identify underlying similarities among disparate national systems.[147]

Ugo Mattei attempts to update these European taxonomies with different criteria.[148] He incorporates an anthropological notion of social control[149] as broader than law. Mattei's classifications also differ from the traditional ones examined and projected by David and Brierley, and Zweigert and Kötz, but only to a limited extent. The methodology of taxonomy applied by Mattei, however, is akin to those it seeks to replace.

Mattei applies the single feature "source of social norms" and identifies three primary ones that form the basis of his taxonomy.[150] In Mattei's view, the "three main sources of social norms or social incentives that affect an individual's behavior" are "politics, law, and philosophical or religious tradition."[151] These criteria then generate three families: (1) rule of professional law; (2) rule of political law; and (3) rule of traditional law. The application of these criteria to the world's legal systems generates categories not terribly different from those previously posited. Mattei's families roughly correspond to (1) Western; (2) developing, and many formerly socialist, countries in Africa, Latin America, and Eastern Europe; and (3) Eastern ("Oriental").[152]

Many interdisciplinary anthropological and sociological classifications are based on societal rather than arguably autonomous legal factors.[153] The shift to societal factors broadens the scope of content.[154] The impulse to classify, however, reduces a complex world to dubiously simplistic categories. Sally Falk Moore notes three of the common classificatory dichotomies in law and anthropology.[155] Maine, Durkheim, and Gluckman differentiate technologically simple and technologically complex societies.[156] Maine divides all systems into kin-based and territorial-based organization.[157] Durkheim distinguishes systems based on evidence of either mechanical or organic social cohesion.[158] Gluckman bases his dichotomy on the two criteria of simple societies with multiplex social relationships and technologically complex societies with single-interest social relationships.[159] Each of these schema focuses on one (or at most two) sociological features and then attempts to develop a social theory of legal differentiations based on that sole factor.[160]

Diamond and Hoebel, for example, in the evolutionist tradition of anthropological-legal classification, view legal systems according to different stages of historical development.[161] Diamond classifies legal systems according to evolutionary characteristics from savagery, through barbarism, to civilization.[162] Hoebel identifies a sequence from simple to complex, decentralized to centralized, and "private" to "public" law.[163]

Rather than examining an entire legal system, Gulliver uses another set of anthropological and sociological differentiations to focus on dispute resolution.[164] Gulliver identifies the polar types of judicial and political dispute resolution.[165] Political dispute settlement is differentiated by the absence of a third-party intermediary (e.g., a judge);[166] thus, resolutions are based on the relative social strength of the parties instead of legal norms.[167] Gulliver then postulates a series of gradations between the two polar types.[168] In addition, Bohannan focuses on dispute settlement, differentiating unicentric, bicentric, and multicentric process models.[169] Gluckman also focuses on differentiating the level of authoritativeness of the judicial intermediary.[170]

Reflective scholars acknowledge that classifications of systems into groups or "families" do "not correspond to a biological reality" but, rather, serve merely as a "didactic device."[171] Because legal systems have so many features that may be shared or unshared by other systems, and because classification schemes tend to place systems into exclusive (not overlapping) categories, most classifications of legal systems have been forced to focus on one- or two-feature theories to justify the classification.[172] Those fitting into the same classification are presumed similar (sometimes equivalent), and those placed in different categories are presumed different (sometimes opposite). In this way, classifications oversimplify similarities and differences by ignoring similarities among systems in different categories and differences between systems in the same categories. As Andrew Huxley remarked, "It is as little use looking for the Buddhist approach to law as it is the Chinese or the European."[173]

Like comparative legal scholars, anthropologists of law tend to choose one axis of differentiation and then attempt to locate whole systems somewhere along that axis based on the isolation of limited differentiating features. The purpose for which the comparison is made, the choice of variable, and the comparative tests chosen for purposes of differentiation are implicitly secondary to the commentator's particular dichotomous or continuous framework. Many of the anthropological classifications may be valuable in identifying important distinctions and describing human experience along the lines of one model or another. They are of extremely limited value, however, especially in societies where polar types and gradations of series (which classifications deem mutually exclusive) actually coexist and may increasingly interact.

For example, most national communities offer some limited combination of alternative forms of dispute resolution. These traditionally include, but are not limited to, a formal litigation system, institutional and/or informal arbitration,[174] other consensual forms of mediation and conciliation,[175] or (where these mechanisms are underdeveloped) self-help and direct negotiation processes. The complementary nature and interdependence of one form or another are not captured by isolating comparisons of litigation systems.[176] For example, direct negotiation takes place within the shadows of adjudication. Conversely, the effectiveness of the alternatives to formal litigation is frequently dependent on the state because the courts are asked to compel arbitration and confirm and enforce arbitral awards. In more unique cases like post-Soviet Russia, the state depends on private actors to enforce judgments.[177] Anecdotal reports suggested that litigants frequently took court judgments to organized crime groups who carry out enforcement procedures.[178] The problem becomes most complicated in societies that operate under more than one legal system at different levels of political organization.[179] Therefore, conventional classification by reference to these patterns of dispute resolution would fundamentally ignore this diversity of phenomena within a system and the interaction between them.

Where other factors are recognized, they are perceived to be more effect than cause.[180] The primary basis for the classification, a socialist economic system or a society of complex technological development, for example, is presumed prior to all other factors, e.g., a judicially controlled legal process. The overly dichotomous nature of these limited-feature classifications occasionally spurs attacks on widely accepted categorical distinctions, such as common and civil law,[181] and claims of effective equivalence between the two systems.[182]

C. INADEQUATE APPLICATIONS OF DIFFERENTIATING CRITERIA

In many classificatory schemes of comparative law, the features chosen to distinguish the categories are inconsistently and judgmentally applied. The leading comparative taxonomies by David and Brierley and by Zweigert and Kötz are vulnerable to this criticism.[183] For example, David and Brierley articulate two conjunctive criteria in order to distinguish legal families: technique and ideology.[184] They are neither "clear-cut," as the authors admit,[185] nor consistently or rigorously applied. The primary reason for their nonapplication is that they are poorly conceived. The first factor is "whether someone educated in the study and practice of one law will then be capable, without much difficulty, of handling another."[186] Even if useful, this technique does not identify anything more than differences among families; it does not necessarily provide insight into which of many potential differences are more or less critical (e.g., different "vocabularies," "different hierarchy of sources," different "methods").[187] The difficulty in adjusting to a new system might be a misleading proxy. For example, an English speaker might find it easier to speak (but not read and write) Chinese (a non-Indo-European language) than Russian (an Indo-European language) because Chinese has a simple noninflective grammar and Russian contains grammatically significant inflections not present in English.[188] Likewise, it is unclear whether an American lawyer would find an easier adjustment to the practice of law in India (a "common law" system) than in Germany (a "civil law" system).

David and Brierley complement the first criterion of technique, itself insufficient in their view, with a second criterion they call ideology.[189] On its face, the second criterion limits the categorical range to two systems, both placed in polar opposition as "entirely different" based on ""opposed" principles. These principles are opposed not only in philosophical but also in political and economic terms. This does not lend itself to capturing much diversity within the range of the legal universe encompassed by their ambitious study. Indeed, notwithstanding the nearly universal impacts of colonialism on the shape of modern legal systems, it would be surprising if all of the legal families in the world today fell neatly into only two categories.

A closer look at the application of the chosen criteria shows that in David and Brierley's classification scheme the two criteria are not consistently applied. David and Brierley do not confine themselves to a typology of two. The first criterion as well as the subcriteria it incorporates are strictly applied to the Romano-Germanic and common law families,[190] but not very rigorously applied to the identification of a separate socialist law family.[191] The second criterion is not applied to the Romano-Germanic and common law distinction but provides the primary basis for differentiating the socialist family.[192] Neither of these appears to be very carefully applied to the "other systems" category.[193] Other implicit criteria seep into the differentiations of Muslim, Hindu, and Jewish law. David and Brierley base their classification on the existence of a belief in "natural law" as a "model" or "ideal," rather than on what is "really observed."[194] Then they claim that law in the Far East is "completely different" because "the very value of law itself has traditionally been put into question."[195] A separate category is created for black Africa and the Malagasy Republic, where "the principal objective is the maintenance or restoration of harmony rather than respect for the law."[196]

D. THE POT CALLING THE KETTLE BLACK

Those who explicitly object to single-feature theories often fall into the trap of employing them. Zweigert and Kötz, for example, are more attentive to problems of classification but in the end fall upon their own swords. They explicitly criticize others for utilization of single-theory models. They comment: "The unsatisfactory feature of most previous attempts is to distinguish the legal families" in a "one-dimensional" way by applying a "single criterion."[197] In their review of the taxonomies of prominent comparatists, they criticize Esmein, Levy-Ullmann, Sauser-Hall, Martinez-Paz, and Arminjon, Nolde, and Wolff for their reliance on single-feature classifications.

Esmein based his classification on "a survey of historical sources, the general structure and particular characteristics of each of these systems."[198] Levy-Ullmann's division was based on "the difference in the sources of law recognized by the continental and Anglo-American systems."[199] Sauser-Hall based his classification on race, arguing that the concept provided an evolutionary basis for law.[200] Martinez-Paz queried how much the legal system had been influenced by Roman law, canon law, or democratic ideas.[201] Arminjon, Nolde, and Wolff based their groupings on "substance," without reference to extrinsic factors, such as "geography" or "race."[202]

Given their insightful critique, within which David's attempted classifications were included, it is surprising that, in the final analysis, Zweigert and Kötz fall victim to their own criticism. Their framework collapses five criteria including historical development, mode of thought, distinctive institutions, sources, and ideology[203] into one: "In our view, the critical thing about legal systems is their style, for the styles of individual legal systems and groups of legal systems are each quite distinctive."[204]

Classifications appear to be so integral to the way comparisons are conventionally made,[205] even those critical of them as a mode of differentiation employ them. As the anthropologists like to quip: there are two kinds of people in the world—those who classify all things into two, and those who do not! The observation exposes both the impulse for binary thinking and the irony that objections to binary classifications nonetheless frequently employ them. For example, Alan Watson's objection to classification as a valid pursuit[206] stresses the (mostly historical) relationships between systems. His emphasis focuses on historical development rather than contemporary problems.[207] Watson's view, in itself, poses difficult comparative problems, not altogether different from the weaknesses he identifies in the work of others. Based on the finding of a historical relationship, Watson implicitly creates a presumption of similarity, which itself tends to prefigure the analysis.[208] Watson criticizes other comparative endeavors for lacking an answer to the question "What method?" but offers no method for comparing systems in the relationship he narrowly defines as worthy of scholarly attention.[209]

E. CONCLUSION

The work of these thoughtful comparatists illustrates the difficulties encountered in conventional classificatory systems.[210] Without questioning the categories as starting points, many exhibit the strong tendency to search for explanations of the *a priori* categories instead of selecting key differentiating features[211] prior to making the categorization.[212] In other words, the comparison tends to take place after the categorization rather than before.[213] Classifications are then justified by reference to a limited number of essential variables. Differentiating criteria are often poorly or inconsistently applied. Finally, criticisms of prior classifications or classification in general tend to suffer from the same weaknesses that they identify in others.[214]

2. Prototypes

Rather than classify entire systems, one may proceed with another type of analytical cross-section: comparative prototypes of a law, process, or institution that are then investigated cross-nationally. Though useful, prototypes of simplified models do not avoid the problems of comparative variable selection.

First, comparative treatments of prototypes may be based on a false and implicit equivalence of parochial prototypes with universals. The prototype is frequently derived from a specific system of geopolitical and economic significance to the comparatist's primary audience.[215]

Second, the prototype is frequently defined too ideally and consequently may lack any real-world example.[216] For example, Martin Shapiro disabuses his readership of the ideal prototype of courts as a guide to comparative jurisprudence.[217] Shapiro defines the prototype by reference to four attributes: (1) an independent judge (2) applying preexisting legal norms (3) after adversary proceedings in order to achieve (4) a dichotomous decision, consisting of a binary finding of right and wrong.[218] Shapiro argues that the prototype fits "almost none" of "what we generally call courts across the full range of contemporary and historical societies."[219] He refutes the prototype by noting significant deviations from the ideal features. If judges are not independent, if norms are not found to preexist decisions, if the norms are not applied after an adversarial proceeding, or if the decisions are mediate and not dichotomous, then, in Shapiro's view, "a study of courts that is essentially the measurement of deviance from a type that is rarely approximated in the real world would appear to be equally fruitless."[220]

Third, prototypes may carry embedded value judgments. For example, in much comparative political science, the underlying substantive purposes served by the comparison remain implicit and thus harder to evaluate. As discussed below, independence of the judiciary is implicitly treated as an unequivocally and absolutely positive attribute of judicial systems, but this implicit goal is not given separate treatment so that it can be assessed in comparison with other potentially competing objectives, including political accountability to the affected society.[221] As in other fields, political scientists proceed to address problems of content and comparative differentiation without necessarily identifying both the potentially positive and negative implications of different dimensions and degrees of independence.[222] As an example to be pursued further in part II, whether absolute independence of the judiciary is a desirable goal is not questioned by reference to other goals, e.g., accountability, that may run counter to independence in its extreme manifestations.

Finally, similar to classification, the use of prototypes appears to be inescapable. For example, Shapiro replaces the prototype of court with a more abstract notion of the conflict resolution triad.[223] Is the triad a universal with real-world application, divorced of hidden value judgments, and nonprototypical in nature. Shapiro's triad is an admittedly heuristic device intended to facilitate understanding of the dynamics of third-party dispute resolution. His triad appears to reflect an arguably parochial concern with judicial independence and political influence in dispute resolution, and in this sense is not value free. Shapiro concludes that "a substantial share of courts and judges seems to be engaging in politics."[224] In this respect, Shapiro replaces one prototype with another,[225] which is equally vulnerable to criticism.[226] By exposing the type as deviant,[227] he implicitly redefines deviant as a type. Thus, prototypes appear to carry many inescapable risks of false universalism, parochial idealism, and embedded value judgments. The choice of a particular prototype may be based on the viewpoint that these are not important risks, or on the ability of the prototype to minimize such risks.

3. Microdistinctions/Macrodistinctions

Beyond taxonomy and prototypes, both the choice of micro- or macrolevels of analysis and the identification of the appropriate unit of comparison pose a third set of methodological concerns.

Macrocomparisons (e.g., legal systems—civil versus common law) may be based on a limited scope of microcomparisons (e.g., source of law doctrines regarding legislative code and judicial decision). Other potentially contradictory microcomparisons may be ignored as irrelevant in the classification of commonly labeled systems. For example, both the U.S.

and Indian legal systems are labeled "common law"; however, this label hides significant differences in the legal systems and processes.[228] Alternatively, irrelevant microcomparisons may be considered significant if they take place among differently labeled systems. Because the U.S. and Egyptian systems are labeled differently, unimportant distinctions may be considered significant.[229]

Scholars, ranging widely from Pound to Tumanov, have touched upon this problem. Pound argued that law, not laws, should be the basis of comparison. "Laws are rules, but law is far more than a body of rules."[230] Tumanov contrasted "comparative law in the narrow sense of the word" (microcomparison) with "comparative law in the broad sense" (macrocomparison) of legal systems, branches of law, or legal institutions.[231] Zweigert and Kötz differentiated the "large scale" (i.e., "the spirit and style of the different national systems of law") from a "smaller one" (i.e., "the ways in which the different systems deal with a single legal institution or legal problem").[232] Most treatments of the distinction between micro- and macroanalysis, however, fail to explore the interrelationships postulated between the whole of the system and the parts of its constituent features, whether between laws and law, or other distinctions between the system and its components.

In many modern cases, legal systems are structured on a legal premise. Constitutions consist of specific provisions that affect the broader questions about systems, sources, and institutional structures, as well as horizontal and vertical interrelationships.[233] For example, a rule stating that conflicts of procedure—whether horizontal (i.e., state versus state) or vertical (i.e., federal versus state) conflicts—should be resolved in favor of the law of the forum in which the case resides effectively allocates decision-making power systemically.[234] It is at once a microrule of federal diversity jurisdiction or state choice of law, and a macroallocation of power to a specific court or polity. One level of analysis divorced from the other is likely to mislead. Therefore, comparisons must be versatile enough to shift between the micro- and macrolevels, while posing questions about their interrelationships. If not, comparisons risk falling into overgeneralization on the one hand (defining the forest while ignoring the trees) and extracontextual specificity on the other (seeing the trees but failing to recognize the forest).

A final consideration in the selection of a specific feature is the level of specificity required to measure its existence or nonexistence. Often the distinguishing factor, judicial independence, for example, is too complex to grasp by reference to one or two features. Terms of employment, training, or ideology may each influence the independence of a judge. Evidence of independence from political interference may take the form of freedom from removal, rigorous training in independent judgment, or a strong personal identification with courageous decision making. Each general factor may be broken down further. For example, just taking terms of employment as one of the general features, appointment, promotion, transfer, salary, evaluation, demotion, or removal may vary in the degree to which each supports or frustrates satisfaction of judicial independence. Assume the appointment process is very political. Once appointed, however, the judge is free from political review. In this case, it is difficult to determine the relative independence of the judge because one does not know how to measure and weigh the respective impacts of two variables together or in relation to others of arguably equal importance.

Comparisons of legal processes pose similar difficulties. Each legal process is a complex configuration of actors and the functions they perform. The collective or individual goals and motivations of the actors vary, as do the disputes subject to the process. Additionally, procedural actors do not operate in a vacuum. They participate within institutional frameworks (those that train, certify, and review the work of professionals) and social contexts affected by economic, political, and cultural factors.[235] Therefore, variable selection has to take account of the many factors that directly and indirectly affect the legal process.

Another example in comparative legal process illustrates these problems. If one is comparing the "adversarial" and "inquisitorial" legal processes of the United States and Germany, one should be attentive to which specific subcategories of legal process one is comparing (e.g., civil or criminal, public or private) and the potential problems in making such a selection. For example, the comparison of public processes in two countries can be misleading if one nation relies more heavily on public than private dispute resolution processes or vice versa. Langbein, for example, in arguing for the comparative advantage of German civil procedure did not make any adjustments for comparative settlement rates in the two systems.[236]

Even if one could justifiably put these difficulties aside and compare formal litigation systems, what variables should be chosen to distinguish adversarial and inquisitorial processes? One distinguishing feature is whether the resolution of civil disputes is under judicial or party control. Yet, this distinction raises as many questions as it answers. Control over what, whom, at which point in time, and to which end are all significant features that may vary in their difference and similarity across dispute resolution procedures falling under either the adversarial or inquisitorial rubric.[237] Numerous macrocharacterizations carry the risk that microcomparisons will not justify the general attributions.

This realization causes one to examine the specific procedures under each model that are either party or judicially controlled, or both. If one breaks the formal dispute resolution process into its constituent functions (initiation and service, evidence taking, law finding, judgment/resolution), one may reach different conclusions about relative degrees of party and judicial control. The conclusions, however, will depend on which particular function or set of functions one deems most important and how generally or specifically they are differentiated.[238] For example, in the German inquisitorial process, initiation, like legal argumentation, is concededly party controlled. Greater, though incomplete, judicial control over evidence taking provides only a limited basis for the characterization of the German process as inquisitorial.[239]

4. Conclusion

The foregoing evaluation of content selection in comparison raises significant problems in the choice of variables. Subpart 1 (Classification) demonstrates that taxonomy frequently prefigures comparisons and hides the comparisons that justify the choice of differentiating variables. Propensities for limited-feature dichotomies cause many to search for explanations of the essential differences between the preestablished categories. Similarly, subpart 2 (Prototypes) examines the use of prototypes in comparative legal studies, including the inescapable problems of differentiating universal from deviant and the risks of embedded value judgments. Subpart 3 (Macrodistinctions/Microdistinctions) raises the problem of choosing variables among alternative micro- and macrofeatures, and the difficulties inherent in modeling the relationships between general and specific legal features and systems.

The foregoing discussion provides a preliminary basis upon which to compare variable choices made through the use of classification, prototypes, and micro/macrodistinctions. In specific legal problems, the choice of variable may help to explain disagreements about law and policy. Whether Germany has an advantage in civil procedure is in part a question of choosing one set of features over another.[240] Whether litigation or alternative dispute resolution is preferable is in part a question of the nature of the disputes to be resolved.[241] Whether nations behave or not is in part a question of which nations are counted and the time frame within which they comply.[242] Furthermore, within the academic debates about comparative law, attention to choices of content provides a rationale for accepting or rejecting differences in classificatory frameworks, the use of prototypes, and micro/macrodistinctions. Improving the choices of comparative content requires a more subtle differentiation and evaluation of the consequences that the choices carry. The discussion now turns attention to the ways in which common methods of categorical differentiation fail to answer questions about the implicit measurements employed in predominantly binary methods of grouping.

C. *Comparative Modes of Differentiation*

1. Categorical Differentiation

The many disagreements about the purposes and content of comparative legal studies overshadow the lack of discussion about how two or more presumably distinct phenomena should be comparatively differentiated.[243] Conversely, disagreements about modes of differentiation risk hiding arguments about what to compare and why.

What are the conceptual alternatives in the differentiation of two or more phenomena? By focusing on differentiation—a method of distinguishing comparative similarities and differences—one can identify six commonly applied cross-referential[244] principles that structure the relationship between two or more concepts or the phenomena they attempt to grasp: dichotomy, overlap, relativity, interdependence, equivalence, and indeterminacy.[245]

Comparative distinctions between common and civil law,[246] inquisitorial and adversarial processes,[247] hierarchical and coordinate ideals of authority,[248] national and international legal process,[249] law and politics,[250] substance and procedure,[251] or East and West[252] all employ at least one or some combination of these differentiating principles.[253] Particularly in classificatory schema, dichotomy and equivalence characterize extreme conclusions of difference and similarity. Commentators who focus on convergence among traditionally divergent systems recognize the overlap among them. Overlap thus captures a subset of variables shared by different systems.[254] As a remedy for the limits of the binary choice of either dichotomy or equivalence, relativity offers an alternative and more nuanced framework for seeing degrees of difference along a continuous spectrum. Further, interdependence may highlight the complementary nature of putatively different features. Finally, postmodernists and "Crits" employ notions of indeterminacy to capture the incommensurability of putatively comparable phenomena.[255]

The choice of categorical principle tends to signify a conclusion rather than a process of comparison that leads to differentiation.[256] Beyond the critique in this discussion, subpart 2 (From Categorical to Threshold Differentiation), below, explores how each principle can be used as a complementary tool in the process of comparative differentiation.

A. DICHOTOMY AND OPPOSITION

Comparative features are frequently treated as oppositional or dichotomous, without allowing for relative variation between the poles. The binary quality of most European comparisons may be reflective of an internal dualism, questionably unique to European intellectual culture.[257] For this reason, within European commentary, dichotomy is possibly the most frequently employed interpretive comparative tool. The models for classifying legal systems and social theories of law all apply some form of opposition.[258]

In application, dichotomy does not provide much explanatory power. Abel takes the position that "[t]he differences we discern among social actions seem to me to be continuous, and therefore unhappily distorted by such either/or characterizations. Moreover, dichotomies curtail further refinement; once you learn that a variable is not present in a given instance, there is little more that can be said."[259] For example, if one employs relative terms in absolute ways, idealization of the feature described can be expected. If no judiciary in the world is entirely independent from external economic and political influence, what measure of independence does one employ? If no formal litigation process is completely controlled either by any parties or the judge or judicial panel, what measure of party control is employed to the distinction between the adversarial and inquisitorial processes? If no national law is perfectly enforced, and (more arguably) few international laws are completely meaningless, what standard of compliance should be used in determining whether and why people (or nations) behave in compliance with the law? Without developing a more continuous framework for differentiation between the described poles, charactcrizations of difference may unfairly distinguish similar phenomena and the characterizations of similarity may blur critical differences.[260]

B. OVERLAP AND CONVERGENCE

When dichotomies are falsified by evidence of common features, overlap becomes a helpful tool. For example, in comparative legal studies, researchers who attempt to grasp convergence stress overlapping characteristics among systems prcviously thought to stand in mutually exclusive contrast.[261] Like overlap, convergence presumes an identification of common features short of total equivalence. Yet, unlike overlap, convergence signifies that two phenomena are moving closer together. In either sense, convergence, whether caused by interaction or the incidental result of parallel development postulates only an increasing resemblance of the two objects.

Merryman, for example, shifts among variables of increasing abstraction in his treatment of convergence. Shifting the levels of comparison allows him to see points of divergence (from one perspective) as evidence of convergence (from another).[262] Merryman contends that the rise of the nation-state is directly related to the disruption of the *jus commune*; yet, he also stresses the unifying effects the nation-state has on smaller units of political organization.[263] Moreover, divergence may also reflect convergence. Merryman discusses the decentralization and differentiation within national governments, by which forces within nations and peoples are attempting to establish their unique identities.[264] These forces of divergence are, from another perspective, points of convergence to the extent that they are shared in the experiences of many national communities. [265]

C. RELATIVITY AND CONTINUITY

As an alternative to dichotomy, a more relative or continuous treatment of phenomena posits differences of degree between opposed poles. Yet, these continuous frameworks provide little guidance for differentiating shades of degree, where most phenomena may descriptively fit.

Many legal scholars have rejected dichotomous oppositions in favor of a more relative scale.[266] For example, Abel proposes a more continuous framework for comparative dispute resolution, including both structural (role allocation) and procedural attributes (functions).[267] By disaggregating roles and functions, Abel effectively avoids the overly simplistic and dichotomous classificatory conceptions of legal process and thereby creates more open-ended and ultimately more fruitful tools for comparative research. Abel's continuous framework, however, identifies no differentiating thresholds on the spectrum between the poles.

Specifically, how should one measure the chosen factors and their effect on transplantability?[268] Eric Stein writes that "any scientific measurement of the degree of their importance would present a more than usual challenge to even the most adventurous 'quantifiers' of the new political science."[269] Still, no alternative approach is suggested. Stein points out that political scientists have exerted great efforts in attempting to treat comparative differentiation more quantitatively. In some of these works, the implicit tests are still crude.[270] For example, some attributes are framed in the form of Likert-type scale, ranging from total (X) to partial (X) to total (−X).[271] Yet, the value of these scales, without more, is far from clear.

These differentiations are valuable for framing neutral and open-ended theoretical baselines[272] or scales bound by polar extremes. It may be useful to presume that reality is likely to fall somewhere between the polarities.[273] In practical application, very few, if any, attributes will be fairly located on absolute extreme ends of the spectrum. Furthermore, because most, if not all, attributes will fall into the "partial" category, the vagueness of that term will hardly be helpful as a tool for distinguishing one partial system from another. This is one of the reasons that the tools of measurement and differentiation for a variety of attributes remain hidden in the majority of comparative evaluations. Vague and relative measures, such as "amount," "extent," "manner," "types," "nature," and "scope" pervade otherwise potentially useful frameworks.[274]

Finally, many of the attributes chosen for comparison may be measured only by reference to even smaller units of comparison. Without further disaggregation, the scales of differentiation will tend to be more judgment based because the measures for each compacted variable will remain implicit or hidden.[275] When more judgment is involved in the comparison, there is greater opportunity for inaccurate characterizations. Where judgment cannot or should not be avoided, the identification of thresholds of differentiation is important to establishing transparency of subjective motivations in the characterization. Without a sense of a specific limitation, relativity does not facilitate a characterization of existence *vel non* of a partially existent variable.

D. INTERDEPENDENCE AND COMPLEMENTARITY

Interdependence is the tool utilized in discussions about the complementary nature of distinguishable concepts or phenomena, even when perceived as oppositional. Rarely is interdependence used for cross-national comparisons. More frequently, it provides a comparative framework for understanding the relationship (not only the more static distinction) between distinctive phenomena. For example, Felstiner utilizes interdependence to explain the utilization of diverse types of dispute resolution. He writes: "Where adjudication and mediation are feasible, avoidance is costly: where avoidance has tolerable costs, adjudication and mediation are difficult to institutionalize. This complementarity has a logical base. The same set of social circumstances that makes one set of processes available frustrates the other and vice-versa."[276] As reflected in Felstiner's view, the complementary nature of two phenomena is still dependent on the variables chosen for comparison. Here again, complementarity holds no key for distinguishing comparative costs in terms of relative feasibility or infeasibility, tolerability or intolerability.

E. EQUIVALENCE AND LIKENESS

Equivalence is frequently posited as a necessary precondition to comparison.[277] For example, the corollary to the "apples and oranges" objection is the claim that apples must be compared to apples. The posited necessity of equivalence is itself tautological and only serves the purpose of emphasizing the importance of finding common denominators as a basis for comparison. Even the comparison of the taste of one apple with the size of another would not be helpful, even though the apples are alike. There are additional problems with the requirement of equivalence or likeness as a precondition to comparison. First, equivalence presumes a comparison has already taken place. In this sense, the starting point is actually a preliminary conclusion that is potentially unjustified because establishing sameness as a starting point hides the process of comparison that leads to that particular point of departure. Second, it is hard to imagine why comparison is useful if one is confirming only the presupposed equivalence of X and Y. Equivalence, in and of itself, does not appear to provide any greater understanding, the basis for reform, or international unification, unless differences are considered as well. For example, Gutteridge exclaimed that "[l]ike must be compared with like,"[278] meaning that one must compare systems of the "same stage of legal, political, and economic development."[279] He does not discuss how one establishes "likeness" or "sameness" as a starting point; nor does he explain how to locate differences, however small, among "like" phenomena.

Gutteridge is not alone in making "sameness" a precondition of comparison. Zweigert and Kötz mistakenly make comparison contingent on "sameness."[280] Tautologically, they state that "[i]ncomparables cannot usefully be compared,"[281] and then continue to overemphasize the need for identical functionality as "the basic methodological principle of all comparative law."[282] The requirement of likeness, if taken to its extreme, would appear to defeat the purpose of comparison itself.[283] As Cappelletti, Seccombe, and Weiler aptly put it, "comparative analysis becomes meaningless in conditions of identity."[284] If comparisons are limited in their content to total, or even near, equivalencies, little, if any, purpose would be served by comparison.

F. INDETERMINACY AND INCOMMENSURABILITY

Conceptions of incommensurability or indeterminacy in both domestic and international contexts and for incommensurability in comparative analyses are increasingly common. Postmodernists and "Crits" argue that cross-cultural comparisons are necessarily skewed because such comparisons are made from a single cultural perspective. Based on the premise that no common measure exists upon which these comparisons can be made, comparisons are therefore incommensurable. The conclusion of incommensurability carries four significant weaknesses.

First, incommensurability is often based on a dichotomous comparative framework.[285] In evaluating the "postmodern" views of Lyotard, for example, McGowan observed that his views oscillate between "an endless proliferation of private languages" and "some fundamental East/West distinction."[286] Second, like the "apples and oranges objection,"[287] conclusions of incommensurability are themselves based on comparisons. Even languages that are presumed incommensurable, such as English and Chinese for example, must be compared to reach that conclusion.

Third, comparisons frequently reveal that the subjects of the study are not incommensurable.[288] For example, comparisons between English and Chinese can be made on the basis of tone, inflection, or the similarities in phrases or sentence structure.[289] These comparisons isolate specific features: whether a tone in a specific word has phonemic value in changing the meaning of the word; whether conjugation and declension are utilized to determine the function of words in relation to one another; or whether there is a focus on sentences or phrases. In the case of the Chinese/English distinction, these criteria are relative. For example, English is more inflected than Chinese but far less than many other Indo-European languages, such as Latin or Russian. The degrees of inflection, and many other features, can be and are comparatively measured by modern linguistics.

Finally, like indeterminacy, taken in its extreme form, incommensurability would tend to undermine comparisons of nearly every type. In a world of increasingly intensified interaction, stressing the incommensurability of law holds little promise. As Huxley has pointed out, this view of incommensurability is "doomed to inhabit a world of unique singularities." [290]

2. From Categorical to Threshold Differentiation

By themselves, categorical modes of differentiation do not provide much theoretical or practical assistance in the process of comparison. These categorical relationships are tenable as conclusions, following careful analysis and synthesis, but less so as starting points because they tend to prefigure comparisons. Current explications of opposition, convergence, relativity, complementarity, likeness, and incommensurability reflect inadequately sharp tools with which to compare and contrast. These blunt tools must be further refined if comparisons are expected to provide guidance and justification in legal decision making and commentary.

Moving beyond their methodological weaknesses, however, may require ultimately using these categorical modes as constructive tools. Notions of opposition, overlap, relativity, complementarity, likeness, and incommensurability may not be wholly satisfactory. Yet, they are not entirely worthless. How, then, might a comparison draw effectively upon each of these modes of differentiation?

First, comparisons may make ample use of opposition by establishing polar extremes that contain relative differences in between. For example, a relatively independent judiciary may be conceptually located somewhere between the extreme poles of total dependence and total independence. Without the polar opposition, relativity itself would not be meaningful.

Second, comparisons may make fruitful use of overlap by establishing multifactored and overlapping comparative classifications. These classifications would allow for one system to belong to one or more categories. Instead of arguing whether socialist law is a legal family separate from common and civil law, one would be able to see the potential coexistence or nonexistence of two or more features. For example, classifications based on the two features X (democratic political system) and Y (free market economic system) would allow classifications of up to four groups: both X and Y, neither X nor Y, X and not Y, and not X and Y.

	Y	-Y
X	XY	X-Y
-X	-XY	-X-Y

As one adds features, the number of possible groupings increases. Although overlapping classificatory schemes do not explain why phenomena are categorized as either X or -X, Y or -Y, breaking up amalgamations of multifeature types or prototypes allows one to see that all features presumed to be interdependent may be considered independently from one another.

Third, comparisons may employ relativity in postulating degrees of difference along a continuous spectrum bound by two poles. Thus, instead of necessitating a black or white assessment, one may see finer distinctions of gray in between. This allows for a finer tool of differentiation and scalar measurements of carefully identified common variables. For example, relativity would not be helpful in determining the difference between an authoritarian political system and a free market economic system.

Fourth, comparisons may use complementarity not only to explore the interdependence of meaning but also to consider whether sharply distinguished features interact in significant ways. For example, a self-description of an independent judiciary is meaningless unless it can be contrasted with a more dependent one. Moreover, a strong democratic system may not be inconsistent with—but supportive of and supported by—a strongly independent judiciary (notwithstanding its theoretically un- or antidemocratic features). Many commentators in modern India, for example, see the judiciary, despite the considerable problems discussed in chapter 5, as the branch of government primarily responsible for the preservation and strengthening of democratic institutions.[291]

Fifth, comparisons may use the principle of equivalence to ensure that variables are compared on the basis of consistent variable choices. Poor civil law systems may be compared with rich common law systems on the basis of (1) wealth; (2) the type of legal system; and (3) the effect of one variable on the other. The selection of equivalent variables will provide a check against certain problems of incomparability.

Sixth, indeterminacy is helpful because it emphasizes the limitations of certainty and objectivity in making comparisons.[292] The questions of which variables to choose, how to measure them consistently, and according to which purpose are nearly impossible to answer in advance of conducting a comparison. Once the comparison accounts for these questions, evaluating and improving the comparison then becomes possible. Incommensurability and indeterminacy, when supported by a comparative evaluation, are useful justifications for humility, but not if they cause one to make perfect the enemy of good.

How then might the chosen variables be compared? Can the method of variable choice draw on the strengths and avoid the pitfalls of the foregoing modes of categorical differentiation? The objective of the following suggestions is not to convince the reader of their superiority but to underline the issues of choice involved in differentiating two or more legal phenomena.

First, one may create a hypothetical polarity to distinguish between two abstract types in their most polarized form. This is a deliberately heuristic tool designed to derive an abstract comparative model from preexisting perceptions of specific phenomena. If the variable differentiating adversarial and inquisitorial legal process (chosen pursuant to a choice of comparative purpose) is the level of party versus judicial control, one might create a simple polar framework. At one extreme of the spectrum, processes are wholly controlled by the judge; at the other end, the judge has no control whatsoever over the process.

Second, having created this abstract polarity, one may presume (rebuttably) that most legal processes fall somewhere between the two hypothetical poles. With certain exceptions, it may be fair to presume that very few, if any, formal litigation processes will exhibit complete judicial control or the total absence thereof. In these cases, compared phenomena will fall somewhere between the two extremes.

If so, a third step that involves more mediate terminology is required to differentiate degrees of difference between the poles. These standards of differentiation may be referred to as thresholds because they help to identify the interpretive line between satisfaction and nonsatisfaction of a given attribute. At the crudest point in the development of a threshold, a standard of primarily (that is, greater than 50 percent satisfaction) can serve as a useful starting point. A threshold facilitates interpretations of how much control is required to satisfy the characterization.

Fourth, one applies observations of each of the chosen features to the threshold standard. Assuming that aggregated generalities are dependent on disaggregated specificities, one may conduct an investigation of each relevant feature (depending on the purpose) independently before reaggregating the specific conclusions as justification for a general characterization. Judicial control over initiation, service, fact- and law-finding, judgment, enforcement, and appeal may vary widely. That fact-finding may be judicially controlled does not necessarily mean that the entire process is controlled by a judge or judicial panel. Once each variable is properly measured, the relationships between them are more easily understood.[293] This set of techniques may better ensure that the comparison is purpose driven, based on a careful selection of general and specific variables, and accurate in its comparative differentiation of disaggregated and reaggregated comparative features.

3. Conclusion

The foregoing evaluation of alternative modes of comparative differentiation raises significant problems in the comparison of two or more phenomena. Once variables have been chosen pursuant to the motivation underlying the comparison, how should the phenomena under consideration be compared and contrasted? The above discussion identifies and evaluates the inadequacy of common categorical approaches to differentiation. However, each mode provides a basis for the further development of more sophisticated interpretive techniques of differentiation. These techniques include use of oppositional polarities, overlapping classificatory models, relative gradations upon spectra of continuity between the poles, complementary relationships among distinguished variables, the equivalence of common denominators, and the recognized indeterminacy of comparative differentiation. The integration and improvement of these techniques and their comparison with those now available may create a stronger foundation upon which comparisons may be better understood, evaluated, and possibly improved.

By identifying and addressing these problems, the foregoing evaluation provides a preliminary comparison of modes of differentiation. Beyond the comparative purpose and content, the mode of differentiation provides a third rationale for the acceptance or rejection of a comparison. Differentiation rationales may be located in specific legal contexts (e.g., who controls service of process), large classificatory schemes projected by the discipline itself (e.g., whether a process is party or judge controlled), or general methodological debates about methodology itself (e.g., the mode of differentiating modes of differentiation). Ultimately, improving these modes of differentiation requires both a comparison and evaluation of these alternative choices.

D. *Conclusion: Implications for Justice Reform*

What, then, are the lessons for justice reform to be drawn from this discussion? As explained in chapter 1, each reform intervention (including those inspired by foreign models) proposes a change from the status quo, e.g., the introduction of a judicial commission to Indonesia or the adaptation of mediation processes to the Indian civil justice process. Reformers bear the burden of persuasion in attempts to convince opinion leaders and participants that such changes (notwithstanding their risks of failure or other costs) will result in an improvement in the system's performance (eradicating political interference and internal corruption or reducing backlog and delay). Each proposal therefore has three elements (even if they are not completely explicated): the aims of the reform; the factors considered critical to the problem and the solution; and a threshold determination that the potential benefits of the reform make them worth the risk or cost. The following discussion in part II of the book illustrates that attending to methodological concerns, therefore, is not merely of theoretical importance.

In Search of Justice Reform

Our opportunities and prospects depend crucially on what institutions exist and how they function.[1]

They will have to go out into the streets and roads and listen to the barking dogs.[2]

Justice reform . . . implies political change in its broadest sense.[3]

4

The Most Neglected Branch

A. The Global Rule of Law Challenge

As discussed in the introduction,[4] many national legal systems have made sweeping commitments to democracy and human rights, to free, knowledge-based economies, and to globalization and the reduction of cross-national barriers. In pursuit of these commitments, countries have generated an enormous amount of new substantive law, including civil rights, criminal justice reform, commercial legislation, constitutional law,[5] and free trade agreements and regional economic unions.[6] The fulfillment of these commitments poses a formidable institutional challenge. The realization of the right to vote, the right to contract and protect property, and the ability to trade with other societies without predatory tariffs or unfair treatment all require institutional adherence to the rule of law.

To fulfill rule-of-law commitments, however, states must be (paradoxically) strong and self-limiting.[7] In order to resolve this paradox, states will have to increase their intellectual and financial investments in impartial and effective adjudication and dispute resolution systems. The courts (and complementary institutions) represent not only the least dangerous[8] branch of government but also the one best able to serve this dual function of strong enforcement and self-limitation.[9] No branch of government is better designed to hold political and economic actors accountable to law or to ensure that commercial and property rights and obligations are enforced through impartial judgment. Judicial institutions thus carry the greatest promise of providing an effective check on political, economic, and cultural threats to the emergence of a democratic, prosperous, and law-based global society.[10] Given this critical role, therefore, institutional vehicles for the effectuating of the rule of law should receive as much priority as the rules themselves.[11]

Yet to perform this critical role, courts (or some functional equivalent to them) must be independent from undue political interference, maintain integrity in the face of private financial pressures, and operate at a high level of efficiency, especially given frequently inadequate human and financial resources. As Amartya Sen has emphasized in a broader context, "Our opportunities and prospects depend crucially on what institutions exist and how they function."[12]

Independence from political interference is necessary to ensure that the state is self-limiting in its effectuation of democratic values and practices. Impartiality in the face of strong financial incentives to favor one party over another is critical to a fair and thus well-trusted dispute resolution capability. Finality is central to the purpose of the justice system to render judgments that are binding on the parties. The interminable delay of enforceable results undermines any positive effect that a particular ruling can have on the parties and others similarly situated.

A large body of national, transnational, and international law, including constitutional law and foundational human rights declarations,[13] deeply engrains these norms. Even where the operable instruments do not explicate these principles, opinion leaders readily interpolate these values. In Indonesia, for example, Article 24, cl. 1, of the Constitution merely states, "Judicial Power is vested in the Supreme Court and such subordinate courts as may be established by law"; yet, some interpret this as an exclusive allocation of judicial power in the court.[14] National codes with extraterritorial application and international treaties reinforce integrity principles.[15] Many procedural systems place a strong value on finality of court decisions (requiring binding determinations within a reasonable time period).[16] The acceptance into law of each value thus reaches far and wide, thereby engraving certain qualities of performance considered necessary to meet widely shared global rule of law objectives.[17]

B. *The Most Neglected Branch*

Notwithstanding the critical role (and broad legal aspirations) of the least dangerous branch, the judiciary is sadly often the most neglected organ of the state. Courts are fragile political institutions, and more resilient political, economic, and cultural forces easily undermine their effectiveness.[18] Judiciaries lack adequate funding, support, training, and protection.[19] As a result, national judicial systems have not been able to keep pace with substantive commitments to democracy, free markets, and globalization.

Political[20] and economic interference[21] with impartiality, and delay in the administration of justice[22] currently undermine the achievement of core objectives in many countries throughout the world.[23] Indeed, an excessively partial or slow process renders fundamental public legal principles ineffectual, eviscerates private legal rights and obligations, cultivates the conditions for corruption,[24] and favors the powerful over the weak. Institutional dysfunction thus undermines equality under the law and corrodes the incentives critical to legal compliance.

Ironically, the new demands imposed on the courts by twenty-first-century commitments to democracy, markets, and globalization tend to further undermine their effectiveness.[25] As courts become more important, the incentives to influence them also grow, and illegal interference persists.[26] In Tanzania, bribes of lay assessors (who are paid the equivalent of $0.45 per sitting), are considered necessary to advance or defend claims successfully.[27] In surveys conducted in Bangladesh, 63% of the respondents indicated that they had bribed judicial officials (70% in cash, and 50% in face-to-face transactions); almost 90% said that it was almost impossible to get a quick and fair judgment without monetary influence.[28] In sum, the law that proscribes corruption has profoundly limited effects[29] on the market incentives for bribery.[30]

Additionally, the growing importance of recently implemented law has also imposed new burdens on courts. New rights create new forms of legally cognizable claims and disputes. In most market-oriented or democratic countries, case filings are on the rise; yet, most countries are not close to keeping pace.[31] In three Latin American countries (Argentina, Ecuador, and Venezuela), disposition times increased from 1981 to 1993 by 85 percent in part because of changes in the market economy.[32] In Russia, between 1987 and 1997, the number of civil cases in the courts doubled from more than 1.8 million to upward of 3.9 million, and "the judiciary has been overwhelmed by a new demand for its services."[33] England and Italy are struggling to combat delay as well.[34]

The failure to satisfy minimum human rights standards in the administration of criminal justice is equally common. According to leading experts, pretrial detention and the use of torture are still extremely widespread.[35] Zero tolerance for terror, strong security measures, limited representation for the poor, weak forensic tools, prolonged detention without an early hearing by a judicial officer, the ease with which common people become insensitive to inflicting pain on others[36] each contribute to the continued use of physical and psychological coercion.[37]

These issues are of critical importance in numerous national contexts, including the most recently notable case of Iraq.[38]

C. Institutional Failure: The Cases of Indonesia and India

A dynamic interaction of institutional factors (both historically rooted and systemically reinforced) contributes to the failure of courts to deliver justice in an impartial and effective manner. Indonesia[39] and India[40] each provide rich examples of court systems struggling to realize the vision of democracy, human rights, and economic development in part through necessary enhancements of judicial independence, integrity, and efficiency. These examples also provide a context for advancing and applying insights on the role of comparative methodology in global justice reform.

1. Interference with Impartiality in Indonesia

A. A BRIEF INTRODUCTION

With a richly diverse history of multiple influences,[41] the Indonesian justice system resembles its civil law counterparts in Continental European countries and their former colonies. Preexisting legal cultures deeply influenced the reception of competing foreign legal sources in different regions of the archipelago,[42] with the Dutch establishing political and legal control over the course of the eighteenth century.[43] Following the Japanese takeover in 1942 and Japan's surrender in August 1945, Indonesia experienced a period of conflict and two military clashes with the Dutch. The ultimate settlement engineered by the United States and sponsored by the United Nations left Indonesia with a fundamental question: What kind of legal system would be best for the country? Contemporary reformers continue to grapple with this fundamental question.[44]

During the Old Order period, the country encountered a choice of three alternative constitutions: a skeletal revolutionary constitution devised in 1945; a federal constitution written in 1949, which was critically perceived as a Dutch effort to continue control by the Netherlands; and a 1950 provisional unitary parliamentary constitution, the Konstituante. This parliamentary period was interrupted by military intervention when, in 1959, President Sukarno dissolved the Konstituante and reinstated the 1945 Constitution.[45]

This move helped to centralize legal and judicial power within the presidency. During the period between 1959 and 1965, known as the era of "guided democracy," law found inconsistent with revolutionary policy was considered nonbinding; for example, a Supreme Court declaration or "circular letter" (which itself was declared unconstitutional in 1968) treated the Dutch Civil Code as a set of mere "guidelines." In making these determinations, the judiciary came under enormous influence from the military through the executive, and its independence was seriously undermined.[46]

B. IMPACTS OF SUHARTO'S NEW ORDER

Guided democracy came to a brutal end with a military coup led by General Suharto that obliterated the Communist Party and killed approximately 500,000 people. Although the political ideology of the new system shifted dramatically from the left to the right, the central importance of the executive branch in Indonesian law and the economy continued to grow, and public institutions, particularly the judiciary, became increasingly degraded and demoralized. Suharto granted wide-ranging powers to a small group of family and inner-circle associates, thus concentrating both political and economic power in very few hands. This dual consolidation of power within the executive rendered the judiciary increasingly vulnerable to political influence and private forms of corruption. As well, the fragmentation of the legal professions increased during this period, pronounced by low standards of legal education, admission to the profession, and ethical conduct.[47] In this way, the executive exercised a monopoly over law, the judiciary,[48] and the legal professions.[49]

C. THE TWO-ROOF SYSTEM

Under the 1945 Constitution, the judicial power was vested in the Supreme Court (Mahkamah Agung) and other judicial organs established by law.[50] The Supreme Court sits at the apex of the Indonesian court system, with the High Courts and District Courts, respectively, at subordinate levels.[51] Fifty-one justices sit on the Supreme Court.[52] A chief justice, a vice chief justice, and several junior chief justices with responsibility over various chambers[53] or functional jurisdictions of the court (for example, the Civil, Criminal, Military, and Administrative Courts) and supervision of personnel serve as leaders of the court's administration.[54]

As executive branch oversight for the court system, the Department of Justice supervises the General and Administrative Courts; the Military and Religious Courts fall under the administrative control of the Department of Defense and Security and the Department of Religious Affairs, respectively. Under Indonesian law, the Department of Justice has control over the nearly 3,000 judges,[55] 15,000 staff, 280 court buildings, and 1,000 official housing units. It is responsible for the judicial budget for infrastructure and back-office support, as well as the terms of employment for judicial (and nonjudicial) personnel: appointment (through competitive examinations), salary, training, promotion, discipline, transfer (which is mandatory), and removal. This system, famously exploited by Suharto to influence judicial decision making, is known as a two-roof system because the judiciary is under the administrative control of the Ministry of Justice as well as the Supreme Court.[56]

D. INSTITUTIONAL CHALLENGES OF *REFORMASI*

The deterioration of the economy during the Asian financial crisis in late 1997 created a destabilizing political crisis. Protests in favor of reform took aim at the more than three decades of autocratic rule by President Suharto, and rioting in the urban centers forced Suharto to turn power over to his deputy, Haharuddin Jusuf Habibie. This marked the beginning of a *reformasi* period. In 1999 under Habibie, Indonesia held the first election since 1955 in which the people could form political parties and participate freely. The Indonesian Democratic Party of Megawati Sukarnoputri (Sukarno's daughter) received a plurality of 34 percent of the popular vote; however, the People's Consultative Assembly (MPR)—the highest legislative body—elected Abduraman Wahid as president and Megawati as vice-president. After several scandals forced Wahid out of the government in July 2001, Megawati Sukarnoputri became the third president of Indonesia after Suharto within a span of only three years.[57]

The *reformasi* period has brought massive legislative reform and institutional changes,[58] with many proposals and drafts to be passed in the near future. The strong impulse to introduce an overwhelming panoply of new laws, ranging from environmental regulation and labor law to consumer and intellectual property protections, created new institutional and procedural challenges for which the judicial system now appears poorly prepared.[59]

Notwithstanding these various legislative reforms and blueprints for the future, corruption continues to undermine the legitimacy and integrity of the court system and the legal professions. Corruption also frustrates the achievement of impartiality in the judicial process and weakens social incentives for compliance with the law. Furthermore, corruption appears nearly intractable because the root causes are deeply embedded in the four decades of institutional neglect that characterized recent Indonesian legal history.[60]

The terms of employment for judges are highly unsatisfactory. Salaries are extremely low, transfers (at times to remote and undesirable locations) are mandatory, promotions are based mainly on lockstep seniority, working conditions are poor, performance evaluation is nonexistent, and support staff and resources remain inadequate. Furthermore, the available disciplinary mechanisms appear to be inadequate. Finally, the lack of transparency and accountability in the judicial process creates ample opportunities for corrupt practices. Court management systems are underdeveloped, and evidence taking is discontinuous and protracted, relying heavily (as in other traditional Continental European–style systems) on the exchange of documents. The process lacks (or has lost) what many other Continental systems have already accomplished (or are on their way to achieving): more pervasive morality, publicity, concentration through event-driven mechanisms, and transparency. Formal alternative dispute resolution is perfunctory; however, informal private processes play a significant role in filling the gap left by ineffectual adjudication functions. Although a new arbitration law was passed in 1999, arbitration and other alternatives to litigation are still very infrequently used, and the institutional capability for formal alternative dispute resolution is generally limited. Enforcement of judgments is ineffectual. The judiciary has no contempt power (or its functional equivalent) over the litigants and no effective authority over the police, and the allocation of such powers is unlikely, given the widespread distrust of the judiciary itself and the risk that a contempt power or its equivalent would be abused. With the noted exception of the new Commercial Court adjudication procedures, court decisions are conclusory and unpublished.[61]

E. INSTITUTIONAL REFORMS: ONE-ROOF AND THE JUDICIAL COMMISSION

New legislation aims at reconfiguring the two-roof system of executive and Supreme Court supervision over the national judiciary. In response to the demoralization of the judiciary under Suharto, a newly legislated one-roof system (under Law No. 35/1999 for implementation in 2004) vests this control exclusively within the judicial branch.[62] In order to manage the potentially overwhelming administrative burdens resulting from this shift in responsibility, Indonesian reformers have undertaken to design a judicial commission to assist with disciplinary oversight, an integrated career system, and permanent legal education for the judiciary. In 2002, Indonesia amended its Constitution in an attempt to meet the country's many challenges, including reform of the judicial system. The Third Amendment to the Constitution established the constitutional basis for a judicial commission.[63]

The commission may serve as an institutional framework for a potentially wide range of reform initiatives. These include the development of a normative code of ethics and disciplinary system of enforcement, administrative support for a personnel management system for the courts, a permanent education and training system for the judiciary, and a research capacity for self-monitoring judicial performance. The particular course of these institutional reforms remains sketchy, however.

In particular, the Blueprint recently published by the Supreme Court[64] is ambivalent on the scope of external control the Court itself appears willing to accept, reflecting the profound predicament between independence without external accountability on the one hand or accountability without independence from external interference on the other. The shaky intellectual foundations of the Indonesian Judicial Commission thus provides an excellent illustration (in the next chapter) of common methodological problems identified in the discussion above: inarticulate aims, inattention to key features, and accordingly naïve reform determinations and strategies.

With the skeletal 1945 Constitution still fundamentally in place, the recent Third Amendment and its broad references to "a framework of guarding and upholding the honor, noble prestige, and behavior of the judge"[65] did little to resolve profound dilemmas in both normative and institutional contexts. The judiciary still appears poorly prepared for the one-roof implementation, and conflicts over the powers, personnel, and procedures of a judicial commission have prevented agreement on critical and inevitable design and implementation questions.

At this intermediary stage, the Indonesian reforms that have been implemented are publicly acknowledged to be insufficient to fulfill the goals of independence and integrity effectively. The pervasiveness of corruption in the District and Supreme Court system has discouraged the successful utilization of the Commercial Court,[66] which is widely considered to be of vital importance to the economic recovery of the country. Unless these profound systemic problems are candidly assessed and creatively solved, the cultivation of public trust, political stability, and economic recovery will be further delayed.

2. Backlog and Delay in India

A. A BRIEF INTRODUCTION

In contrast to the Indonesian system, the Indian justice system[67] resembles its common law counterparts.[68] Influenced by the British model of civil justice process from which it evolved,[69] the Indian courts reflect a coordinate, pyramid structure of judicial authority,[70] emphasize formal procedural justice dominated by litigants of equal status engaged in adversarial processes,[71] and provide binding, win-lose remedies.[72] The British system supplanted traditional rural forms of Indian dispute resolution,[73] which involved respected adjudicators in an arguably more conciliatory, less formal process, and greater flexibility in remedial action.[74] In contrast, the Indian system now places a laissez-faire emphasis on party-controlled litigation processes, formal adversarial proceedings, and legal remedies generally confined to binary win-lose legal outcomes.[75]

A politically independent[76] judiciary applies both federal and state law under a unified federal system[77] and administers the formal civil justice process.[78] The Supreme Court sits at the apex of the federal system; the High Courts, one in each state, serve as the highest state fora in both civil and criminal matters. Every state is subdivided into several districts, each with a District Court (sometimes called a Sessions Court) designated as the principal civil court of original jurisdiction, under which sit a number of lower courts, including the reinstated *panchayats,*[79] whose powers differ greatly from state to state.[80]

Generally, the Code of Civil Procedure of 1908 (itself a derivation of the British Judicature Acts) and subsequent amendments govern the civil justice process.[81] A typical civil proceeding consists generally of several adversarial, party-controlled stages, including pleadings, a determination of jurisdiction, trial, judgment and decree, appeals (including revision and review), and execution.[82]

B. IMPACTS OF THE ADVERSARIAL SYSTEM

The practical application of this adversarial system in India has achieved mixed results.[83] Some observers have emphasized the positive role played by a strong Indian judiciary in increasing the accountability of democratically elected officials.[84] Yet, others believe the adversarial procedural justice system in India has failed from its inception[85] and is in need of sustainable reforms.[86] Notwithstanding the system's civil service of court administrators, an independent judiciary, a rich supply of professional legal talent, and a modern procedural code, it also exhibits a general failure to manage effectively the dispute resolution processes of a democratic, socially diverse, and newly market-oriented society.[87] Specifically, inefficient court administration systems, excessive judicial passivity in an adversarial legal process, and severely limited alternatives to a protracted and discontinuous full trial frustrate several goals of the adversarial process itself. Inefficiency in court administration denies timely access to legal dispositions. Excessive party control places those seeking legal redress in an unequal position because respondents can abuse and delay the resolution procedures with impunity. Finally, the unavailability of alternatives to litigation clogs the system. Many cases awaiting judgment are no longer contentious, and long-awaited judgments are often difficult to enforce.

These civil justice processes have failed to administer justice in a timely manner. The adversarial model appears poorly designed to meet the needs of a rural population with widespread poverty, illiteracy, and unfamiliarity with formal legal procedure.

C. BACKLOG AND DELAY AND THEIR CONSEQUENCES

Delay is a common problem;[88] yet, India appears to be at the extreme end of a wide-ranging scale. The problem is hardly new.[89] Growing pressures to bring civil justice to the largest democracy and seventh-largest market in the world, however, amplify the problem to a deafening level.[90] The formidable demand for greater political accountability in public administration and the consequences of post-1991 market reforms each place ever-greater pressure on the civil justice system.[91] An estimated backlog of 24 million cases[92] and delays averaging twenty years (requiring an estimated "324 years to clear the backlog")[93] currently undermine the effective enforcement of substantive civil and commercial rights.[94]

As both a daunting symptom and an aggravating cause, widespread and profound backlog and delay[95] frustrate the fundamental priorities of a law-based society. Protracted delays erode public trust and confidence in legal institutions and act as significant barriers to India's chosen path to social justice and economic development. The inability to enter final legal decisions within a reasonable time renders state action functionally immune, turns obligations to perform contractual duties into effective rights to breach with impunity, and devalues remedies eventually provided. In sum, the inability to resolve disputes in a timely manner eviscerates public and private rights and obligations.

D. CAUSES OF BACKLOG AND DELAY

In India, backlog and delay derive from many factors. Court administration systems lose track of matters, events, records, and evidence. Case processing is discontinuous, fragmented, protracted, and excessively permissive of adjournments, provisional ex parte procedures, and appeals.[96] Settlements are rare, and few alternatives to trial are available or well developed. Litigation is still viewed as the primary means of dispute settlement (not to mention dispute escalation). Finality is elusive. Appellate rights are excessively permissive. Cases linger beyond the life span of the original parties, thus triggering additional hearings to satisfy notice and process requirements for new rights holders directly affected by the judgment. Provisional and postjudgment remedies for failure to comply with final judgments are additionally inadequate to deter noncompliance.[97]

Indeed, the typical life span of a civil litigation presents a sad picture. Records of new filings are kept by hand, and documents filed in the courthouse are frequently misplaced or lost among other paper. Lawyers crowd the courtroom and wait for their cases to be called. Even when called, judicial attention is frequently deferred by innumerable adjournments: the witness is not available, the party is not present, the lawyer has not arrived, or a document is not yet available. When the case is heard, a judge orally summarizes testimony for a court reporter. There is little likelihood that this judge will be the same one to issue a decision because judges are transferred more quickly than legal dispositions are made. Judges are so underpaid and overworked that they often adjourn and delay the preparation of a case, if only to put off the demands of reaching a decision.

Streamlining procedures that enable the judge to frame the issues are rarely effectuated. Likewise, sanction power to impose costs for frivolous conduct is seldom exercised.[98] Interim injunctive relief is routinely granted, but long delays in hearing the contentions of those enjoined persist. Commonly made interlocutory appeals fracture the case into many parts and effectively stay the trial. The absence of alternatives to litigation makes a full, discontinuous trial necessary, regardless of how long a full trial may take. Once a judgment is reached, the truly hard work of enforcement and execution begins. These compounding problems engender despair among pessimists and overwhelm even dedicated optimists, while public tolerance appears to be waning.

E. PROCEDURAL REFORMS: COURT MEDIATION

To address these concerns, in 1999 Parliament promulgated several amendments to the Civil Procedure Code of 1908. Among these many amendments, Section 89 and Order X (1A) provided for court-annexed alternative dispute resolution (ADR). Under the new provision, the court directs the parties to choose among several ADR mechanisms, including *lok adalat,* arbitration, conciliation, and mediation.[99] Section 89 contemplates that the judge (presumably the judge assigned to the case) should first determine whether there exist "elements of a settlement which may be acceptable to the parties."[100] If so, second, the court "shall formulate the terms of settlement and give them to the parties for their observations." Third, "after receiving the observations of the parties, the court may reformulate the terms of a possible settlement" and refer the same for arbitration, conciliation, or judicial settlement, including through *lok adalat* or mediation.[101] These provisions, drawn from the conciliation provisions of the Arbitration and Conciliation Act (1996), are based on the United Nations Commission on International Trade Law (UNCITRAL) model law, itself derived from mainly the European practice of conciliation.[102]

Based on widespread opposition to the amendments from the practicing bar, the amendments were suspended indefinitely. In July 2002, however, Parliament decided to put the amendments, including Section 89, into full effect. Following the effectuation of Section 89, a bar association in Tamil Nadu brought a constitutional challenge in the case of *in re Salem Bar Association.* In a panel decision written by Chief Justice Kirpal in late October 2002, the Supreme Court upheld the constitutionality of the law and established a five-person committee to study the reforms and to make recommendations on the need for any amendments or additional rules to facilitate implementation of the reforms.[103]

Conflicts within and between the bar and the bench over the role of these reforms and the impact they may have on collective or individual professional interests continue to stall widespread implementation. Even with strong initiative in several important pockets of the judicial system, the judiciary and the bar appear poorly prepared and postured to move the reforms forward to meet the country's challenge. As of May 2003, no court in the country had implemented a formal Section 89 proceeding. In other words, four years after the major antidelay legislation in the country, no responsive changes have taken place. Without substantial relief from backlog and delay, India will not be able to realize fully its legal commitment to democratic and liberal economic policies.

Similar to Indonesian justice reform, the infirm intellectual foundations for Indian mediation described in the next chapter illustrate common methodological problems: inarticulate goals, inattention to important design questions, and unchallenged theories of institutional or behavioral change. For purposes of present discussion, however, it suffices to note that, notwithstanding the broadly negative political and economic implications of backlog and delay for Indian society,[104] the planned adaptation of mediation (and other devices) as a solution to these profound problems remains unrealized.

D. Conclusion

These brief observations of Indonesia and India reflect the significant difference between the expectations and actual performance of judicial institutions.[105] The gap may be growing as a result of quick normative, and slow institutional, change. Without responsive ways of bridging this gap, judicial systems will be trapped in an endless pendulum swing between high hope and bitter disappointment. To avoid this trap, two lessons should be kept firmly in mind.

First, the legal commitments that set in motion a process of democratization, privatization, and globalization, without adequate investments in institutional development, may make matters only worse, at least in the shorter term. Law takes on greater importance; legally cognizable claims increase; more people come to the courts expecting justice; and the stakes in the outcome rise. (The only phenomenon that flattens this higher demand is the negative feedback of continued failure of the judicial system: if litigants distrust the system or find it ineffective, they will pursue private, extralegal strategies or simply abandon their cases or lump their legal injuries.)[106]

Second, substantive commitments are easier to achieve than institutional reforms. Developing institutional performance means changing behaviors that are difficult to affect without structural changes in incentive structures (and the feedback systems by which agents react to these changes and opportunities).[107] Common (implicitly comparative) assumptions of either perfect enforcement or uniform imperfections in enforcement trivialize the importance of primary agents in the legal process. The next chapter sketches the major impediments to effective reforms of the most neglected branch.

5

Between Rocks and Hard Places

Beyond the daunting nature of the problems to be surmounted, why does reform in so many countries, including Indonesia and India, appear to be so elusive? Why does the mere passage of a new law not immediately translate into a successful change in institutional behavior? Why do reforms often fall victim to the very forces of corruption and delay they are designed to address?

The following discussion outlines a number of significant impediments to effective reform (with particular emphasis on poor comparative understanding of the nature of the problems and their solutions), the common failures that result, and the perplexing dilemmas these conditions pose for reformers.

A. Impediments to Reform

Multiple sources of misunderstanding (many derived from faulty comparisons), severe resource limitations, and obstacles to effective, collective action all impede responsive reform processes. If these impediments are ignored by comparative theories of institutional change, dismissed as "mere resistance," or accepted as unalterable, reform initiatives like those in Indonesia and India will likely fail.

1. Common Sources of Comparative Misunderstanding

A. RASH ASSESSMENTS

Reformers frequently harbor rash judgments of the underlying problems and fail to appreciate what may be functional justifications for the phenomena they criticize. For example, anti-independence measures may aim to regulate an entirely venal judiciary.[1] Corruption may flourish as a response to the inefficiencies of a tenured civil service and an invasive, excessively bureaucratic, or extortionist regulatory system.[2] Delay may be a sign of the system working hard to get it right without cutting corners. Adjournment cultures may develop because it is really hard to get to court on time when one has to travel great distances and notification systems are poor.[3]

For example, the British complained about the long delays in the courts of colonial Tanzania.[4] In the context of certain social conditions, prolonged delays in the assertion of claims could be justified by the practical inability to collect from obligors in the near future. As Sally Falk Moore has pointed out, British colonial authorities wrongly attributed delays in prosecuting civil actions to incompetence rather than to the economic conditions of rural life.[5] Moore notes the wisdom of the Chagga saying "[I]t is no use claiming a cow from a man who does not have one."[6] One may reasonably wait to prosecute a claim "until the original debtor's son or grandson prospers."[7]

B. UNDERESTIMATING POWERFUL INTERESTS

Problems persist in part because they serve the interests of powerful politicians, monopolists, and professional elites (including lawyers themselves).[8] Political leaders rarely appreciate the benefits of limits on their own power. Rich families and corporations may prefer to purchase justice than to subject their legal disputes to impartial decision making. Lawyers paid by court appearance (a common practice) have strong incentives to protract litigation into a series of fragmented, discontinuous proceedings. Therefore, reforms meet substantial resistance from those who benefit from the status quo. Those in support of reform may risk their careers and personal safety. Ample security for those working on sensitive reform initiatives is rarely, if ever, available. Shortsighted comparative analyses of the ostensibly apolitical nature of court reform,[9] coupled with excessive optimism to effect change, are likely to result in deep disappointments.[10]

C. LIMITED SELF AWARENESS OF ACTUAL PERFORMANCE

Reform proposals based on inaccurate self-assessments are not likely to have a positive impact in addressing critically important problems. This is particularly the situation in systems where there is a large deviation between law and practice. Self-awareness depends on candor, quantitative empirical tools, and qualitative assessments. Unfortunately, powerful interests may repress candid assessments, and very few reforming communities have an adequate set of empirical tools, and even where both are available, most quantitative analysis is often deficient in qualitative thinking. In Indonesia, for example, corruption is considered the norm, not the exception, of everyday judicial behavior; however, because of its unlawful character, there is currently no empirical understanding of the precise nature, breadth, or depth of corrupt practices in the judicial process. In India, the empirics of delay are nearly as weak. To date, there is no reliable national data on backlogs and little empirical insight on the nature of the different cases and their disposition times.

D. MYOPIC VIEWS OF INTERRELATED PROBLEMS

Reformers tend to see specific problems in isolation from others. Political interference, corruption, or delay may be perceived as separate problems. These manifestations of institutional failure, however, are mutually reinforcing. Insecure terms of employment make judges more vulnerable to corruption and less likely to combat delay with sufficient industry. Political interference and delay are also conducive to corruption because these conditions give court administrators (e.g., from the Ministry of Justice to the court registrar) the ability to extract rents for altering outcomes or pushing matters forward or back. If judges are corrupt, the legitimacy and integrity necessary to give them more independence are lacking, and the incentives to preserve or even create delay increase. Thus, in a vicious cycle of interrelated problems, solving one problem seems to require solving them all simultaneously. Yet, solving them all seems entirely impossible because resources are insufficient and conflicts generated by the reforms themselves impede the necessary forms of collective action.

E. INEXPLICIT AIMS

Successful reforms presuppose an articulation of specified goals or objectives. These aims, however, are often inexplicit, imprecisely relative, or (when applied) in conflict with others of arguably equal importance. For example, the stated goal of judicial independence in Indonesia begs many questions: independence from whom, for what, through which measures, to which degree? Will one-roof reforms in Indonesia replace dependence on the executive with dependence on court hierarchies or a new judicial commission? Are one-roof reforms justified equally for administrative and decisional functions? As another example, the effort to reduce backlog and delay and produce a more efficient process in India seems clear enough. Several questions, however, need be addressed. What is meant by "delay"? Do references to delay mean any amount of time or "too much time?"

If independence in Indonesia is not an absolute goal, which measures will achieve the right degree: independent authority over judicial selection, promotion, discipline, transfer, court or case management, management of court resources, or budget and accounting? Or to take the Indian example, how much time should a particular case take to adjudicate? Is the mere reduction of time necessarily efficient?[11] That would depend on the quality of the social outcome produced over the reduced time period (compared to the longer one). Flipping a coin may produce a quick, but arbitrary, outcome, one that would be inefficient in the sense that the time needed, however short, produces no particular social value beyond an arbitrary result.

Independence reforms in Indonesia that insulate the judiciary from potential sources of interference may simultaneously reduce its accountability for corrupt behavior. Similarly, delay reduction reforms may conflict with broader goals to increase access for the society to justice. Perfunctory processes with the political goal of resolving disputes are not necessarily just. The failure to explicate, define, or reconcile potentially conflicting goals renders the success of reforms more elusive.

The frequently embedded, vague, and conflicting aims of contemporary justice reforms and the resulting inability to define and monitor success profoundly impede their implementation. The inability to articulate and reconcile competing aims thus weakens reform processes.

The Blueprint for an Indonesian judicial commission and other policy papers recently published,[12] for example, fail to provide a consistent explication of the desired outcomes of the outlined initiatives. Missing objectives range from the intrinsic qualities of judicial performance reformers seek to inculcate (impartiality), to the social products to be produced (normatively forceful decisions) or the outcomes of better judicial performance for society (predictability of legal regulation of commerce, enforcement of fundamental rights, mediating tensions between the center and the regions). Although this is an understandable consequence of historical circumstances in Indonesia, the inability to articulate objectives clearly and consistently weakens the entire reform enterprise in three critical respects.[13]

First, the absence of objectives makes it more difficult to inspire support and confidence for these costly endeavors. Translating proposals into real benefits for the judiciary, the political branches, and the society at large helps to get necessary buy-in from the career judiciary, to attract the necessary budgetary allocations (from Parliament and foreign donors), and to cultivate sufficient public support for the judiciary (as a primary, though frequently overlooked, source of professional pride in the office and political will to invest in judicial institutions).

Second, without clearly articulated objectives, the anticipated or actual success or failure of any particular proposal cannot be measured. The best (or even second-best) proposals for the judiciary, from selection to discipline, education to training, transfer to promotion, budgetary accountability to flexibility, are nearly impossible to justify without a clear notion of what is to be achieved, what social outcomes judges are expected to produce (discovery of truth, settlement of disputes, normative pronouncements on critical issues) and to what end (predictability for commerce, peace in society, or social equality and fundamental rights). Within particular areas of discussion, this common problem limits the ability to assess particular proposals. Without a compass of aims to guide the reform, any particular change in direction appears arbitrary, thus rendering reforms that are much more difficult to sustain.

Third, without articulating intrinsic or instrumental values (some possibly in tension with others), it is difficult to get a sense of priority. For example, are strong independence measures necessarily consistent with accountability through discipline and supervision? Is substantive law training as important as programs on the art of decision making? The Supreme Court's recently published papers on reform do not express a strong sense of priority.[14] The current reform plans thus offer little guidance. Accordingly, strategic choices on both scope and sequence of particular interventions are difficult to make or justify. For example, the Blueprint defers discussion of the basic norms of judicial behavior, whether purely ethical canons of integrity or more general notions of competence. Questions of institutional allocation of disciplinary matters (to the Supreme Court, a commission, or criminal justice system), the particular process to be applied (formal or informal, private or public), the sanctions to be applied (prison, dismissal, demotion, salary reduction, mandatory transfer, public or private admonishment, required retraining) cannot be answered intelligibly without clear expectations of minimum ethical and competent behavior and the correlative risks of over- or underenforcement.

F. POOR DESIGN CHOICES

Broad exposure to alternative models and specific features capable of adaptation and manipulation liberates contemporary thinking, punctures local dogmas, and liberates reformers to think beyond overly simplistic models. In-depth exposure to the variety of other systems (both real and contemplated) also provides legal reformers with a comprehensive check-list of detailed considerations to be addressed in a sustainable reform initiative. Many legal communities, however, have been severely isolated from this comparative exposure and have little basis for imagining the range of possible alternatives. Many are closed to the idea of drawing on the experience of all but a few nations with whom they identify (e.g., the United States, former colonial powers with whom origins are shared, or neighboring countries with similar value systems or levels of development).[15] The common isolation or narrow focus of legal communities produces a parochial perspective that limits the comparative range of conceivable remedies. Parochial perspectives also lead to the unwitting, wholesale acceptance of foreign models.

The procedural design for mediation in India provides a vivid example of this problem. Section 89 of the Civil Procedure Code contemplates that the judge (presumably the judge assigned to the case) should first determine whether there exist "elements of a settlement which may be acceptable to the parties."[16] If so, the court then "shall formulate the terms of settlement and give them to the parties for their observations."[17] Third, "after receiving the observations of the parties, the court may reformulate the terms of a possible settlement"[18] and refer the same for arbitration,[19] conciliation, judicial settlement, including through *lok adalat* or mediation.[20]

These provisions, drawn almost verbatim from the conciliation provisions of the Arbitration and Conciliation Act (1996),[21] based on the UNCITRAL model law, itself derived from mainly the European practice of conciliation, raise several issues that reflect a lack of consideration of basic design choices. First, the timing (after written statement, when parties are examined, before framing of issues, or as a precondition to an application for *ad interim* relief) of Section 89 through a case management proceeding of some kind remains an open question. An answer to the question of timing depends on an assessment of when the perceived incentives for settlement are highest (as a function of a sense of jeopardy or the early mutual gains of saving costs).

Second, it is unclear how the judge will determine whether there are sufficient elements of a settlement to justify the investment of time. Every case has elements of settlement; however, these are difficult to identify without reviewing the case and questioning the parties about their underlying interests. Without further guidance, these cost-benefit decisions will be difficult to make. This difficulty may be resolved either by using Order X (1a), which simply authorized the court to direct the parties to one of several alternatives,[22] as a primary and independent mechanism for triggering a choice of alternative dispute resolution (ADR) venues or by sequencing the types of cases in which Section 89 processes will be employed as a matter of course (rather than discretion). The use of Order X, however, has not yet attracted serious, independent attention.[23]

Third, if the Section 89 judge is the same one who presides over the trial, the parties are not likely to share observations that would narrow the differences between them. There is no Section 89 provision for the confidentiality of these observations, and even if there were, the parties would be understandably reluctant to express weaknesses in their positions or to suggest compromise for fear of appearing weak to the other side. Assignment of a special Section 89 (or settlement) judge within the court and ensuring the confidentiality of the party observations may help to alleviate these concerns; however, the small number of judges in most courts (one or two) may preclude the specialization as settlement judges.

Finally, it is unclear what impact the specific terms defined by the judge will have on a subsequent settlement through mediation or other techniques. If the settlement discussions lead the parties away from or beyond the specified terms, they may worry about the enforceability of the settlement agreement. In contrast, if they constrain their negotiations to the specified terms, the likelihood of settlement may be significantly diminished. Again, instead of the judicial conciliation process contemplated by Section 89, treating Order X (1a) as an independent provision for triggering Section 89 ADR options (a–d) may provide a quicker, cleaner, or more versatile bridge to mediation and other Section 89 alternatives that promote settlement. Order X is frequently overlooked, however, as a potential solution to some of these procedural problems.

G. WEAK THEORIES OF INSTITUTIONAL CHANGE

Common approaches to reform design vary widely from a more internally driven reform by negation of putative causes or externally motivated reform by transplantation of foreign prototypes. First, reforms conceived as blunt negations of the status quo are not likely to be successful.[24] For example, wresting control from the executive branch over administrative authority over the courts will not necessarily lead to impartial decision making in Indonesia. The mere establishment of greater controls on the management of cases or the growth of consensual alternatives to trial may not necessarily have any positive impact on backlogs in India.

Second, foreign models, as merely copied or transplanted into the system, are equally unlikely to render success. The argument that transplants are easy and common (though based on substantial historical evidence) profoundly undervalues the relationship between law and external social objectives.[25] The success of foreign models is frequently exaggerated. Most judicial commissions or councils (inspiring the Indonesian reforms) have not achieved their stated objectives,[26] and it is far from clear whether the adoption of mediation (inspiring the Indian reforms) has been critical to the reduction of backlog and delay. Furthermore, the adoption of foreign models as prototypes, i.e., package deals to accept or reject (but rarely to alter) leaves reformers with fewer options for picking and choosing among features consistent with the needs of local circumstances. Instead of disaggregating functional features of new institutions (commissions,[27] mediation systems), reforms frequently come with a prototypical dogma (e.g., the executive and legislative branch should have no representation in a judicial commission,[28] or mediation must be purely facilitative).[29] Furthermore, institutions are frequently grafted onto other institutions without comprehensive consideration of the system in its entirety (e.g., the use of the judicial commission for integrity violations without considering the criminal justice process in Indonesia as an alternative, repressive anticorruption strategy).[30] Such reforms often lack any workable theory of institutional or behavioral change. Here, too, the Indonesian judicial commission and Indian mediation reforms provide useful illustrations.

(i) Indonesian Blueprints The Blueprint for an Indonesian judicial commission does not express any working or testable theory of institutional or behavioral change. Which factors are likely in which time frame to tip judicial behavior to the desired set of outcomes: eradicating corruption, increasing technical competence, work efficiency, or the publication of normative resolutions of key legal issues?[31] Which effective combinations of incentives and deterrents or limits on opportunities for illicit be-

havior, such as increases in salaries or more repressive disciplinary interventions, will have an effect on ethical behavior?

The current Indonesian judicial reform strategy offers weak responses to these questions of scope, timing, and success indicators. First, the overwhelming scope of issues to be addressed creates a serious predicament. On the one hand, reforms may take a fully comprehensive approach and get stretched way too thin. Trying to do everything often means not accomplishing anything particularly well. On the other hand, reforms may be more selective and therefore necessarily ignore key areas, which, if left unattended, will undermine useful efforts elsewhere. These current reform plans do not address this problem or determine which of these many initiatives (the commission, judicial training, human resources policy, or financial management) will make the greatest impact (without easily being undermined by less attention to other areas).

Second, and related to scope, timing is critical. Whatever is done must be pursued according to a particular time frame. Assuming that everything cannot be achieved at the same time (due to limitations of focus and resources), different initiatives must be sequenced in an intelligent way (i.e., by reference to priorities, higher-impact/lower-risk interventions, cost, or other factors). With some exceptions,[32] the current plans do not address timing questions. Indeed, a quick survey of the Supreme Court policy papers and their appendices (with tables noting the term of reform activities) shows a very high percentage of proposals timed for the same moment (i.e., one year after the one-roof transfer).[33] Notwithstanding the lack of sequencing, the choice of a time for these important initiatives is itself problematic. In particular, the Blueprint defers serious strategic planning decisions (including the sequencing of reform activities) to a point in time that may be way too late. Without much explanation (limited time, limited resources), the vast number of concrete steps are to be taken up to one year after one-roof unification. The Blueprint acknowledges the lack of a transitional reform process in contrast to the "mounting homework";[34] however, the documents do not themselves achieve what they say is most needed. In architectural terms, the judiciary will work under one roof in August 2004, without having built the necessary foundation and weight-retaining walls to support that enormous administrative burden.

Finally, the articulation of success indicators leaves a great deal to be desired. As emphasized above, this is largely a consequence of the failure to articulate objectives. In particular, the Blueprint and related policy papers tend to express success indicators in terms of decrees and the establishment of programs, instead of the impacts from these programs. This provides a superficial set of indicators, and also leaves open the question of workable monitoring devices capable of determining whether the interventions are working well or not (e.g., achieving greater justice for society, increasing competence, reducing corruption, recruiting greater talent, increasing public trust, resolving more cases, spending money more efficiently, or gaining greater discipline in budgeting).

(ii) Indian Mediation as Diversion of Caseload Similarly, the introduction of mediation into India, inspired and guided heavily by U.S. influence, is presumed to be an effective remedy to backlog and delay. One Supreme Court justice expressed the sentiments of many when he opined: "I sincerely feel that even if 25% of the cases pending in the courts are resolved through ADR mechanism, the judiciary would be able not only to control the docket explosion but also clear the backlog."[35] Even though few challenge this conclusion, a more thorough examination of the comparative theory implied in this view of the reform would be worthwhile.[36]

Imagine the legal system in the metaphor of a funnel designed to sift through small and large stones in an effort to produce precious gems. If the society pours stones into the wide mouth of the funnel at the top, the system will process them through a narrow channel, producing the gems through the narrow mouth at the bottom. Assume that the stones en masse represent all of the legally cognizable disputes in society, and the gems that come through the narrow neck represent judicial decisions as the articulation of public norms that then guide the society in its public and private behavior. Further assume that the purpose of the funnel is to find and process the gems, not (by itself) to resolve every single dispute in the society.

Now imagine that, because of the sheer scale of the number of disputes in society and the unchanged, narrow neck of the funnel, the stones (and even smaller jewels) are creating a bottleneck, and too many disputes put into the funnel are not allowing the valuable ones (those worth the public investment of the courts) to pass through the system within an expected time period.

Generally, legal systems apply three strategies to this bottleneck. First, they try to prevent more stones from entering the funnel, but here they often try to do this by imposing increases in court costs or creating other incentives (cost shifting) to prevent claims from entering the system. Such prevention measures (court costs in particular—the cause of disturbances by the bar in the spring of 2003 in the state of Gujarat) are crude and unjust tools for preventing backlogs. They are crude because they do not contemplate that either cases of great normative value may never get to the courts because the claimant cannot afford the costs or cases of no normative value brought by parties who can afford the costs may still clog the system. They are also unjust simply because for poor litigants these costs impede access to the justice system.

Second, legal systems employ alternative dispute resolution techniques to divert cases from the narrow neck of the funnel. Alternatives create valves, escape hatches, exits from the system, thus (or so the theory goes) taking pressure off the system by moving cases out before they need to be processed at trial or through appeals.

Third, legal systems employ streamlining, tracking, and other interventions to manage the internal operation of the courts (court management) and the particular cases (case management). These mechanisms require infrastructural improvements (e.g., court technology for case and event tracking) and cleverly calibrated investments of invaluable court time to manage cases efficiently.

In the early stages of these efficiency-driven reforms (aside from the undesirable litigation-prevention techniques described above), court systems may face a troubling paradox. As the society internalizes the signal that the system is working more efficiently, those who would not have bothered with filing litigations (for fear of cost or the time involved) may newly seek the court's services. This means that at least in the early stages antibacklog measures may actually increase court filings. This phenomenon is similar to the paradox of traffic reduction strategies. City planners create wider, better, more versatile networks of roads and highways, which then gives a greater incentive to more people to drive on them. Thus, antitraffic interventions can result in more traffic.[37] The inability to understand the dynamics of the interaction between the reforms and the behavior of litigants and their lawyers carries a large risk of frustrating at least the expectations, if not the overarching goals, of any particular change. The successful introduction of court mediation in India may inspire a crushing demand from people who would otherwise have internalized their legal injuries. Thus, here too, Indian mediation reform reflects weak theories of institutional change.

H. UNDERESTIMATING COLLECTIVE ACTION PROBLEMS

In this last regard, frequent conflicts between individual and collective interests demand critical attention. Generally, reform depends heavily on the participation of local legal opinion leaders and practitioners. Short of full occupation and micromanagement by a foreign power or international institution, external pressure and assistance can go only so far toward this end.[38] The communities in most need of effective reform, however, tend to have the lowest levels of participation in the reform process.[39] Without widespread participation in reform by primary participants in the operation of the system, the risks of nonimplementation or unintended consequences substantially increase.[40]

As Linn Hammergren put it, "Justice reform also implies political change in its broadest sense."[41] Reform therefore depends on a political strategy that can overcome the powerful forces in support of the status quo. Few experts in judicial systems have the political sophistication to develop a political strategy, however, and reformers thus have difficulty aligning political leadership at the top with the demand for change at the street level.

Communities that have not had the opportunity to determine the design of their own legal system have a comparative disadvantage in reform. Legal cultures[42] accustomed to exclusively top-down reform tend to be passive in developing their own views and complacent in holding authorities accountable to plans for implementation. Common failures result in part from the failure to understand the internal dynamics of the judicial process from the bottom up. Court reform in Indonesia or India that does not contemplate the incentive structures underlying professional behavior is not likely to succeed.[43]

Systems that reward corruption and delay more than they do integrity and efficiency create nearly insuperable conflicts for reform minded individuals. Alone, they are nearly powerless to effectuate change. The single judge who refuses a bribe or the individual lawyer who expedites a case against the wishes of his client is unlikely to make a significant impact on systemic behavior, and resource deficiencies, political insecurity, and top-down political cultures impede the necessary forms of collective action.

For example, the path to mediation reform in India is riddled with obstacles that arise from the vantage point of participants in the justice process. Exposure within the legal community to these facilitated negotiation processes, though spreading rapidly, remains limited. Judges harbor understandable apprehensions about the relationship between mediation and the formal judicial process and deep skepticism over the application of mediation to a wide variety of Indian legal disputes (particularly outside the commercial area). Furthermore, lawyers see alternative dispute resolution (ADR) as a code for an "alarming drop in revenues." Settlement means fewer court appearances and a reduction in fees for service. Lawyers may object to ADR because of the resulting opportunity costs they associate with resolving matters (and thus losing the ability to charge clients for their work over many years). As previously noted, legislated reforms of the civil procedure code were immediately suspended in consequence of nationwide lawyer strikes because the views, practices, and interests of the system's key participants were not taken into account in developing the reform.[44] Comparative research in Europe has shown that the neglect of taking lawyer compensation schemes into account may completely undermine civil justice reform aimed at containing cost or delay.[45]

I. IGNORING RESOURCE LIMITATIONS

These normative, conceptual, empirical, and political problems are compounded by severe deficits in the human and financial resources a judicial system can attract through either the public or private sector.[46] Human resource deficiencies are critical, and ignoring them is thus perilous. Lawyers in many societies are still at a relatively low rung of professional rankings, and legal educators struggle to attract talented students. This is changing in many dysfunctional systems, particularly those transitioning to a new market system; however, the talented students attracted to law, in Russia for example, are interested in transactional settings far removed from the practical operation of the courts. Judicial positions are far less desirable than one would presume (from a U.S. context, in which the role of the judge in society produces a form of psychic income that is unavailable to judges in systems that give them weaker civil service roles).[47]

Even if one could solve these recruitment problems, limited financial resources pose an additional impediment. Experts bemoan the low level of public financing in the courts; however, beyond intentional neglect, political institutions may be reluctant to invest in institutions that function so partially or poorly. Lawyers in these systems complain about the way they struggle to make a living, and judges always complain about their salaries as substantially less than those of the bar. It is unlikely, however, that a legislature or clientele would reward a judiciary or bar when there is very little perceived social value rendered by their services. These resource problems are both cause and consequence of the conditions reforms aim to redress.

J. CONCLUSION

Given these impediments and conditions, reforms frequently fail. Failure may take at least three different forms. First, reforms frequently render disappointing results. Judicial commissions or councils aimed at improving judicial performance for example, appear vulnerable to the same problems they are designed to address: political interference, corruption, and bureaucratic delay.[48] Case management and alternative dispute resolution reforms in the United States have not demonstrated any appreciable, multidistrict, universal impact on savings of cost or time.[49]

Second, interventions for one purpose frequently undermine other equally important objectives. Strong judicial independence measures, such as the one-roof reform in Indonesia, may further insulate the judiciary from anticorruption and other accountability measures.[50] Efficiency measures, for example, that integrate alternative dispute resolution may undermine values of publicity (because settlements are confidential) and normativity (because no judgment is produced to shape the law applicable to others).[51]

Third, reforms may completely backfire. According to a former chief justice of the Indian Supreme Court, the court's refusal to allow the executive branch to play any role in judicial promotions has led to more interference, not less.[52] Severely repressive anticorruption measures, such as in the People's Republic of China, may drive illicit behavior further underground and enhance those with power and discretion in those systems to extract rents from those vulnerable to attack.[53] Additionally, as discussed above, efficiency measures may have a paradoxical effect: by making the courts and appended processes more attractive to disputing parties, reformers may unintentionally attract larger numbers of litigants who would otherwise have settled or lumped their disputes. Thus, antibacklog measures may unintentionally create new backlogs.[54]

Accordingly, the frequency and probability of reform disappointments pose an additional impediment: the psychological internalization of likely failure. The mere expectation of reform failure deflates the political and financial support necessary to motivate institutional and behavioral changc. After repeated failures, rhetoric in support of reform rings hollow, and desperation turns into hopelessness.

B. Comparative Dilemmas in Justice Reform

Given the discouraging conditions, urgent needs, and the conceptual, financial, and political obstacles, reformers (at a systemic level) and participants in reform (at an individual level) frequently face a series of vexing dilemmas, i.e., undesirable choices between sets of at least two unsatisfactory alternatives. These dilemmas range widely in their variety: from undesirable design to method choices, from social dilemmas to metadilemmas (i.e., unsatisfactory choices of antidilemma strategies).

In designing their reforms, should reformers in Indonesia stress judicial independence or accountability in the formation of a judicial commission?[55] Should Indian justice reformers emphasize settlement to reduce disposal times regardless of outcome or adjudication accompanied by severe delays in the adaptation of mediation to the legal process? Which design of a judicial commission in Indonesia or mediation systems in India will do best to realize shared aims?

Each choice presupposes a set of implicitly comparative methodological issues. In the choice of a reform strategy or method, how should valuations of independence and accountability or justice and delay reduction be comparatively weighed and maximized? Do reformers in Indonesia sufficiently understand the nature of corruption by reference to key factors in the judicial system (ethics or incentives) or do Indian leaders appreciate the many complex factors that contribute to the country's notorious delays (the unmet need for courts or their dysfunction) and a national backlog of nearly 25 million cases in order to move forward with responsive reforms? Should reformers draw on foreign expertise (which is drawn from different and thus potentially misleading systemic contexts) or local expertise (which by its nature is parochial and less integrative of global experience)? Should reformers work from the top down (concentrating on centers of power and authority that might be too far removed from the realities on the ground) or from the bottom up (focusing on critically important behaviors, without cultivating the support of leadership within paternalistic political cultures)? How much must reformers understand (through qualitative empirical research) about the judicial system before they make recommendations in order to limit these failures?

Finally, with potentially conflicting goals and imperfect information, at which point or threshold do leaders or participants decide to support or resist reform? To what extent should reformers invest resources in support of reform (without sufficient levels of demand) at the risk of waste? Or should they wait for demand to bubble up (when the percolation of demand may itself require an infusion of resources)? Should reform be more a supply-side process of providing computers and training or a demand-side approach that listens to what people in the system say they need? What are the comparative risks of moving ahead with vague valuations and imperfect valuations underlying shaky reform proposals compared to the ever-escalating costs of maintaining the status quo?

These valuation, information, and threshold problems present a series of comparative design and method dilemmas for the reformer. From this perspective, each fork in the road to reform can be seen as presenting a choice of (at least partially) undesirable pathways to reach a particular reform objective.

The following discussion sketches and illustrates three different types of dilemmas frequently confronted by reformers. Chapter 6, below, will outline and apply a series of antidilemma strategies. The discussion will continuously draw upon a variety of national examples, with a particular focus on the Indonesian and Indian reform contexts.

1. Design Dilemmas

A. INDEPENDENCE OR ACCOUNTABILITY

Many legal experts deem judicial independence and accountability[56] (a code word for anticorruption, anti-incompetence, or antidelay) to be mutually contradictory or defeating.[57] Judicial elections (in many U.S. states),[58] disciplinary systems (as advanced in Indonesia),[59] retraining certification requirements (as pursued in the country Georgia),[60] or court management interventions (as applied in Israel)[61] may be seen in certain corners as potentially serious limits on judicial independence. On the other hand, internal disciplinary systems (watchmen watching the watchmen)[62] in Turkey,[63] life tenure (regardless of ineffectiveness and inefficiency) in Italy,[64] or individual independence of the judge to manage a calendar or caseload (regardless of delay) in the United States before

1980[65] may badly undermine the quality of judicial performance. Accordingly, reformers confront a strongly perceived dilemma, if not a conceptual dichotomy, between enhancing judicial independence (at the expense of accountability) and enhancing accountability (at the expense of independence).

B. JUSTICE OR SETTLEMENT

Both reformers and scholars in the United States[66] and beyond[67] regard delay as a critical problem in the administration of justice. Over the past decade, reports of excessive delay come from a diverse set of national environments, including Chile,[68] the Czech Republic,[69] Italy,[70] Egypt,[71] Hungary,[72] the People's Republic of China,[73] and the United Kingdom.[74] Delay tends to discount the value of legal claims, imbalance the leverage of claimants and respondents, corrode public trust in judicial institutions, create perverse incentives for noncompliance with public and private obligations, and fertilize the medium for corrupt practices.

Many systems struggle to bring justice to the broader society through a neglected court system. Only a subset of legally cognizable claims reaches the courts, and even those linger for years, awaiting public pronouncements of normative judgments that resolve the formal dispute. The condition of backlog and delay and the use of consensual alternatives to trial present a perplexing design dilemma. Should the courts emphasize settlement to reduce delay while simultaneously forsaking the publicity and normativity that judgments produce? Or should the courts shun alternatives while meritorious cases remain buried in the interminable queue? Is settlement (private, confidential, interest-based, calibrated results) anathema to justice through judgments (normative, public, position-based, win-lose outcomes)? Furthermore, as observed above, is there a relationship between antidelay reform and the likely increase in delay, when successful reforms attract more people in search of justice to the courts, thus putting additional administrative pressure on insufficient resources?

2. Method Dilemmas

A. INCREMENTAL OR SYSTEMIC

Reformers also recognize issues arising from the chosen scope and sequence of a reform. To what extent should the reforms be sequenced gradually[75] as increments or aggressively pursued on a comprehensive, systemic basis?[76]

Narrowly defined reforms seek to reform systems in increments. Incremental reforms are less costly, may be more easily controlled to render success, and tend to manage expectations effectively by postponing the ambition for systemic reform. Pilot projects, strategic sequencing, and procedural (even interstitial) innovations short of legislation frequently appeal to reformers for these reasons. Pilots permit learning from mistakes short of a nationwide failure. Strategic sequencing of small to big reforms allows capacity to be built over time. Interstitial administrative procedures rarely require a time-consuming legislative process. For each of these reasons, incremental reform is perceived as desirable.

Notwithstanding the popularity of gradual approaches, however, incremental reforms tend to fail for systemic reasons. Ethics training for judges and lawyers in a corrupt system do little to reverse the underlying motivations for the receipt, if not solicitation, of bribes. The appointment of outsiders may not permeate the corporatist culture of a career judiciary. Mediation pilots do not touch upon the underlying reasons and motivations for furthering delay. Where incentives of judges, lawyers, and at least one of the parties are weak, mediation is unlikely to succeed. Failure at incremental approaches leaves reformers wondering whether they should have been more ambitious and less superficial in the scope of intervention.

The downside of incremental strategies, however, does not mean that systemic reforms are necessarily a superior alternative. Systemic reform (including attempts to start from scratch) is extremely difficult to carry out in practice. First, the resource requirements are staggering. Second, the assumptions underlying the effective replacement of old with new wine are frequently false. The architecture of the proverbial new bottle may be changed, but the old wine may carry the same taste. Even in cases where court personnel can be fired, it may be naïve to presume that new personnel are available, learn quickly enough to take their place, and will avoid deeply internalized behavioral patterns. Finally, shock therapy (as in the notoriously Russian example of more shock than therapy) underestimates the need to prepare for sudden change. True, changing from the left side to the right side of the road cannot be done gradually (without causing head-on collisions even in the early stages); however, each country that has made the change successfully spent ample time preparing the roads and population for the sudden switch. For these reasons, the choice of incremental or systemic change produces a dilemma for thoughtful reformers. Each alternative, however desirable, carries significant risks of failure.

B. TOP-DOWN OR BOTTOM-UP

Will reform begin from the top down or proceed from the bottom up? Top-down interventions may ensure the support of the government or key opinion leaders; however, resistance among participants in the judicial system can easily undermine the intended implementation. Anticorruption reform in Indonesia may do little to alter incentives on the ground for honest behavior and, by increasing the disincentives without addressing underlying conditions, may drive illicit activity further underground. Likewise, antidelay reforms in India may instigate protests and harden unwillingness to participate in newly designed procedures. Bottom-up, grassroots reform efforts, on the other hand, may fall on deaf ears. Without foundational legislation and budgetary allocations for necessary costs, without the professional and political security provided by the government's imprimatur, without the assent of leaders in patriarchal political cultures, bottom-up processes may stagnate on the bottom with no upward movement whatsoever.

C. EXTERNAL (FOREIGN) OR INTERNAL (DOMESTIC)

Method dilemmas also perplex the use of foreign assistance or financial assistance. Should reforming communities draw on foreign expertise (based on perceived foreign advancements in reform theory or experience in successful reform efforts)? Leaders and experts from foreign countries exhibiting strong judicial independence and integrity or short disposition times and rigorous mediation systems may be in much demand. Or should reformers shun foreign expertise as of dubious value based on overblown theoretical claims and falsely celebrated views of foreign success?

Notwithstanding the seemingly insatiable interest among elites in foreign models and big-name experts, this critique of external approaches to justice reform is forceful, even within the United States.[77] Many observers have illuminated difficulties encountered in failures of the "law and development" movement of the 1960s and 1970s.[78] Deeply influenced by this critique, Franck admonished (some thirty years ago): "What is needed is help given and taken, with mutual respect, and without strings, to promising projects, backed by responsible individuals and institutions."[79] More than twenty-five years ago, Merryman effectively summarized these problems in a review of law and development scholarship. He cited four critical weaknesses in the export of American legal models to the developing world: (1) unfamiliarity with the host legal system; (2) the absence of a respectable theory; (3) immunity from consequences and an artificial access to power; and (4) a resulting tendency to project and impose U.S. attitudes and ideas.[80]

More than a dozen years ago, Alvarez revisited these issues, albeit a bit more optimistically, in a thorough review of "rule of law" programs administered by USAID in the 1980s.[81] Most recently, in *Aiding Democracy Abroad: The Learning Curve,*[82] Tom Carothers skillfully captured the common features of a diverse range of democracy-aid projects funded by the U.S. government, more specifically USAID, as an external model. Specifically, he identified several related problems in the external model, including a lack of humility,[83] superficial assessment,[84] simplistic modeling,[85] a misplaced emphasis on ends rather than process,[86] and weak evaluative tools[87] and commitments.[88] Given the weight of this critique, is there any role for foreign experts, whose expertise, however arguably strong, is, in a word, almost always foreign?[89]

The dilemma of whose advice to seek or accept is related to the practical issue of cost. The process and implementation of effective reform (especially that contemplated by foreign experts from wealthy countries) can be expensive. Frequently, both internal and external sources of financial support are required. Domestic matching or counterpart funding or in-kind contributions of time and resources reflect a positive internal commitment to reform. Internal sources by themselves, however, are often insufficient. Thus, reforming communities need to draw on available external funding from the "donor community." Understandably, the donor community requires assurances that money invested in reform is well and effectively spent. This dynamic frequently poses a catch-22 scenario. The host community needs resources and expertise to develop an implementation strategy worthy of donor funding. The donor community, however, conditions funding on the development of an effective and credible reform strategy.

D. RESEARCH OR REFORM

Recently, it has become fashionable to insist that justice reform have an empirical basis.[90] As argued above, self-awareness of the nature of the problems in their practical operation is undeniably critical to reform. The equivalence of empiricism with statistics, however, leaves much to be desired. Statistical empiricists tend to favor examining phenomena that are easily measured. Thus, there is a strong tendency to avoid exploring qualities that are difficult to quantify or operationalize. That is, despite the immediate benefits of the data, the deficiency of complementary, qualitative assessments often raises more questions than the data can answer. For example, a recent World Bank study in Argentina and Mexico found far less backlog and delay than previously estimated because of a great number of cases that were eventually "abandoned."[91] The study, however, does not express any evaluation of the merits of those dropped cases, any diagnosis of why they were dropped (e.g., an early failure at obtaining injunctive relief, an internalization of the likelihood of an endless delay, the litigants ran out of money used to pay off the registrar to keep the case moving), or of the social or economic effect of their abandonment (noncompliance with contract and property rights, increase in the risk and cost of doing business).[92] Notwithstanding the merits of gathering data to support or refute mere perception, without a qualitative evaluation, it is far from clear what to make of these "empirical" findings.

The limits of current methodologies for knowing the phenomena to be addressed and the limited information available leaves reformers with an additionally perplexing dilemma: whether to move forward without an adequate understanding, thereby increasing the risks of failure, or to maintain (at least temporarily) the status quo until further research is completed, thereby increasing the opportunity costs of inaction in the face of pressing needs.

3. The Social Dilemma of the Individual and the Collective

Beyond these design and method dilemmas, a common social dilemma impedes reform. As discussed above, reforms often accentuate a conflict between the interests of the individual (or some group of individuals) and the collective. It would be difficult to find an Indonesian who believes that corruption is good for the country. Likewise, the Indian population, including judges and lawyers, if asked, would be universal in its condemnation of delay in the courts. No one (beyond providing more empathetic accounts) justifies or defends the staggering backlog or protracted disposition times as a positive condition. If everyone agrees, why does reform still seem so impossible?

What people want for the collective and how they actually behave as individuals (and why) pose distinctly different questions. Individual judges, lawyers, and litigants in India, Indonesia, and elsewhere act according to a set of conditions and incentives that run counter to the reduction of delay, corruption, and other problems in the justice system, even while recognizing that this unsatisfactory level of performance is not in their collective interest. This creates a social dilemma in which the pursuit of individual interests compromises collective values and the pursuit of collective aims may not be in the individual (at least short-term) interest of the system's primary participants.

C. Conclusion

These critical observations underline how difficult it is to work through such predicaments. The seemingly insuperable obstacles, expected failures, and the perplexing nature of design, method, and social dilemmas (depressingly) reinforce deep pessimism about the prospects for reform. Even well-justified pessimism, however, is not an option for reformers: to give up conceptually what is so difficult to achieve financially and politically is to doom hundreds of millions of people to a society that offers no meaningful access to justice. The following chapter, therefore, is an attempt to breathe new conceptual life into the suffocating, narrow space between the rocks and hard places of justice reform.

Employing many of the analytical tools developed in part I, chapter 6 offers two novel contributions to contemporary thinking about justice reform. First, the discussion explores the metaphor of emergent systems as an antidote to the submergence of the most neglected branch described in chapter 4. Second, it articulates a series of antidilemma strategies in an attempt to drive a wedge between the perceived rocks and hard places of many justice reform initiatives. Throughout the discussion, greater attention to the clarification of aims, the selection of key features, and attention to decision-making thresholds will shed light not only on the infirmities of contemporary reform but also on more promising paths ahead. With these two modest contributions, chapter 6 might help justice systems to emerge from their many troubling dilemmas.

6

Emergence from the Dilemmas

With the foregoing conceptual, economic, and political impediments to reform and the predicaments they create, the emergence of justice reform appears extremely unlikely. How will judicial systems like those of Indonesia, India, and so many other countries emerge from these nearly paralytic dilemmas of justice reform? And what help, if any, is greater attention to methodological comparisons of alternative designs and methods of reform?

This chapter provides a set of preliminary, modest answers to these two pressing questions. Proceeding from the description of the neglected condition of submerging judicial systems in chapter 4, part A examines the very process (and metaphor)[1] of emergence, with an emphasis on the self-organizing properties of legal cultures. The metaphor serves as both a source of humility and inspiration for global justice reform initiatives. In response to the types of dilemmas that frequently perplex justice reform efforts, part B presents a series of conceptual and social strategies that might help to improve, if not transcend, the apparently constrained and unsatisfactory choices. Instead of a recipe book of myriad solutions to common problems, this discussion presents conceptual strategies intended to address deep predicaments and to enhance the quality of particular reform decisions. These strategies draw on insights advanced in chapter 3 that stress the importance of defining clear aims, choosing the right variables, and identifying thresholds for distinguishing (and here choosing) among alternatives.

A. Emergence

Reformers are often blind to the self-organizing dynamics of legal cultures. The notion that justice systems are less permeable to intervention from above or from without is anathema to the work of both leaders within the system and experts external to it. Therefore, reformers tend to think that leadership and correct designs are vital, thus underemphasizing the leadership qualities of the "followers," the primary participants in the system, and the peer-to-peer social processes of interaction that institutionalize desirable practices. For this reason, it may be helpful to emphasize, by way of a provocative metaphor drawn from a broad body of nonlegal literature,[2] the emergent (or here submergent) qualities of legal cultures.

In emergent systems,[3] (e.g., schools of fish or ant colonies)[4] relatively primitive agents produce a higher level of intelligent, systemic behavior. In contrast to the extraordinary emergent properties of simple biological organisms, institutions responsible for administering justice appear to have submergent properties, in which relatively intelligent agents[5] (e.g., judges, lawyers, citizens) produce a lower level of systemic behavior: frequent political manipulation of judicial decision, systemic corruption, massive delays, and so on. What are some examples of emergent systems, and why are they at all analogous to justice systems?

1. Celebrating Slime

Imagine a small maze with four possible routes, and planted pieces of food at two of the exits.[6] Now picture slime mold in the maze. (Slime mold is a very primitive organism with no centralized brain of any kind.) What are the chances that the slime mold, with no apparent cognitive resources, will find the most efficient route to the food? Practically nil? Hopeless?

Remarkably, in an experiment designed two years ago by a Japanese scientist, Toshiyuki Nakagaki, the slime mold solved this puzzle.[7] Who knew that slime mold could move?!? Scientists have long observed slime mold moving along a forest floor as conditions in moisture and temperature change. Under inhospitable conditions, slime mold act as single organisms, but when the weather is cooler, they enjoy a larger food supply and move as a coordinated group, exhibiting characteristics of a single entity.[8]

How does slime mold do this? It releases a substance known as cyclic AMP, which, when released by each cell, sends signals to its neighbors, resulting in a system of positive feedback. For many years, scientists looked for a kind of leading cell that ordered the other cells to begin aggregating, but no one could find evidence of the putative pacesetter.[9]

Nearly thirty years ago, however, Evelyn Fox Keller (a physicist and biologist) and Lee A. Segel (an applied mathematician), drawing on Alan Turing's use of mathematical patterns to show how complex organisms organize themselves without any master planner, demonstrated that the slime mold emerged from simple to complex, from individual to group behavior.[10] This was among the first discoveries in a new body of work ranging from the social science of city culture to artificial intelligence that grasps emergent systems.[11]

Emergent systems solve problems by drawing on masses of extremely simple elements. From a systemic point of view, these simple elements are dumb: they have no perspective on the collective, nor can they individually design or command group behavior. They are bottom-up systems in the sense that the simple agents on one basic level together produce behavior that as a whole performs tasks on a higher level of sophistication.[12] For example, ants create colonies;[13] urbanites create neighborhoods;[14] simple pattern software recognizes voice or handwriting and even recommends new books.[15]

2. The Analogy

The reader is correct at this point to be deeply skeptical. Did the foregoing discussion just draw some crude analogy between slime and lawyers? Did the author call judges stupid? What does any of this possibly have to do with justice reform? In response, five specific aspects of the slime mold experiment are instructively analogous to the challenge of justice reform.

A. THE PERCEIVED IMPOSSIBILITY OF JUSTICE REFORM

Most readers would never guess that such a simple organism of slime mold could actually solve the maze. Similarly, for the reasons outlined in chapter 5, the chances of effective justice reform in many countries are equally low.

What are the chances that within, say, a ten-year period the Indonesian judicial system will become independent from political interference, rid itself of systemic and systematic manifestations of private corruption, and bring under control a backlog of more than seventeen thousand cases in the Supreme Court?[16] Most observers and participants in the system would respond: the chances are low, and the situation, notwithstanding more recently positive signs, is still "desperate"—if not entirely hopeless.[17]

What is the probability of India's efforts to tackle its overwhelming backlog of 24 million cases and average delays of up to at least twenty years to final disposition,[18] while it struggles to maintain the traditional independence and integrity of its judicial system? Most observers and participants would throw up their hands in despair and internalize the impossibility of success through a growing sense of hopelessness and apathy.

Thus, the first aspect of the analogy is the apparent impossibility of effective justice reform.

B. THE PACESETTER HYPOTHESIS

Of the many impediments to reform, one of the most frequently identified is the lack of political will or leadership.[19] This complaint echoes from common jabber in the corridors of paternalistic political cultures where people defer to the most senior authority for his signal before taking action. In Indonesia, the choice of a Supreme Court chief justice in 2000–01 was considered absolutely critical to the prospects of judicial reform, and the delays in that appointment suspended any progress toward important court reform initiatives.[20] Many experts both outside and within the Indian courts believe that civil justice reform in India will not progress even slightly without an explicit commitment from the chief justice of the Supreme Court. That is, in thinking about reform (or the movement of slime across the forest floor), people are in constant search for a leader as the key to success.[21] Just like the early scientists attempting to solve the slime mold puzzle, reformers continue to look for a pacesetter in the high ranks of the government or judiciary itself to inspire and command effective justice reform.

C. THE VALUE OF BOTTOM-UP PERSPECTIVES

Most observers view a justice system or process on a scale or macrolevel above the actual local behaviors of each of the actors in the system: judges, registrars, administrators, lawyers, clients, the press, politicians, businesspeople, citizens, foreigners, NGOs, and so on. This perception renders a very abstract and formal approach to thinking about the system and its characteristics of independence, integrity, or efficiency.

Observers tend to see independence as the power of judicial review or secure terms of employment (e.g., tenure).[22] Legal experts evaluate integrity by reference to disciplinary systems, codes of ethics, or the number of complaints launched.[23] Reformers comprehend efficiency as annual rates of disposition (how many cases in; how many out) and the operational systems utilized (court and case management for event tracking and accountability).[24]

This top-down or outside-in way of looking at systems provides useful frameworks for capturing a mass of complex, detailed information. Unless top-down, external perspectives are sobered and complemented, however, by a strong dose of bottom-up, internal observation, they tend to be very misleading. In the wide field of comparative characterization, as discussed in part I, binary distinctions of adversarial/inquisitorial, civil/common law, impartial/partial, or fast/slow systems provide frequently misleading views of the entire legal process (e.g., the increasingly strong judicial role in managing adversarial processes, the use of case law as *jurisprudence* in Continental European systems, the anecdote of the extremely time-consuming case that overshadows the typically short one). Secure terms of office provide no guaranty of independence. The mere existence of a disciplinary system provides no assurance of ethical compliance. Data on case disposition rates and times do not measure efficiency, i.e., the value of the social good produced by the particular time and investment.[25] Thus, independence, impartiality, and efficiency depend on some combination of less frequently postulated factors.

Understanding these systems and their practical operation with greater accuracy requires raising basic questions from the ground up: who does what, when, with what level of preparation and resources, and to what effect? Without this kind of bottom-up understanding, we are likely to misunderstand the behavior of the collective system on a higher (or, as I have suggested, possibly even lower) level. Again, using the analogy of emergent systems, if ants produce colonies, and urbanites produce neighborhoods, it may be fair to say that litigants, lawyers, clerks, and judges produce judicial systems and their legal cultures.

The failure to look at systems from the bottom up or the inside out carries significant peril in attempted reforms. For example, court reformers may focus only on new processes of court or case management or alternative dispute resolution, and may not think about the likely behavior of lawyers in response to these innovations. Indeed, comparative research in Europe has shown that the neglect of taking lawyer compensation schemes into account may completely undermine civil justice reform aimed at containing cost or delay.[26]

More affirmatively, the bottom-up perspective has incalculable value in generating new perspectives on age-old issues. Take, for example, the work of Hernando de Soto on access to property rights: had he never taken to the street to hear the barking dogs, he would have not have appreciated the property systems of the poor, albeit outside the shadow of the law.[27] The pathbreaking work of Amartya Sen on development as freedom also looks at issues from the vantage point of the very poor and their actual freedom to survive, to receive nourishment, health care, or an education, or to participate in the polity.[28]

D. LIMITED SYSTEMIC UNDERSTANDING

Are legal actors really as simple or (systemically speaking) stupid as slime? Well, in biological terms, they obviously are neither primitive nor dumb. Yet, as discussed in chapter 5, actors in the legal process have a limited understanding of systemic dynamics. Even the smartest observer of the judicial process is not sufficiently sophisticated or intelligent to understand fully its many complex and self-organizing properties. Thus, arrogance about having a better design or method may be nothing more than an unrealistic command approach doomed to failure. That is to say, no judge or lawyer or other actor working in the system has a full picture or sense of the system as a whole; they experience it in a solipsistic way, guided by their own vantage point and motivations.

Should we expect lawyers or judges to work in ways that they see as contrary to their own professional interest (the age-old agent of the court problem) in order to meet the higher needs of the system as a whole?[29] As certain as we are of an affirmative answer to that question, we should not be surprised if actual behavior falls short of this normative goal. Explaining the shortfall requires a candid distinction between local, individual behavior (and the deeply internalized incentives that shape it) and the global effects such behavior has on the system as a whole. In this sense, lawyers, judges, and others (including especially academics looking on from a distance) have limited understanding from a systemic point of view. Indeed, the individual incentives in some judicial systems are so adverse to widely shared collective values and aims that they may be characterized as submergent. For example, India features an independent judiciary, a well-educated bar, a modern procedural code, and a democratic, market economy. The system, however, produces a quality of systemic behavior that falls far below the positive characteristics of intelligent actors and well-designed codes. The challenge for reformers is to enhance the conditions (or, as students of emergence like to say, "tune the parameters") under which collective intelligence may grasp and multiply local capacities while simultaneously surmounting individual limitations.[30]

E. THE MAZE OF REFORM

Finally, the maze is a useful metaphor for the reformer because there is no straightforward route or algorithm for achieving multiple (and sometimes conflicting) objectives. Indeed, each route seems to offer the likelihood of failure, significant costs, or unintended consequences. To make matters even more daunting, instead of the simple maze used for solving the slime mold problem, we are talking about something much more complex (like the one Harry Potter navigates in the fourth book).[31] It is not merely the relatively simple matter of hunting for food at one or two target points. Indeed, the maze of judicial reform contains multiple exits for those attempting to attain specific, sometimes conflicting, and frequently elusive justice objectives. Navigating the path toward one goal may distance reformers from still another. As a result, reformers are presented with a series of undesirable choices or dilemmas, including determinations of reform design and method, as well as the most profound obstacle of all: the social dilemma of individuals whose short-term self-interest is inconsistent with the articulated values of the collective.

With the foregoing analogy in mind, how might justice systems take the path of the slime mold and emerge from the dilemmas of justice reform? Can ostensibly impossible puzzles be solved through the self-organization of simple (even stupid) participants? Without forsaking the potential value of leadership in social systems, can societies also recognize that leaders emerge only under social conditions that are conducive to or demand their particular role? Can they take full advantage of pursuing bottom-up perspectives in our diagnosis of the pathologies and our prescriptions of the cures? Can they start from a presumption of relative individual stupidity and ignorance and work more collaboratively and with greater humility to create better systems? Can collective, emergent behaviors get reformers through the maze of dilemmas (described in chapter 5) they confront in reform?

B. Comparative Antidilemma Strategies

What are the different ways in which dilemmas (design, method, social) can be approached? The legal literature on reform appears to be silent on the issue. Political scientists and economists explain reform failure as a function of the interests of powerful actors who take advantage of the political process.[32] Dilemmas, especially the paradigmatic one of the two prisoners, are noted frequently in discussions diversely ranging from Native American casinos,[33] to Chinese accession to the WTO,[34] but it seems that even when the dilemmas of reform are central to the inquiry, the subject attracts no serious or formal consideration.

1. Ignoring Competing Values

A first, somewhat crude, and conclusory option is to ignore the dilemma as such. One may dismiss as trivial the competing values that make the preferred option less than fully satisfactory. In other words, the risk of failure of an incremental or systemic approach or the interests of the individual in contrast to the overriding values of the collective could be simply ignored.

Indonesian disciplinary systems for judges may appear to compromise judges' independence, especially if they are themselves subject to abuse. Public admonishment, suspension, and removal are powerful sanctions that could be abused to coerce judges to act in a partial way. Judges in systems like that of Indonesia who have been subjected to such political interference in the past appear (at least initially) to tend to view independence as an absolute value and thus dismiss the value of accountability or overvalue in this view the importance of independence (as a judge once reportedly claimed, even from the law itself).[35]

Similarly, proponents of Indian mediation, as noted above, may trivialize, if not completely ignore, the loss of publicity and normativity, two fundamental benefits of public adjudication. Conversely, opponents may ignore the intrinsic or instrumental values of mediation in attempts to reduce backlogs that prevent public adjudication from proceeding.

2. Sweetening the Deal with Side Payments

A second option is to improve one of the alternatives through incentives or side payments. In other words, when faced with unsatisfactory choices, one may sweeten one of the alternatives. Greater external investments in either an incremental or systemic approach can increase the likelihood of its ultimate success. Finding innovative ways to reward individuals (even through psychic income of honors and awards) for their internalization of social costs in the interest of the collective may help to circumvent the obstacle posed by social conflicts between individual and collective interests.

Indonesia, for example, is an expansive archipelago, with many undesirable, remote venues in which judicial personnel are needed. A mandatory transfer system ensures nationwide coverage of judicial personnel. Mandatory transfers, however, may be subject to abuse of the individual judge's independence. Yet, on the other hand, the rejection of mandatory transfer may mean that some jurisdictions will lack the necessary judicial personnel to operate the justice system. One way to overcome this dilemma is to provide extra incentives (side payments) (e.g., promotions, perquisites, extra housing and education benefits) to judges willing to undertake hardship assignments.

Likewise, lawyer compensation schemes and judicial evaluation methodologies do not currently contemplate rewards for settlements. Lawyers fear that mediation and ADR more broadly will mean an "alarming drop in revenues." In determining whether to promote settlement, judges may be influenced by the quantitative system for evaluating their performance, one that does not count settlements. In order to overcome dilemmas arising from these disincentives, mediation may be sweetened by helping lawyers and clients work out monetary compensation systems for successful settlements and by incorporating settlements as at least an equal quantitative measure of court disposition performance.

3. *Tous les Deux*: Pursuing Both Options

A third option is to attack the strength (or dichotomous nature) of the either/or statement in the articulation of the dilemma. Dilemmas may be falsely characterized as presenting mutually exclusive choices between alternatives X and Y, when both may be pursued to achieve the overall objective.[36] Indeed, incremental reforms may be structured along a plan for systemic change, and individual and collective interests may be considered in parallel (and correctly as interdependent) in an attempt to maximize one by enhancing the other.

Independence measures are not necessarily exclusive of all other accountability measures. Indeed, reformers can mitigate the downside of any one measure by combining it with others, such that independence measures parallel accountability interventions, with one counterbalancing the other.

In Indonesia, as well as many other judicial systems, for example, life tenure may be structured to coexist with strong external controls on corruption. Self-appointment may be designed to coexist with strong and transparent certification standards. Independent control of a judicial calendar may be implemented to coexist with case- and event-tracking methods that create greater accountability in the handling of that caseload. Analogously, mediation is not necessarily exclusive of other measures to strengthen the public adjudication system, including court and case management, cost-shifting devices to discourage frivolous litigation, or new investments in human resources to meet the demands of an exploding population, a high-growth economy, and strong democratic values.

4. Finding a Third Way

A fourth option is to attack the exclusivity of (or rigidity of the boundaries set by) a strong either/or choice, i.e., the choice of two options, no more. Reformers (ranging from Buddha[37] to Blair[38]) frequently look for a third way. In pursuit of this approach, reformers may segment subsystems (more radical than incrementalism and more conservative than shock therapy) or work with subnational-level interest groups as intermediaries between the individual and the national collective.

The issue of judicial appointments provides another example in the independence/accountability context. Reformers may face the dilemma of choosing between (X) judicial self-appointment (strong on independence but weak on accountability) and (Y) executive appointment (strong on accountability but weak on independence). Instead of being forced to choose between these unsatisfactory alternatives, X and Y, reformers in search of a third way, Z, may view legislative appointment as the best of three options (stronger on independence than executive appointment, and stronger on accountability than judicial self-appointment).

As another example, mediation reformers concerned about abuse and exploitation of unsophisticated litigants may insist on a more evaluative, court-supervised form of judicial settlement as the best means of achieving interest-based solutions that are also well within the range of probable legal outcomes. Judicial settlement would provide the advantages of legal oversight to avoid abuse while advancing benefits of a consensual, confidential, interest-based mediation process.

5. Attacking False Polarities

A fifth option is to recognize that the putative polarity in many perceived dilemmas is false. X or Y choices are often posed (improperly) as polarities (where $X = -Y$ and $Y = -X$). This is the primary reason that logicians admonish against the use of rhetorically created oppositions and prefer instead to use negatives (X and $-X$, or Y and $-Y$). Albeit distinct from each other, incrementalism is not the opposite of a systemic approach, and the individual is not the opposite of the collective.

Either/or statements may be more productively phrased as independence or not independence, accountability or not accountability, and so on. Accordingly, independence measures may be contrasted with those that frustrate independence (rather than those that necessarily advance accountability). Stated differently, accountability is not the opposite of independence; anti-independence is. This insight allows for a much greater array of alternatives that fall within four (instead of two more limited) categories of mechanisms and measures that

- Advance Independence, *Not* Accountability (I, $-A$) (partially desirable)
- Advance Accountability, *Not* Independence (A, $-I$) (partially desirable)
- Advance Independence *And* Accountability (I, A) (most desirable)
- Advance *Neither* Independence *Nor* Accountability ($-I$, $-A$ (least desirable)

This analysis provides a much broader range of reform options. Recognizing, for example, that independence and accountability not only are functions of horizontal political relationships among the branches of government but also are influenced by vertical relationships between state and society further supports this conceptual approach. For example, a free press simultaneously can establish greater accountability of judicial institutions to society and through publicity of the process of judicial determinations cultivate greater public trust, itself a source of independence for the judiciary from the other political branches.

Likewise, the common distinction between positions and interests in dispute resolution does not mean that interests are the opposite of positions. Notwithstanding the advice of many mediation experts to shun position-based bargaining and focus primarily (if not exclusively) on a determination, prioritization, and maximization of the parties' interests, a legal position is one of a party's many interests (a source of overlap in a Venn diagram).[39] Therefore, interests and positions may overlap, in the same way that independence and accountability measures do.

6. Divide and Conquer: Aggressive Distinctions

A sixth option of aggressive distinctions may further advance the ability to resolve reform dilemmas. This might be called a divide-and-conquer approach. The goal or cluster of features (independence) may be divided further (or disaggregated) into different subaims or subfeatures. The process of disaggregation helps to resolve dilemmas that are conceptualized too generally. Thus, reform interventions may be broken down into subcategories of strategies that pursue alternatively smaller or larger changes (e.g., a gradual approach to mediation, coupled with a systemic approach to court management), and individual and collective interests can be further divided into different types (e.g., pecuniary, reputational, justice, efficiency, and so on). Breaking down aims and features helps to sharpen antidilemma approaches.

For example, reformers can easily divide and conquer the independence/accountability dilemma by asking why we seek these objectives and how: independence from whom, for what, and by which particular mechanism?[40] Decisional independence may be distinguished (though not necessarily entirely separated) from administrative independence. Individual independence may be distinguished from collective or corporate independence. The independence to conduct oneself lawfully in the judge's personal life may be distinguished from the independence to commit crimes with impunity. Independence as a shield from political interference (through self-appointment, proscriptions against forced transfers, salary protections, exclusively internal disciplinary authority and power to remove) may be distinguished from independence as a sword to curb political branch excesses (judicial review of a violation of civil rights).[41] This allows us to distinguish functional forms of potential interference: from administration on the one extreme to the act of adjudication on the other.

Analogously, "mediation" is a code word for a diverse cluster of features: the type of case to which it is applied; the identity of the neutral; his or her role; the structure of the proceedings (private caucusing, joint sessions); the neutralizing communication skills (reframing, agenda setting, acknowledgment); the bargaining strategies (integrative, mutual gains, distributional); and outcomes (from peaceful separation to a continuation of a mutually beneficial relationship, from monetary settlements to new forms of cooperation unrelated to the underlying cause of action). By disaggregating this cluster or a conceived prototype of mediation, reformers can more easily pick and choose features that help to maximize objectives (e.g., picking cases where litigants are unlikely to be exploited or cases that are so routine there is no loss of normativity if the case settles). It would be an overly constraining mistake to presume any particular cluster as essential or necessary to any one set of circumstances or conditions (whether in individual cases or larger systems).

7. Grasping Relativity of Benefits and Harms

In addition to the divide-and-conquer strategy, opportunities arise from the rejection of arbitrarily binary assignments of absolute 0 or 1 values. One approach is to embrace the relativity of goal satisfaction in degrees of benefits and harms in the pursuit of multiple objectives. There is not always a bright line that bifurcates the gradual from the sudden or the narrow from the broad in justice reform. Furthermore, if the absolute pursuit of one interest subverts another upon which it is at least partially dependent, the maximization of goals will be less than full.

Measures that advance independence in judicial systems like that of Indonesia do so in relative, not absolute, ways.[42] To what extent does a life-tenure system enhance independence? Judges with tenure may not lose their jobs, but they may be deprived of resources (such as salary or a sufficient administrative budget), subject to discipline or removal, or vulnerable to public pressure through political statements or media attention. That is, a life-tenure system does not in itself guarantee full, or even sufficient, judicial independence. To what extent does an external disciplinary system enhance accountability? External systems may suffer from unsatisfactory resources, blocked access to information, or limited protection from corruption in their own processes. That is, an external disciplinary system by itself is no guaranty for establishing full or even partial accountability.

Likewise, the tension between public adjudication (based on legal rights) and consensual settlement (based on party interests) and the values realized or undermined may be thought of in relative terms. The availability of mediation, alone, does not mean that every case will settle consensually, thereby putting an end to adjudication and its primary consequences of normative judgment and publicity. The emphasis on strong public adjudication, on the other hand, is not necessarily inconsistent with the desire to have more cases settle consensually. Clear, final judgments allow parties in dispute to get a more predictable sense of the likely outcome, in this way providing realistic information and a baseline for those involved in settlement negotiations.

Thus, the net result of any reform measure is an empirical question (about which we know much too little) that (if we knew more) would render answers in quantifiably relative rather than absolute terms. What is the importance of this modest insight? Consider the first example in more detail.

Recognition of the relative continuum from the negative to the positive value opens up the possibility that some measures may advance or detract from multiple objectives (independence and accountability or justice and settlement) more than others. Therefore, to take the example above, within the two (out of four total) subsets of goal satisfaction categories, i.e., (I, −A) and (−I, A), there may be reforms that advance independence much more than they detract from accountability and measures that advance accountability much more than they detract from independence. (It also stands to reason that some reforms may detract from independence more than they advance accountability and detract from accountability more than they advance independence.) If the values of independence and accountability were each put on a common scale ranging from −100 (complete attack on independence) to 100 (full independence), and if the value (positive or negative) for each measure along these two scales were aggregated (though that presents a value choice in its own right, as explained further below), the reformer would be able to see by tallying up the scores (whether explicitly through numeric valuation schemes or implicitly through more rhetorical characterizations) which measures to advocate and which to reject on their capacity for maximizing objectives and minimizing harms. Probabilistic thinking about the likelihood of the relative harm can be similarly calculated. Thus, a 10 percent chance of severe harm may reduce a serious concern of interference with an important value to a more minimal one and thus change the calculation of comparative costs and benefits.

8. Picking the Poison: Making Tough Value Choices

What if none of the foregoing options is available, and the dilemma is an undeniably strong and inescapable one? Let's suppose that incremental and systemic approaches are mutually exclusive, that the individual's and collective's interests are necessarily at odds, that an independence measure necessarily (and to the same degree) frustrates accountability (and vice versa), or that mediation is necessarily inconsistent with fundamental goals of a justice system. In such cases, an eighth option for dealing with dilemmas is available. The reformer must choose between mistakes, harms, or errors that result from each of the two alternatives. For example, criminal justice procedures carry two potential harms: the risk of acquitting a person guilty of the crime (Type I Error) and the risk of incarcerating an innocent person (Type II Error) (which incorporates Type I Error because conviction of the innocent usually means nonprosecution of the guilty). Thus, standards for what searches are reasonable, whether confessions should be admissible, or how the burden of proof may be understood (and evaluated, though not exclusively) as a choice of (or mitigation of) Type I or Type II Errors.

Where two policies are necessarily mutually destructive, the reformer simply has to make a value choice of which error is better to avoid in the context of the particular system. In Indonesia, this choice boils down to the comparative harms of private corruption as a result of strong independence protections with the lack of effective accountability measures, or political interference with judicial decision making due to strong accountability measures that compromise judicial independence protections. In India, this means the choice between protracted delays that undermine justice as a result of insistence on a complex procedural system and the loss of normative, public judgments that inform the law because of an emphasis on consensual settlements.

9. Explicating Evidentiary Thresholds for Reform

The clear demarcation of the foregoing value choices, however, is rare. The relativity of benefits and costs, coupled with the (relative) ignorance of the nature of systemic problems or the precise effects of any particular reform design or method pose an additional evidentiary problem. As pointed out in the previous discussion of research/reform dilemmas, the choice between (1) going forward with higher risks of failure derived from incomplete information and (2) holding back out of caution with the consequence of prolonging suffering presents a serious predicament in reform. Similar to the debate over the imminence of threats sufficient to justify military intervention,[43] global warming,[44] or the adjustment of rigorous scientific protocols for anti-AIDS drugs,[45] justice reform encounters (but with less attention) the common problem: where to set the evidentiary threshold.

Should the risk that a judicial commission will become a source of political interference or corruption prevent reformers from moving ahead with design and implementation? Should the risk that mediation might be undermined by lawyers and litigants, hide too much negligent conduct from public view, or even increase backlog and delay counsel reformers to hold back? With imperfect information about the problems to be addressed and the effects of the reform interventions, reformers and opponents make determinations on the basis of (frequently implicit) answers to these (rarely posed) questions. Greater attention to explicating implicit, relative, evidentiary burdens of proof might help reformers to manage their ignorance of the facts and choose which mistake they would rather make.

10. Confronting the Metadilemma

The identification of alternative strategies and a comparative evaluation of them raise an even deeper philosophical problem. To the extent that the alternatives themselves are unsatisfactory in some respect, they present a kind of metadilemma, that is, a dilemma over how to deal with dilemmas. This does not mean that each option is equally unsatisfactory in general or especially in different sets of circumstances. Diverse circumstances may counsel minimizing the harms of one option or another; sweetening one option with side payments; attacking the strength of the either/or statement; broadening the boundaries that define it; finding new space for a third way; pursuing division or relativity measures; making hard value choices about which error is more important to avoid; and setting thresholds that help reformers and participants to decide whether to support or resist specific measures.

There is no absolute or universal solution to this vexing methodological problem. To navigate past the obstacles it poses, it appears that explication itself provides a necessary starting point.[46] Beyond its arguable philosophical importance, this process of explication may help advance reform in three ways. First, it opens a much wider range of potential strategies designed to avoid either paralysis (for fear of making any mistake) or catastrophe (pushing ahead for fear of failing to act in the face of pressing needs). Second, it causes leaders and participants to ask which strategies are being employed, and thus explication exposes them for critical evaluation. Third, it may help the society to develop in the longer run ways to distinguish between better and worse approaches to reform dilemmas in different contexts.

In this final sense, a methodology for managing dilemmas may help to bolster both the theory and practice of different approaches to reform. Given the critical contemporary need for improving judicial performance worldwide and the impediments confronting reformers engaged in that project, an intellectual investment in exploring the nature of dilemmas and how to deal with them is potentially worthwhile.

11. Taking Collective Action on the Social Dilemma

In dealing with these dilemmas, the use of the word "reformer" has been applied quite loosely. This word choice may have given the false impression that the reformer is a single individual or decision maker. In most cases, reform (or least a triggering decision) appears to be determined by one person (the chief justice of the Supreme Court, a minister of justice, leader of the parliament, or a prime minister or president). As the study of emergent systems demonstrates, however, in an organized, complex social system,[47] the views, practices, and interests of each participant may be critical, particularly in interactions with others. Each actor exhibits an individual (and through interaction collective) sense of self-awareness, assessment of the problems, openness to change, level of creativity, courage to take risks, appreciation of personal and professional dilemmas in making a commitment to change, and strategy (including tough value choices) for dealing with these dilemmas. Even the most passive followers may lead by creating an implicit demand for (or lack of interference with) a particular direction they are willing to traverse without a fuss.

With these perspectives, each participant in reform may face at critical times a social dilemma, that is, an undesirable choice between maintaining current practice (with perceived professional/personal gain at the cost of the system) or changing actual behaviors (with systemic gains but perceived professional/personal losses). Imagine a lawyer in Indonesia representing an indigent client accused of a serious crime. Should she pay off the police to gain access and violate her ethical duty to the system? Or would it be more ethical to resist the bribe at the expense of the client's interests? Imagine an attorney in India who can manipulate the system for a client who has defaulted on a loan and postpone collection for fifteen years. Should he represent the client zealously at the expense of the system's performance? Or should he expedite the matter, forcing the client to incur greater costs but saving the system from another case clogging the system and slowing it down for other meritorious adjudications?

Short of a commanding theoretical solution, societies need practical strategies for these types of social dilemmas in part because complex, organized systems defy top-down, command-control solutions.[48] Nonthreatening, open-ended communication about the nature of the social dilemma and the values at stake may do more to advance reform than any particular resolution advanced by a single leader or individual. Experimental research shows that (in addition to side payments, which are not always available) nonthreatening communication may create more cooperative behavior (by creating conditions for internalization of the social costs).[49] It may be useful to recall that in the paradigmatic case of the prisoners' dilemma, the two detainees were not allowed to confer.[50] Without this restriction, a more collaborative, bottom-up process of individual and collective self-assessment and problem solving may help to break down the constraints imposed by social dilemmas in justice reform.

Reform, as emphasized in the foregoing discussion, often fails precisely because it is in fact threatening. If those eventually subject to the reforms, however, have a voice in their design and can articulate their concerns in advance of reform determinations, defensive behavior can be substantially mitigated. More collaborative studies organized around internal agents thus have begun to address the weaknesses Merryman exposed in the law and development movement more than twenty-five years ago. Inside-out (rather than outside-in) and bottom-up (rather than top-down) reform processes foster a greater familiarity with the actual conditions of the host system and its many participants; are more likely to supply a respectable theory of agent behavior; reduce immunity (enjoyed by outsiders in particular and even high-level officials on the brink of retirement) from the consequences of reform; and minimize the harmful projection of foreign attitudes and ideas.[51] Furthermore, these collaborative approaches have begun to show preliminary results.[52]

This emphasis on collective communication celebrates the accomplishments of the slime mold, applies what can be learned from emergent systems, and attempts to facilitate a more robust reform strategy. The individual reform capacities and smaller battles of each participant in the legal process are integral to the larger one, and this is what makes the bottom-up perspective so important to the area of justice reform. To emerge from the dilemmas of reform, the collective participation of individual actors is essential because no individual is smart enough or absolutely in possession of the (frequently conflicting) values of the community. Reforms based on the pretense of greater knowledge than is actually possessed may do more harm than good.[53] Even if such knowledge existed, the realization of whichever plan or design would be heavily dependent on active participation and practices of the community at large.[54]

In other words, judicial systems may overcome their submergent conditions only through sharing and thereby improving the limited navigational tools of their participants. Collectively, systems may thus emerge through the many rocks and hard places of dysfunctional systems and their pathologies. For better or worse, this form of collaborative peer-to-peer communication appears to be the only way for the slime mold to move or for justice reform to proceed. The more participatory and collaborative exploration of dilemmas and the positive or negative feedback from these alternative antidilemma strategies may help to develop more intelligent strategies for the improvement of justice systems globally. That may be the only way that reformers can demonstrate that our legal systems are at least as smart as aggregations of slime mold. That may be the only path through which we might emerge through the maze-like puzzle of justice reform.

C. Conclusion

Emphasizing the complexity of these various interactions (between the individual and the collective, or between the structure and performance of a system) poses a formidable challenge to the integrity of comparative reform theories or approaches. The probability that individual dynamics will make a systemic difference and that large-scale design can alter local incentives makes the comparative enterprise risky. Where aims, variables, and thresholds for decision making vary widely across systems, (longitudinal) lessons derived from one national context for use in another carry a high risk of falsehood (both false negatives—where proposals fail one place but would succeed in another—and false positives—where proposals succeed in one environment but would fail in another). Furthermore, even where proposals are not driven by the perception of foreign success, (latitudinal) domestic reform interventions require predictions about the future (always a risky business). The dynamics are complex, and reforms are thus vulnerable to disappointments, backfires, and unintended consequences. Shedding light on the infirmity of these comparative theories is likely to cast serious doubt on noble pursuits to solve shared, serious problems. Simultaneously, however, critical candor about the necessity and limits of the explicated comparative theories may also help the proverbial emperor realize that he should put on some clothes. In other words, the development of comparative methodology is a dual-use technology: it facilitates both candid criticism and potentially reconstructive and more effective approaches to vexing problems.

7

Conclusion
The Prospects for a Comparative
Methodology in Global Justice Reform

Part I of this book focuses on the weaknesses of comparative methodology. Chapter 2 evaluates explanations of the comparative method. Its part A emphasizes the importance of comparison in legal decision making and commentary. Its part B points out the general inadequacy of current explanations of the comparative method. Finally, its part C considers alternative justifications for the specific lack of attention to methodological problems and concludes that the complex nature of comparison best explains comparison's methodological underdevelopment. Chapter 2 illuminates the need for greater attention to comparison as the theoretical foundation of comparative legal studies. Chapter 2 also notes the practical significance of comparison for contemporary legal decision making, especially in an era of globalization.[1]

Chapter 3 generates a preliminary framework for comparing (and distinguishing) comparisons by raising three basic interrelated questions about purpose, content, and modes of differentiation. Specifically, its part A illuminates difficulties with the identification and specification of purposes, and explores the consistency of these explicit purposes with assertions of autonomy for comparative law as a discipline. Its part B critiques common methods of variable selection. In particular, it addresses the use of classification, prototypes, and micro- and macrolevels of analysis. Part C illuminates issues raised by competing modes of differentiation and measurement. In sum, chapter 3 provides a suggestive framework in which comparisons may be compared and differentiated based on the motivating purpose, chosen content, mode of differentiation, and their interrelationships. In sum, part I represents an important step beyond traditional treatments of the comparative method as mere comparison but cautiously stops short of developing in detail a comparative methodology capable of justifying the acceptance or rejection of alternative comparisons.

Part II of this book explores comparative methodology in the context of global justice reform. Chapter 4 sketches the global context in which institutional failure within the most neglected branch is disturbingly common, noting the contradiction (and interrelationship) between ambitious normative commitments and neglected public institutions. The discussion highlights multiple factors of common institutional problems (political interference and corruption, as well as backlog and delay) in the context of two significant contemporary national reform initiatives: the development of a judicial commission in Indonesia and the introduction of legal mediation to India.

Chapter 5 identifies key features in reform failure and the predicaments they create. Its part A identifies several common sources of comparative misunderstanding (rash judgments, underestimates of resistance, limited self-awareness, myopic views of single-factor theories, obstacles to the selection of key factors, and inflexibility in design), limited resources, and collective action problems, and the consequentially common failure of many reform initiatives. Its part B outlines different types of dilemmas (design, method, social) encountered in reform. These unsatisfactory choices include purportedly binary distinctions between judicial independence and accountability or justice and settlement; between incremental and systemic sequencing, top-down and bottom-up political processes, external and internal expertise, research and action-driven reforms; and the social dilemma individuals face when their personal or professional interests are perceived to be inconsistent with those of the collective. Together, these problems create a nearly insuperable set of predicaments for judicial systems in search of reform.

In response to the challenge posed by chapters 4 and 5, chapter 6 advances a set of navigational tools for judicial systems to use in attempts to emerge from these many dilemmas. Its part A explores five useful aspects of the emergence metaphor, which itself has pervaded a diverse body of nonlegal literature from biology to urban planning. Part B sketches a series of antidilemma strategies, illustrating them with examples again drawn primarily (but not exclusively) from Indonesian and Indian contexts.

Together, parts I and II of the book underline the importance of developing a comparative methodology capable of providing a deeper set of justifications for accepting or rejecting comparative reforms of law, legal institutions, or processes. The inquiry also cautions, however, against prematurely crystallized rationales for distinguishing comparisons (good from bad) or the selection of any one approach to common dilemmas in justice reform initiatives.

In general, the full step ahead to the development of a comparative methodology for global justice reform carries significant peril. First, by developing an abstracted methodology or strategy divorced from the context in which comparative work is done, there is a significant risk that it will not address the needs of the process of comparison in reform practice. Complaints that methodologists themselves do not practice what they preach are to be expected. Second, metacomparison is subject to an infinite regress. If comparisons can or should be compared, why not continue with comparisons of comparisons of comparisons, and so forth? Thus, each key to comparative legal studies appears itself to be locked beneath yet another layer of methodological questions. Third, others may sensibly avoid the development of a graduated methodology by claiming that "a little methodology is a dangerous thing."[2] Accordingly, thoughtful scholars may conclude that the value of the search for methodology is of dubious value.[3] Fourth, conceptual approaches complement or detract from equally important political, cultural, and financial considerations and though important remain one dimension among many. Finally, as methodological rationales become stronger, rejections of comparisons may serve to chill innovative approaches that do not follow the prescriptive dictates of the methodology.[4] This is of particular sensitivity in the area of reform. A common justification for the resistance to legal change, from steps to reduce global warming to pilot programs in single-gender public education, is the claim that not enough is known. It will be important to qualify the dictates of greater methodological development against the sense of urgency arising from the dysfunctional condition of court systems.

Notwithstanding these specific perils of advancing methodological rules, further investigation of these conceptual problems and strategies must be weighed against four potential rewards. First, the questions and criticisms raised by the examination of the comparative method and the framework for comparing purposes, content choices, and modes of differentiation serve to advance comparative legal discourse beyond method to one of method choice.[5] It may also eventually lead to the methodological development of greater discipline in support of the claims of legal science. Second, by illuminating and engaging the disagreements on methodological grounds, it may become easier to explain the value of comparative scholarship, evaluate the satisfaction of its objectives, and if necessary, improve upon its methods. Third, by focusing on comparison itself as an integral part of legal decision making and commentary, including reform determinations, the discussion may stimulate permeations of unnecessary boundaries between comparative law (implicitly defined by its focus on what is foreign) and ostensibly noncomparative (i.e., purely domestic) legal subjects.[6] Finally, by realizing that comparison involves three distinct, yet related, types of choice (the why, what, and how), even an inconclusive search for methodological rationales and antidilemma strategies may open a wide array of unforeseen channels of fruitful comparative inquiry and choice in reform. New approaches to maximize the benefits and minimize the harms of judicial independence and accountability or justice and settlement may become possible with these reconstructive tools.

All told, then, comparative methodology does not merely represent a hurdle for reform proposals to surmount by requiring them to explicate and defend the comparisons upon which they rely. It also represents an essential intellectual foundation for the creativity that is so urgently needed. Greater investments in comparative methodology accordingly may lead to an appreciation of broader and more innovative comparative possibilities, including in particular the creative use of comparison to work through paralyzing dilemmas. In this sense, methodological inquiry provides a rich set of creative vehicles for enhancing comparative understanding of ostensibly incomparable phenomena in service of reform. These vehicles carry the promise of enhancing the range and adaptability of reform proposals to address pressing needs. Accordingly, the global need for judicial systems to function free of political interference, untainted by private corruption, and without unreasonable delay calls for greater attention to comparative methodological inquiry and strategy.

Which are greater: the potential risks or the benefits of comparative methodology in global justice reform? It may be too early to say, given the preliminary nature of the project; however, contemporary global trends, the challenges they pose, and the creative powers of these tools may tip the balance toward advancing the methodological investigation of comparison in a wide array of legal reform contexts. Trade and capital liberalization and expanding communication and transportation technologies facilitate interaction among heterogeneous communities worldwide. Patterns of human activities extending across political borders have expanded the breadth and depth of community conflicts.[7] Thus, the global need to compare the national, transnational, and international law and institutions responsible for dealing with these conflicts has become ever more pressing. Communities with different legal sensibilities may be expected to continue to generate inconsistent and, indeed, conflicting comparisons of the relevant law and authorized institutions. How should these conflicts be resolved or accommodated? How should decision makers and commentators navigate an expanding global sea of cresting legal alternatives under both local and global pressures? How should judicial and other dispute resolution institutions be reconfigured to meet these challenges? As these comparisons become seemingly ever-more difficult, better ways to compare become both critically necessary and potentially useful.[8] In this way, deeper inquiry into the nature and tools of comparative methodology may serve to help meet the pressing challenges of global justice reform.

Notes

NOTES TO CHAPTER I

1. Peter Medawar, *Pluto's Republic* (New York: Oxford University Press, 1984), 116.

2. Alasdair MacIntyre, "Incommensurability, Truth, and the Conversation between Confucians and Aristotelians about the Virtues," in *Culture and Modernity: East-West Philosophic Perspectives*, ed. Eliot Deutsche (Honolulu: University of Hawaii Press, 1991), 121.

3. Mark Blaug, *The Methodology of Economics: Or, How Economists Explain* (Cambridge; New York: Cambridge University Press, 1980), 47.

4. As of January 2000, out of the 191 countries in the world, 120 countries have electoral democracies. See World Forum on Democracy, "List of Electoral Democracies," available online at http://www.fordemocracy.net/electoral.shtm. The first World Forum on Democracy (WFD) took place in Warsaw, Poland, in June 2000, and included an international gathering of scholars, civic and religious leaders, labor and business leaders, and former government officials from more than eighty countries.

5. United Nations, "International Covenant on Civil and Political Rights," 16 December 1966, 999 UNTS 171.

6. World Trade Organization (WTO), "General Agreement on Tariffs and Trade 1994," 15 April 1994, 33 ILM 1125 (cited hereinafter as GATT).

7. See, e.g., William P. Alford, "Making the World Safe for What? Intellectual Property Rights, Human Rights and Foreign Economic Policy in the Post-European Cold War World," *N.Y.U. J. Intl. L. & Pol.* 29 (1996–1997): 136–40 (describing the efforts of the United States to get the People's Republic of China to adopt and enforce laws protecting intellectual property).

8. See Paul Masson, *Globalization: Facts and Figures* (Washington, D.C.: International Monetary Fund, Policy Discussion Paper No. 4, 2001), 2, 9–10. See also Tatyana P. Soubbotina and Katherine A. Sheram, *Beyond Economic Growth: Meeting the Challenges of Global Development* (New York: World Bank, 2000), 113, and United Nations Conference on Trade and Development, *FDI Inflows in Millions of Dollars,* available online at http://www.un.org/reports/financing/profile.htm (estimating an 18 percent increase in the U.S. dollar value of inflows of foreign direct investment, from US$1.075 trillion 1999 to $1.270 trillion in 2000); see also Sebastian Edwards, "Capital Mobility, Capital Controls, and Globalization in the Twenty-first Century," *Annals* 579 (2002): 261 (analyzing the effects of economic openness and increasing capital mobility on the economic growth).

9. Intergovernmental Panel on Climate Change, *Methodological and Technological Issues in Technology Transfer,* ed. Bert Metz et al. (Cambridge; New York: Cambridge University Press, 2001), available online at http://www.grida.no/climate/ipcc/tectran/ (finding that total international financial flows supporting technology transfers across Organization

for Economic Cooperation and Development (OECD) countries in 1998 exceeded US$300 billion in 1998, compared to slightly more than US$100 billion in 1990). Globalization is both a cause and a consequence of cross-border technology transfers. See Lester C. Thurow, "Globalization: The Product of a Knowledge-Based Economy," *Annals* 570 (2000): 19 (arguing that globalization is one of the effects of new technological developments, e.g., microelectronics, computers, robotics, telecommunication, new materials, and biotechnology).

10. The value of world merchandise exports grew by 12.5 percent, reaching US$6.2 trillion in 2000, which tripled the amount in 1999. Further, growth in trade volumes more than doubled for the major regions of the WTO. Asia and the transition economies recorded the highest export growth among the major regions and the largest increases in imports. In Western Europe, trade grew by 10 percent, double the amount of the preceding year; in North America, the growth of imports exceeded that of exports for the fourth consecutive year. WTO, *International Trade Statistics 2001* (Geneva: World Trade Organization, 2001), 1–2, 19 (Table I.2: Growth in the Volume of World Merchandise Trade by Selected Region, 1990–2000). See also U.S. Census Bureau, "Goods and Services Deficit Increases in May 2002," July 19, 2002, available online at http://www.census.gov/indicator/ www/ustrade.html (Graph and table reflecting U.S. International Trade in Goods and Services: March 2000 to March 2002).

11. By the mid-1990s services accounted for almost two-thirds of the world's GDP, up from about half of the world's GDP in the 1980s. Soubbotina and Sheram, 52. World exports of commercial services rose by 6 percent in 2000, reaching US$1.4 trillion. WTO, 2; see also Lic. Patricia Hernandez-Esparza, "Accounting Services for the 21st Century," *U.S.-Mexico L. J.* 8 (Spring 2000): 11–20 (arguing (1) that globalization has increased the need for a multidisciplinary practice approach with complex and sophisticated services and (2) that few traditional legal practices have the global reach necessary to adequately meet the needs of rapidly expanding multinational companies).

12. See Tomas A. Lipinski, "The Developing Legal Infrastructure and the Globalization of Information: Constructing a Framework for Critical Choices in the New Millennium Internet—Character, Content and Confusion," *Richmond J. L. & Tech.* 6 (1999): 19 (arguing that the "commodification" of information has jettisoned the policy issues of the right to control and access information into the dynamics of the marketplace).

13. With each decade beginning 1931–40, immigration to and emigration from the United States have both steadily increased. Immigration increased from 528,000 during that decade to 7,338,000 during 1981–1990. U.S. Department of Justice, *1999 Statistical Yearbook of the Immigration and Naturalization Service* (Washington, D.C.: U.S. Government Printing Office, 2002), 239, available online at http://www.ins.usdoj.gov/graphics/ aboutins/statistics/FY99Yearbook.pdf. Emigration during those two periods increased from 649,000 to 1,600,000, respectively. Ibid. From April 1, 2000, to July 1, 2003, the United States had a net international migration of approximately 4,190,277 people. U.S. Census Bureau, "Cumulative Estimates of the Components of Population Change for the United States and States: April 1, 2000 to July 1, 2003," available online at http://eire .census.gov/popest/data/states/tables/NST-EST2003-04.php.

14. For a description of legal globalization, see Hiram E. Chodosh, "Globalizing of the U.S. Law Curriculum: The Saja Paradigm," *U.C. Davis L. Rev.* 37 (2004): 843–68, 844–48 (describing scale and nature of globalization and its relationship to law).

15. See Amy Chua, *World on Fire: How Exporting Free Market Democracy Breeds Ethnic Hatred and Global Instability* (New York: Doubleday, 2003), 145 (noting, for example, that Sierra Leone "was a classic case of the collision between markets and democracy").

16. For a forward-looking examination of the relationship between comparative law and conflict of laws, see Benedicte Fauvarque-Cosson, "Comparative Law and Conflict of Laws: Allies or Enemies? New Perspectives on an Old Couple," *Am. J. Comp. L.* 49 (2002): 426 (arguing that the "growing influence of fundamental rights . . . has radically changed both disciplines as well as their mutual relationships."). See also Friedrich K. Juenger, "The Need for a Comparative Approach to Choice-of-Law Problems," *Tul. L. Rev.* 73 (1999): 1324–26 (noting the perils of parochialism).

17. David J. Gerber, "Centennial World Congress on Comparative Law: Globalization and Legal Knowledge; Implications for Comparative Law," *Tul. L. Rev.* 75 (2001): 950 ("We might expect the field of comparative law, therefore, to be replete with efforts to comprehend globalization and its impacts on law and to develop strategies for dealing with them. . . . So far, however, comparatists have paid relatively little attention to these influences and their implications.").

18. H. Patrick Glenn, "Centennial World Congress on Comparative Law: Comparative Law and Legal Practice: On Removing the Borders," *Tul. L. Rev.* 75 (2001): 1002 (observing phenomenon of "comparative legal practice" as a "rapidly expanding field of legal practice").

19. For an assessment of the role of comparative law in the last half of the twentieth century in the Europeanization of private law, see Mathias Reimann, "The Progress and Failure of Comparative Law in the Second Half of the Twentieth Century," *Am. J. Comp. L.* 50 (2002): 685 (noting that comparative law "has been a resounding failure . . . as a field of inquiry."). See also Markku Kiikeri, ed., *Comparative Legal Reasoning and European Law* (Dordrecht; Boston: Kluwer Academic Publishers, 2001), 1 (arguing that "comparative law seems to be at the heart of modern European law."). For a report on the use of comparative law in the courts, see Ulrich Drobnig and Sjef van Erp, eds., *International Congress of Comparative Law (14th). The Use of Comparative Law by Courts / XIVth International Congress of Comparative Law* (The Hague; London: Kluwer Law International, 1999), ix (noting in the preface, "In our quickly integrating world, comparison of the various divergent national laws is of ever-growing importance.").

20. See P. John Kozyris, "Comparative Law for the Twenty-First Century: New Horizons and New Technologies," *Tul. L. Rev.* 69 (1994): 167:

> [T]he utility of the comparative method is beyond dispute. Comparative law not only provides alternative solutions to be used in legal reform but also gives us a better understanding of our existing law. In short, it is an indispensable tool of legal science. In addition, the internationalization of transactions and the increasing applicability of foreign law make comparative law an indispensable tool of the legal practitioner.

21. Roscoe Pound, "What May We Expect from Comparative Law?" *A.B.A. J.* 22 (1936): 58–59. Dean Pound reiterated this question nearly two decades later in another article. Roscoe Pound, "Comparative Law in Space and Time," *Am. J. Comp. L.* 4 (1955): 72 ("[W]hat, then, is to be compared? It comes down to what we mean by the term Law.").

22. A snow shovel may be an indispensable tool in the snowy winter months; however, to serve its purpose, the tool must be of sufficient quality (e.g., strength, size, design, weight, durability), and the person using the tool must know how to shovel with strength and skill.

23. Parts A, B, and C of chapter 3 articulate some preliminary suggestions for dealing with the identified problems.

24. For an excellent series of critical essays on comparative law, see Annelise Riles, ed., *Rethinking the Masters of Comparative Law* (Oxford; Portland, Ore.: Hart Publishing, 2001).

25. Chapter 2, part C articulates and assesses alternative explanations for the lack of methodological attention to the fundamental questions raised in this book.

26. Reimann, 686 ("The most embarrassing theoretical weakness is the continuing lack of an understanding of what it really means to compare.").

27. See Ladislav Holy, ed., preface to *Comparative Anthropology* (New York; Oxford, U.K.: Blackwell, 1987) (analyzing "the present standing of comparison in social anthropology"); Amitai Etzioni and Fredric L. Dubow, eds., *Comparative Perspectives: Theories and Methods* (Boston: Little, Brown, 1970), 17–41 (essays on "[w]hat to compose to what and how to do it"); Clifford Geertz, *Local Knowledge: Further Essays in Interpretive Anthropology* (New York: Basic Books, 1983), 167–234; Sally Falk Moore, *Law as Process: An Anthropological Approach* (London; Boston: Routledge and Kegan Paul, 1978) (discussing the way the law changes in different cultures); Leopold Pospisil, *Anthropology of Law: A Comparative Theory*, 2d ed. (New York: Harper and Row, 1992), 39–96 (identifying universal attributes of "law" for purposes of cross-cultural comparison).

28. See Gary King, Robert O. Keohane, and Sidney Verba, *Designing Social Inquiry: Scientific Inference in Qualitative Research* (Princeton: Princeton University Press, 1984), 212 ("The comparative approach—in which we combine evidence from many observations even if some of them are not very close analogies to the present situation—is always at least as good and usually better than the analogy."); Adam Przeworksi and Henry Teune, *The Logic of Comparative Social Inquiry* (Malabar, Fla.: Robert E. Krieger Publishing Company, 1982), 13 (addressing challenge of introducing "systemic factors into general, theoretical statements and to retain the systemic context" of comparative measurement); Arend Lijphart, "Comparative Politics and the Comparative Method," *Am. Pol. Sci. Rev.* 65 (1971): 682–85, available online at http://links.jstor.org (focusing on the comparative method as a strategy for finding relationships among variables rather than as the first step of measuring the variables before exploring relationships, and differentiating it from statistical methods on the basis of number of cases). For a more quantitative approach, see John R. Schmidhauser, ed., *Comparative Judicial Systems: Challenging Frontiers in Conceptual and Empirical Analysis* (London; Boston: Butterworths, 1987); Jennifer A. Widner, "Comparative Politics and Comparative Law," *Am. J. Comp. L.* 46, no. 4 (Fall 1998): 740 (reflecting "on the problems of meeting the demand for comparative research in law, based on observation of the field of political science, which has faced some of the same challenges in recent years.").

29. See Rodney Needham, *Counterpoints* (Berkley: University of California Press, 1987); Charles Kay Ogden, *Opposition: A Linguistic and Psychological Analysis* (Bloomington: Indiana University Press, 1967); Mark Durie and Malcolm Ross, eds., *The Comparative Method Reviewed: Regularity and Irregularity in Language Change* (New York; Oxford, U.K.: Oxford University Press, 1996).

30. See, e.g., Charles Tilly, *Big Structures, Large Processes, Huge Comparisons* (New York: Russell Sage Foundation, 1984) (arguing for comparative historical research in explaining momentous social changes).

31. James S. Coleman, "Metatheory: Explanation in Social Science" in *Foundations of Social Theory* (Cambridge: Belknap Press of Harvard University Press, 1990), 1–26; Michael Armer and Allen D. Grimshaw, eds., *Comparative Social Research: Methodological Problems and Strategies* (New York: Wiley, 1973, published under the auspices of the Institute for Comparative Sociology); Melvin L. Kohn, ed., *Cross-National Research in Sociology* (Newbury Park, Calif.: Sage Publications, 1989); Charles C. Ragin, *The Comparative Method: Moving beyond Qualitative and Quantitative Strategies* (Berkeley: University of California Press, 1987) (arguing for Boolean techniques of qualitative comparison); Else Øyen, ed., "The Imperfection of Comparisons," in *Comparative Methodology: Theory*

and Practice in International Social Research (Newbury Park, Calif.: Sage Publications, 1990), 8–18 (noting the theoretical poverty of comparative research).

32. See Blaug (advocating falsificationism as ideal of economic methodology); Bruce J. Caldwell, *Beyond Positivism: Economic Methodology in the Twentieth Century* (London; Boston: George Allen & Unwin, 1982) (advocating methodological pluralism); Deirdre N. McCloskey, *The Rhetoric of Economics* (Madison: University of Wisconsin Press, 1988) (criticizing methodological, and exploring rhetorical, foundations of economics).

33. Many other disciplines are currently struggling with similar methodological issues. See, e.g., Reed K. Storey and Silvia Storey, *The Framework of Financial Accounting Concepts and Standards,* Financial Accounting Series 181-C (Norwalk, Conn.: Financial Accounting Standards Board, 1998). This piece explains:

> [A]s accounting has matured and its role in society has increased, momentum in developing accounting principles has shifted to those accountants who have come to understand what has been learned in many other fields: that reliance on experience alone leads only so far because environments and problems change; that until knowledge gained through experience is given purpose, direction, and internal consistency by a conceptual foundation, fundamentals will be endlessly reargued and practice blown in various directions by the winds of changing perceptions and proliferating accounting methods; and that only by studying and understanding the foundations of practices can the progress be discovered and the hope of improving practice be realized. (p. 3)

34. See generally Peter Medawar, *Pluto's Republic* (New York: Oxford University Press, 1984).

35. "Methodology" is used here to denote more than its common usage as "more method or technique." "Methodology" is used here as it is defined by Blaug, "the rationale for accepting or rejecting [the] theories or hypotheses," and is the distinguishing feature of a science. Blaug, 47.

36. See Riles, 1 ("Comparison, as a creative or scientific, pragmatic or utopian act, a method and a project, is one of the most ubiquitous and yet undertheorized dimensions of modern knowledge.").

37. See MacIntyre, 121, quoted in Andrew Huxley, "Golden Yoke, Silken Text," *Yale L. J.* 106: 1885–1950, 1932 n. 307 (1997) (book review) (reviewing Rebecca Redwood French, *The Golden Yoke: The Legal Cosmology of Buddhist Tibet* (1995) and R. P. Peerenboom, *Law and Morality in Ancient China: The Silk Manuscripts of Huang-Lao* (Albany: State University of New York Press, 1993)) (arguing that we have no neutral standpoint from which to compare opposing legal standards).

38. This process of "metacomparison" carries a philosophical problem of infinite regression. If one should compare comparisons, the questions should be posed: Why not continue with a comparison of comparisons of comparisons (a "meta-metacomparison")? When comparing comparisons, one might ask, what purposes are to be served, what content of comparisons should be selected to compare, and what modes of differentiation and rationales should be selected and applied? The choice not to engage this level of meta-metacomparison may appear arbitrary; however, to proceed to the meta-metalevel without having satisfactorily explained the metalevel would be impractical and unproductive at this point in the development of the inquiry. If one has not developed a way to compare comparisons, a comparison of compared comparisons is not likely to be fruitful.

39. John C. Reitz, "How to Do Comparative Law?" *Am. J. Comp. L.* 46 (1998): 618 (attempting "to list the most important characteristics of good comparative scholarship"). Even if one argues that the projected value of methodology is undesirable or impractical, the view against methodology is likely to be based on methodological

justifications. Antimethodologists alternatively argue that methodology is irrelevant because no one pays attention to its rules or because methodology is too constraining of potentially valuable research conducted through unconventional means.

40. Medawar, 116.

41. MacIntyre, 121.

42. Blaug, 47.

43. In search of methodological explanations, this book examines each of these three interrelated and overlapping stages of development. Methodological rationales (the third stage) presuppose a framework for comparing one comparison to another (the second stage). The comparison of comparisons in the second stage presupposes an explanation of comparison as an intellectual process (the first stage). Notwithstanding this sequential progression, it may be useful to consider how advanced understanding of a presumably later stage might shed light on an earlier stage of understanding. For example, it may be necessary to compare comparisons (the second stage) in order to understand the nature of comparison itself (the first stage). Also, the development of methodological rationales for accepting and rejecting comparisons (the third stage) may aid in articulating more purposeful, content-specific, and differentiable comparisons of comparisons themselves (the second stage).

44. See, e.g., Francois Venter, *Constitutional Comparison: Japan, Germany, Canada and South Africa as Constitutional States* (Cape Town; Cambridge, Mass.: Kluwer Law International, 2000), 257 ("[G]lobalization and the information explosion have brought us to the point where full knowledge of one national constitutional system is incomplete knowledge: the comparative perspective is indispensable.").

45. The first part of the book draws from Hiram E. Chodosh, "Comparing Comparisons: In Search of Methodology," *Iowa L. Rev.* 84 (1999): 1025–1131.

NOTES TO CHAPTER 2

1. For example, in the late 1990s critics hailed the pop sensation Oasis as the new Beatles. See Mathew Zuckerman, "Squashing These Comparisons Like Squashing a Beatle," *Asahi Shimbun/Asahi Evening News,* Feb. 12, 1998, 1 ("It's easy to take potshots at a band that in some quarters is being rated as the new Beatles—'More like the new Herman's Hermits,' a friend muttered in the pub the other day—but there is some truth in the comparison. The question is, how much?").

2. Around the same time, avid users of the all-time, best-selling computer game, Myst, were confronted with its sequel, Riven. The availability of the sequel has generated a storm of technical and nontechnical comparisons. See David Thomas, "All in the Game: Driven by Riven to Superlatives," *Denver Post,* Oct. 31, 1997, A3 ("But looking under the hood and making technical comparisons between the games doesn't do justice. Because where Myst could feel sterile and stagnant, Riven feels alive.").

3. See American Association of Law Schools, *Law School Rankings May Be Hazardous to Your Health: A Message to Applicants from Law School Deans,* 1998, 1 (stating that, based on a recent Rand study, law applicants are urged not to supplant their own judgment with commercial law school rankings because "rankings leave many important variables out of account, arbitrarily weight others, and are generally unreliable as a guide to those qualities of different schools that an applicant should consider when applying to law school"); "Law Methodology, FYI," *US News and World Report: 1998 Annual Guide, Best Graduate Schools,* Mar. 2, 1998, 48 (responding to legal educators by agreeing that "rankings should not be applicants' main source of information," but disagreeing with allegations that the rankings "ignore important factors like faculty quality and curricula,"

based on survey questions that asked "academics and lawyers [to] take such factors into account").

4. See Ann Doss Helms and Laurie Lucas, "Preparing for the Unthinkable," *Press-Enterprise* (Riverside, Calif.), Jan. 11, 1998, D1:

[P]reparing for the unthinkable. No one likes to think about [death]. But for parents, choosing a [guardian] for their children is an ultimate act of responsibility. Such decisions require a complex weighing of multiple comparative considerations and factors. For example: When they come to our attention, such incidents can launch a mental inventory, which often goes something like this: The sister in San Francisco is too far away, and the brother-in-law who [is] single is out of the question. Another sister lives nearby, but her husband drinks a lot. Our parents are getting old. We have friends who seem like ideal parents, but could we ask such a favor?

5. For a pre-9/11 perspective on this question, see Steven Lee Myers, "Whether to Bomb Is the Easy Part," *New York Times,* Feb. 1, 1998, A4 (pointing out advantages and disadvantages of all of the military options for the United States in Iraq and emphasizing that "[m]ost important, this country must decide what its objective really is, how to accomplish it and what the risks are.").

6. The role of comparison in personal identity is of significant interest. Vivian Curran began her thoughtful article on the émigré approach to comparative law with a quote from Thomas Mann: "Denn nur durch Vergleichung unterscheidet man sich und erfährt, was man ist, um ganz zu werden, was mann sein soll" (For only through comparison does one distinguish oneself and experience what one is, so that one can become completely what one should be.) (Curran's translation). See also Vivian Grosswald Curran, "Cultural Immersion, Difference and Categories in U.S. Comparative Law," *Am. J. Comp. L.* 46 (1998): 43. Amitai Etzioni and Fredric L. Dubow, the editors of *Comparative Perspectives: Theories and Methods* (Boston: Little, Brown, 1970), begin the collection thus: "Comparisons play a central role in our daily lives, in logic, and in substantive theories." Etzioni and Dubow, vii.

7. See Douglas R. Hofstadter, *Gödel, Escher, Bach: An Eternal Golden Braid* (New York: Basic Books, 1979), 26 (defining intelligence by essential abilities, inter alia, "to recognize the relative importance of different elements of a situation; to find similarities between situations despite differences which may separate them; to draw distinctions between situations despite similarities which may link them").

8. See Curran, "Cultural Immersion," 47 (stressing the role of comparison in human cognition).

9. Hofstadter, 26 (including with the essential abilities of intelligence "to synthesize new concepts by taking old concepts and putting them together in new ways").

10. See John Henry Merryman, "Comparative Law and Scientific Explanation," in *Law in the United States of America in Social and Technological Revolution,* ed. John N. Hazard and Wenceslas J. Wagner (Brussels: Emile Bruylant, 1974), 84 (describing the difference between a descriptive and prescriptive statement: "[T]he difference is fundamental; it is the difference between the is and the ought.").

11. See Neil K. Komesar, *Imperfect Alternatives: Choosing Institutions in Law, Economics and Public Policy* (Chicago: University of Chicago Press, 1994), ix and passim (arguing that even though institutional comparison is imperfect and difficult, the evils of not doing so are much worse).

12. Basil S. Markesinis, *Always on the Same Path: Essays on Foreign Law and Comparative Methodology,* vol. 2 (Oxford; Portland, Ore.: Hart Publishing, 2001), 58 ("[R]eal differences, be they in language, aesthetic values, or the law, provide the kind of contrasts

and yardsticks which allow one to understand and rethink one's own ideas, rules, and institutions, and, on occasion, be converted to the alien ones.").

13. See Merryman, "Comparative Law and Scientific Explanation," 81–82 (describing the need for comparison). Each of the propositions discussed by Merryman, whether explanatory, general, specific, or prescriptive, involves comparison: between nations with and without constitutional courts, between community property and noncommunity property jurisdictions, between developed and nondeveloped legal systems, between the presence and absence of procedures for controlling administrative legality, between controlling or not controlling administrative legality, or between the presence or absence of the obligation of wrongdoers to pay compensation to their victims. Ibid. See also Donald L. Horowitz, "Foreword: Compared to What," *Duke J. Comp. & Int'l L.* 13 (2003): 1 ("human cognition is inexorably based on comparison of one phenomenon with another").

14. See Konrad Zweigert and Hein Kötz, *An Introduction to Comparative Law,* 3d ed., vol. 1, trans. Tony Weir (New York: Clarendon Press, 1998), 8 (recognizing that "all legal history involves a comparative element").

15. The current controversy over proposals to repeal the independent counsel law provides a topical example. See Linda Greenhouse, "Blank Check; Ethics in Government: The Price of Good Intentions." *New York Times,* Feb. 1, 1998, Sec. 4, p. 1. ("[C]ost-benefit analysis is also a comparative exercise. The absence of an independent counsel law would have costs of its own.").

16. Mark Blaug has illuminated and bridged the role of comparison in statistical inferences (the Neyman-Pearson Theory) and legal burdens of proof in jury trial:

[A]ny statistical test of a hypothesis always depends in an essential way on an alternative hypothesis with which it is being compared, even if the comparison is only with an artifact, [the null hypothesis]. But that is true not only of statistical tests of hypotheses but of all tests of "adductions." Is Smith guilty of murder? Well, it depends on whether the jury presumes him to be innocent until proven guilty, or guilty until he can prove himself to be innocent. The evidence itself, being typically "circumstantial" as they say, cannot be evaluated unless the jury first decided whether the risk of Type I error (conviction of innocent people) is smaller or greater than the risk of Type II error (acquittal of guilty people). (p. 21).

17. Leopold Pospisil, *Anthropology of Law: A Comparative Theory,* 2d ed. (New York: Harper and Row, 1992), 39–96 (identifying universal attributes of "law" based on the study of multiple legal cultures).

18. For example, consider a proposal for a more independent judiciary in Country X. Putting aside potential disagreements in understanding the various meanings of "judiciary," the term "independence" raises some fundamental comparative questions. Which purposes (in contrast to others) might be better served by an independent judiciary? For example, an argument for an independent judiciary might emphasize independence from recognized political authority, yet discount the alternative objective of accountability to the public. Which type of independence should be examined (independence from political branches of government or economically powerful criminal organizations)? Which terms of employment evidence political or economic independence? Once chosen, according to which spectrum of relative differences should they be measured?

A comparison of two models illustrates the point that comparisons of this type are riddled with methodological questions of purpose clarification, variable selection, and differential measurements. Consider the following, albeit crudely stated, contrast between two competing models of judicial independence. Model A employs a political process for appointment; yet, once appointed, judges have life tenure. Model B selects judges through competitive examination; however, judges may be removed for political reasons. First, a comparative choice of models requires a determination of the greater potential risk to judicial independence (ideological screening mechanisms in the selection process largely avoided by Model B, or the threat of removal for politically unpopular decisions largely avoided by Model A). Second, to answer the question of which judiciary is independent requires a choice of comparative variable(s): selection or tenure. If the comparatist (e.g., from B) considers selection as the primary feature of independence, Model A would not represent an independent judiciary. On the other hand, if the comparatist (e.g., from A) thinks that life tenure is the most significant index of independence, Model B would not represent an independent judiciary. Furthermore, the question "how independent?" requires a balance with other goals, e.g., accountability, depending in part on the functional powers of the judiciary to review the actions of other branches of government. It also requires a relative measurement of the role of political interference either in A's appointment system or B's removal system. That is, it requires a more detailed look at the appointment or tenure regime itself. This examination would illuminate the specific criteria for selection or the grounds for removal, the institutions responsible for applying these criteria, and the process through which they are applied. Therefore, the selection of any particular model depends on the motivating purpose, choice of variable, and standard of differentiation. Thus, a decision on how to design an independent judiciary relies heavily on the quality of its comparative underpinnings. See Komesar, 125 ("[T]he same structural elements and safeguards that produce independence and evenhandedness produce systemic biases in adjudication and limitations on the competence and physical capacity of the adjudicative process."). See also chapter 4, infra.

19. See Komesar, 273 (criticizing "the failure of many legal scholars to pay careful attention to the comparative institutional characteristics of the courts").

20. See Oscar G. Chase, "Legal Processes and National Culture," *Cardozo J. Int'l & Comp. L.* 5 (1997). Chase argues that

> the relationship between national culture and dispute resolution processes . . . takes on new urgency with the acceleration of globalization; . . . the principal institutional differences between the American and German procedures implicate and reflect different and deeply held attitudes about the appropriate relationship between individuals and authority. The German system . . . reflects a willingness to accept structures of authority that are inimical to the more individualistic Americans. (1–2)

See also John H. Langbein, "Cultural Chauvinism in Comparative Law," *Cardozo J. Int'l & Comp. L.* 5 (1997): 41 (arguing that Chase wrongly bases his views on "ethnic stereotypes about the individualism of Americans and the authoritarianism of Germans").

21. But see State v. Kargar, 679 A2d 81 (Me. 1996) (dismissing criminal charges against Afghani refugee; holding that although defendant's kissing his son's penis fell within the literal definition of gross sexual assault, conduct was an accepted cultural practice as a sign of love and affection for a child, defendant's conduct was not sexual, and the child was not harmed).

22. See John Henry Merryman, "On the Convergence (and Divergence) of the Civil Law and the Common Law," *Stanford J. Int'l L.* 17 (1981): 357 (exemplifying the scholarly examination of the topic).

23. See John Henry Merryman, "How Others Do It: The French and German Judiciaries," *S. Cal. L. Rev.* 61 (1988): 1865 ("[D]o we have something to learn from French and German practices? Is their system better than ours?").

24. Langbein has lamented that "the study of comparative procedure in the United States has little following in academia, and virtually no audience in the courts or in legal policy circles." John H. Langbein, "The Influence of Comparative Procedure in the United

States," *Am. J. Comp. L.* 43 (1995): 545; see also Ernst C. Stiefel and James R. Maxeiner, "Civil Justice Reform in the United States—Opportunity for Learning from 'Civilized' European Procedure Instead of Continued Isolation," *Am. J. Comp. L.* 42 (1994): 147 (arguing for civil justice reform). For a purely domestic comparison, see James Kakalik et al., *Just, Speedy and Inexpensive? An Evaluation of Judicial Case Management under the Civil Justice Reform Act* (Santa Monica, Calif.: RAND Institute for Civil Justice, 1996), 26 ("[B]ecause case management varies across judges and districts, we were able to assess the effects of specific procedures and techniques on time to disposition, costs, and attorneys' satisfaction and views of fairness. This assessment clearly shows that what judges do to manage cases matters.").

25. See Owen M. Fiss, "Against Settlement," *Yale L. J.* 93 (1984): 1076 (explaining the frequent imbalance of power between parties to a lawsuit); Andrew W. McThenia and Thomas L. Shaffer, "For Reconciliation," *Yale L. J.* 94 (1985): 1660 (arguing Fiss "attacks a straw man"); see also Owen M. Fiss, "Out of Eden," *Yale L. J.* 94 (1985): 1670 (arguing contentions of McThenia and Schaffer are "just beside the point"); Carrie Menkel-Meadow, "For and Against Settlement: Uses and Abuses of the Mandatory Settlement Conference," *UCLA L. Rev.* 33 (1985): 512 (arguing that requiring all cases to go through a mandatory settlement process would be a mistake); Judith Resnik, "Many Doors? Closing Doors? Alternative Dispute Resolution and Adjudication," *Ohio St. J. on Disp. Resol.* 10 (1995): 211 (discussing the interrelationship between claims made for ADR and views of adjudication).

26. See also Curtis A. Bradley and Jack L. Goldsmith, "The Current Illegitimacy of International Human Rights Litigation," *Fordham L. Rev.* 66 (1997): 320 (addressing the "legitimacy of international human rights litigation in U.S. courts"); Curtis A. Bradley and Jack L. Goldsmith, "Customary International Law as Federal Common Law: A Critique of the Modern Position," *Harv. L. Rev.* 110 (1997): 815 (criticizing the use of federal common law in international law litigation in domestic courts); Harold Hongju Koh, "Is International Law Really State Law?" *Harv. L. Rev.* 111 (1998): 1826–27 (responding to Bradley and Goldsmith's criticisms and examining whether federal common law legitimately governs international law).

27. See Joel P. Trachtman, "Introduction: Toward Comparative Analysis of Institutions for International Economic Integration," *Nw. J. Int'l L. & Bus.* 17 (1996–1997): 351 (posing questions of comparability: "Are these entities [the European Union, the North American Free Trade Agreement, and the World Trade Organization, for example] comparable on any dimension? Do the tremendous differences in the goals of these entities, combined with the tremendous differences in their composition, structure, and legal culture, make folly of any attempted comparison?"); see also J. H. H. Weiler and Joel P. Trachtman, "European Constitutionalism and Its Discontents," *Nw. J. Int'l L. & Bus.* 17 (1996–1997): 355 (Identifying trappings of time-bound, simple metric, and other failings of cross-legal comparisons, yet arguing that "the European Union should no longer be viewed as sui generis or nirvana").

28. See H. L. A. Hart, *The Concept of Law* (Oxford: Oxford University Press, 1961), 209 (arguing that international law lacked both "secondary rules of change and adjudication which provide for legislature and courts" in domestic legal systems and a "unifying rule of recognition specifying 'sources' of law and providing general criteria for the identification of its rules"); Hans J. Morgenthau, *Politics among Nations: The Struggle for Power and Peace,* 4th ed. (New York: Knopf, 1967) (putting forth a theory of international politics based on realism); Terry Nardin, "Ethical Traditions in International Affairs," in *Traditions of International Ethics,* ed. Terry Nardin and David R. Mapel (Cam-

bridge: Cambridge University Press, 1993), 13 (stating that "international law is 'not really law,' because it cannot be enforced").

29. See Louis Henkin, *How Nations Behave: Law and Foreign Policy,* 2d ed. (New York: Columbia University Press, 1979), 47 (noting that "almost all nations observe almost all principles of international law and almost all of their obligations almost all of the time").

30. See generally Thomas M. Franck, *Fairness in International Law and Institutions* (Oxford: Clarendon Press, 1995); Thomas M. Franck, *The Power of Legitimacy among Nations* (New York: Oxford University Press, 1990); Harold Hongju Koh, *Why Nations Behave: A Theory of Compliance with International Law* (forthcoming); Jose E. Alvarez, "Why Nations Behave," *Mich. J. Int'l L.* 19 (1998): 303; Harold Hongju Koh, "Transnational Legal Process," *Neb. L. Rev.* 75 (1996): 181; Harold Hongju Koh, "Why Do Nations Obey International Law?" *Yale L. J.* 106 (1997): 2602 n. 9 (reviewing Abram Chayes and Antonia Handler Chayes, *The New Sovereignty: Compliance with International Regulatory Agreements* (1995) and Franck, 1995).

31. See Ronald Coffey, Interventions in Securities Decisionmaking: Methodology and Analytics (1992), 1 (unpublished manuscript) (on file with author):

Legal methodology confronts our most primitive issue, namely: what patterns of thought and what sorts of apprehensions and judgments are (and ought to be) eligible or required as components of justifications for (or against) governmental intervention in the form of directives and prohibitions specifying the conditions under which property rights will be awarded or liability imposed through a variety of sanctions.

32. See American Bar Association, *An Independent Judiciary: Report of the ABA Commission on Separation of Powers and Judicial Independence* (Washington, D.C.: American Bar Association, 1997) (cited hereinafter as ABA Report) (quoting from the Judicial Conference of the United States that "if the federal courts alienate the public and lose its support and participation, they cannot carry out their appropriate role"). See ibid., 43 (stating, "Maintaining the Appropriate Balance Between Independence and Accountability is of Critical Importance to Our Democracy").

33. See Henry T. King and Theodore C. Theofrastous, "From Nuremberg to Rome: A Step Backward for U.S. Foreign Policy," *Case W. Res. J. Int'l L.* 31 (1999): 47 (criticizing the U.S. position against formation of the permanent international criminal court).

34. See Cuban Liberty and Democratic Solidarity (Libertad) Act, U.S. Code, vol. 22, secs. 6021–6091 (1996) (hereinafter cited as Helms-Burton Act) (providing punishment for corporations that have purchased property that the Cuban government has expropriated from U.S. citizens).

35. See Coffey, 8 (noting that "by presenting partial justificative analyses, a rulemaker or commentator is unaccountable to his audience").

36. See Curran, "Cultural Immersion," 44: "[C]omparative law as a field should be able to offer valuable contributions, given that it is the one field which by definition has always dealt with and analyzed the other, the different. Yet comparative law in the United States has seemed largely impervious to the current theoretical debate surrounding the role of the other, the marginalized, within our own legal culture." See also Vivian Grosswald Curran, "Dealing in Difference: Comparative Law's Potential for Broadening Legal Perspectives," *Am. J. Comp. L.* 46 (1998): 658 (pointing out the benefits of an emphasis on "difference" and "otherness").

37. See Peter Medawar, *Pluto's Republic* (New York: Oxford University Press, 1984), 132 (observing that "[a] scientific methodology, being itself a theory about the conduct of

scientific enquiry, must have grown out of an attempt to find out exactly what scientists do or ought to do").

38. See Kozyris, 166 (quoting Schlessinger: "Comparative law is not really 'law' like international or domestic law but is only a method."); Pedro A. Malavet, "Counsel for the Situation: The Latin Notary, A Historical and Comparative Model," *Hastings Int'l & Comp. L. Rev.* 19 (1996): 392 ("Comparative law is not a body of rules and principles. Primarily, it is a method, a way of looking at legal problems, legal institutions, and entire legal systems.").

39. The arguable exception to this observation is "choice of law" because a choice implies a comparison of alternatives prior to making a choice. For example, "comparative impairment" is a doctrinal approach to choice of law which attempts to determine which state interests would be more (or most) impaired by application of another state's law. See generally William Baxter, "Choice of Law and the Federal System," *Stan. L. Rev.* 16 (1963): 1.

40. See Friedrich K. Juenger, "American Jurisdiction: A Story of Comparative Neglect," *U. Colo. L. Rev.* 65 (1993): 1 ("Comparative law, or, as some prefer to call it, the comparative method can serve a variety of purposes."); see generally Kozyris, 167; Malavet, 392.

41. For example, Christopher Whelan's claim that "[t]here has been for some time a substantial but largely theoretical body of literature proposing ground rules for proper application of the comparative method" still remains unpersuasive unless by the phrase comparative method one excludes the method of comparison itself. Christopher J. Whelan, "Labor Law and Comparative Law," *Tex. L. Rev.* 63 (1985): 1426 (citations omitted).

42. Critical reviewers of comparative scholarship have frequently experienced disappointment from justifiably heightened expectations. See generally Martha A. Fineman, "Review: Contexts and Comparisons," *U. Chi. L. Rev.* 55 (1988): 1431 (reviewing Mary Ann Glendon, *Abortion and Divorce in Western Law* (1987)).

43. For an exceptional treatment of comparative method in work on comparative legal professions, see Robin Luckham, "The Political Economy of Legal Professions: Towards a Framework for Comparison," in *Lawyers in the Third World: Comparative and Developmental Perspectives,* ed. C. J. Dias et al. (Uppsala and New York: Scandinavian Institute of African Studies, 1998), 287.

44. See Alan Watson, *Legal Transplants: An Approach to Comparative Law,* 2d ed. (Athens: University of Georgia Press, 1993) (emphasizing the absence of discussion on the topic of what the comparative method is: "What is this method or technique? The student will find that the question tends to remain unanswered.").

45. See Hiram E. Chodosh et al., "Egyptian Civil Justice Process Modernization: A Functional and Systemic Approach," *Mich. J. Int'l L.* 17 (1996): 879–90 (noting the general absence of a rigorous comparative methodology in civil justice jurisprudence).

46. See Guyora Binder, "Institutions and Linguistic Conventions: The Pragmatism of Lierbe's Legal Hermeneutics," *Cardozo L. Rev.* 16 (1995): 2182 (citing Robert W. Gordon, "Legal Thought and Legal Practice in the Age of American Enterprise 1870–1920," in Professions and Professional Ideologies in America, ed. Gerald L. Geison (Chapel Hill: University of North Carolina Press, 1983), 84) for the proposition that "the comparative method consisted of looking to the practices of other civilized nations") (citations omitted).

47. Should one assume a position of distance or proximity to the subject at hand? See Gunter Frankenberg, "Critical Comparisons: Re-Thinking Comparative Law," *Harv. Int'l L. J.* 26 (1985): 447–48, 454–55 (discussing the role of distance in comparative law). The chosen perspective may be considered external to (outside) or internal to (inside) the subject studied. What appears external, however, may grow out of an internal experience, and

what appears to be internal may draw on variables chosen from bodies of thought external to the subject. Lasser argues that his internal approach (though not perfect) is better than the external approach of Damaska, but three points of skepticism should be raised. First, his use of literary theory as a way to get at underlying similarities does not emerge from within the subject of French judicial decisions he studies (and compares). Second, his primary inquiry emerges from a contrast with American judicial decisions that is at least partially external to the French. Third, it is not necessarily more clear from the inside what is relevant or worthy of analysis. Mitchel de S.-O.-l'E Lasser, "Comparative Law and Comparative Literature: A Project in Progress," *Utah L. Rev.* (1997): 474–80; see also Karen Engle, "Comparative Law as Exposing the Foreign System's Internal Critique: An Introduction," *Utah L. Rev.* (1997): 366 (noting that external caricatures of French law are perpetuated by self-descriptions: "What many French jurists (including the ones that seem to be the most listened to) say about their own system perpetuates the myth"); George P. Fletcher, "The Universal and Particular in Legal Discourse," *BYU L. Rev.* (1987): 340 (attacking the functionalist perspective and praising H. L. A. Hart's "innovative suggestion that in seeking an account of legal experience, we consider the internal as well as the external point of view"); W. Cole Durham, "Foreword: Comparative Law in the Late Twentieth Century," *BYU L. Rev.* (1987): 328 (arguing that Fletcher poses "an important corrective to excessive functionalism, but he overstates the point").

48. See F. Eggan, "Some Reflections on Comparative Method in Anthropology," in *Context and Meaning in Cultural Anthropology,* ed. Melford E. Shapiro (New York: Free Press, 1965), 366 ("[T]he comparative method is not a 'method' in the broad sense, but a technique for establishing similarities and differences."); Moore, *Law as Process,* 136 (quoting the same).

49. See William Ewald, "Comparative Jurisprudence: What Was It Like to Try a Rat?" *U. Pa. L. Rev.* 143 (1995): 1896 (stating that "the primary object of study for comparative law should be the philosophical principles that lie behind the surface of the rules."); William Ewald, "The Jurisprudential Approach to Comparative Law: A Field Guide to 'Rats,'" *Am. J. Comp. L.* 46 (1998): 701 (summarizing and clarifying the 1995 article); see also Joachim Zekoll, "Kant and Comparative Law: Some Reflections on a Reform Effort," *Tul. L. Rev.* 70 (1996): 2719 (expressing disagreement with Ewald's criticisms and suggestions for reforming the discipline).

50. For example, Andrew Huxley has drawn a preliminary connection between the conclusions of comparative research and the choice of comparative content or variables. Huxley, 1924 ("In my view, the conclusions of a typical comparative law project are prefigured by the researcher's choice of what to compare."); see also Eric Stein, "Uses, Misuses—And Nonuses of Comparative Law," *Nw. U. L. Rev.* 72 (1977): 198 (claiming that "the specific question of how the law maker should employ [comparative method in the sense of German Rechtsvergleichung] to suit his purpose remains").

51. See Pierre Legrand, "How to Compare Now," *Legal Studies* 16: (1996): 232 (discussing the interactions of European legal transactions; the question is hardly new, but alternative answers are scarce); Pound, "Space and Time," 76 ("Now how are they to be compared? What is to be the measure or what are to be the measures of comparison?"). Myres McDougal complained over forty years ago that the "greatest confusion continues to prevail about what is being compared, about the purposes of comparison, and about appropriate techniques." Myres S. McDougal, "The Comparative Study of Law for Policy Purposes: Value Clarification as an Instrument of Democratic World Order," *Am. J. Comp. L.* 1 (1952): 24.

52. C. N. Kakouris, "Use of the Comparative Method by the Court of Justice of the European Communities," *Pace Int'l L. Rev.* 6 (1994): 268 fn. 3, 282–83; see ibid., 282–83

(describing the "quasi-harmonization" brought about by the Court of Justice of the European communities).

53. Ibid., 268 n. 3.

54. See discussion infra at chapter 2. B. 3. Merryman argues that "certain kinds of activity sometimes loosely associated with comparative law actually involve no comparison." Merryman, "Comparative Law," 82.

55. Watson, *Legal Transplants,* 11 (citing to Lawson's observation that "I do not see how a comparison between two laws can be systematic") (quoting W. W. Buckland and A. D. McNair, *Roman Law and Common Law: A Comparison in Outline,* 2d ed. (Cambridge: Cambridge University Press, 1952), xii). It must be pointed out here that both Watson and Lawson may have envisioned (and then quickly rejected) the notion of a universally settled way of conducting comparative research suitable to all scholars. Watson explains further: "At least there is no single system, no set of criteria which would be useful for all purposes, or acceptable to all scholars." Ibid., 11 fn. 5.

56. H. C. Gutteridge, *Comparative Law* (Cambridge: Cambridge University Press, 1946), 72–87.

57. Ibid., 75–82 (discussing the identification of sources); ibid., 82–87 (discussing the identification of materials).

58. Ibid., 73.

59. Ibid. This requirement would undermine contemporary efforts to model underdeveloped legal systems on more developed ones.

60. See Rudolf B. Schlesinger et al., *Comparative Law: Cases, Text, Materials,* 6th ed. (New York: Foundation Press, 1998), 1–43.

61. Ibid., 2.

62. See ibid., 3–6; Greenspan v. Slate, 12 NJ 426, 97 A2d 390 (1953) (holding parents liable for medical services rendered to child in emergency based in part on foreign authority of Continental European civil code provisions).

63. Schlesinger et al., 14–16.

64. Ibid., 21–29.

65. Ibid., 29–47.

66. Ibid., 47–52.

67. John Henry Merryman, David S. Clark and John O. Haley, *The Civil Law Tradition: Europe, Latin America, East Asia,* 2d ed. (Charlottesville, Va.: Mitchie, 1994).

68. René David, *Grands Systèmes de Droit Contemporains,* 3d ed. (1969); René David and John E. C. Brierley, *Major Legal Systems in the World Today: An Introduction to the Comparative Study of Law,* 3d ed. (New York: Free Press, 1985).

69. Mauro Cappelletti, *The Judicial Process in Comparative Perspective* (Oxford: Clarendon Press, 1989).

70. Mirjan R. Damaska, *The Faces of Justice and State Authority: A Comparative Approach to the Legal Process* (New Haven: Yale University Press, 1986).

71. See David, *Grands Systèmes,* 23–24 (discussing the concept of legal families, or le groupement des droits en familles).

72. See Cappelletti, xiv (describing the phenomenological-comparative approach as phenomenological because it studies "observable facts and events" and "comparative" because of its interest in societal problems "shared by various countries"). Thus:

> [T]he phenomenological inquiry proceeds to examine the methods — rules, processes, institutions, etc., adopted by those countries to solve that problem, often with the end result of designing 'models' of the various types of solution thus adopted. . . . [T]he various solutions can be evaluated, not indeed in any absolute sense, but in relation to their efficacy or impact in solving the problem with which

the entire research began. Value judgments such as "progressive or backward," even "just" or "unjust," can then be used with a degree of objectivity—in relation, that is, to the demonstrated adequacy or inadequacy of a given solution to address the particular problem involved. Ibid., xviii–xix.

73. See Damaska, 16–46 (contrasting hierarchical and coordinate ideals in the organization of authority); ibid., 71–96 (contrasting the reactive and activist state).

74. Ibid., 66 (discussing the commensurability of the hierarchical and coordinate ideals):

I have also implicitly suggested the difficulty of comparing procedural problems across the divide that separates them. Otherwise similar forms of justice in the two institutional settings may differ in ways not easy to define, and forms of justice natural in one setting can elude description in terms of categories habitual in the other. Surely, Continental and Anglo- American lawyers find it more difficult to develop a common language in matters of procedure and evidence than in other areas of the law. Some problems of relating the divergent outlooks deserve a cursory review.

Damaska goes on to explain that because his "study seeks to illuminate differences more than to identify common grounds, I shall not inquire here whether a scheme can yet be formulated in which procedural conventions in the two settings of authority can be made easily translatable." Ibid., 68–69.

75. McDougal, 29–30.

76. Ibid., 30.

77. Ibid., 34.

78. Ibid., 30.

79. Ibid., 35.

80. McDougal, 35.

81. Ibid., 37.

82. Stein, 209–10.

83. Ibid., 215. One explanation for the non-use of the comparative method is the lack of common understanding about what it entails. Conversely, there may be so few academic-practitioners of any, no less the, comparative method that comparisons of the sort contemplated by these writers have not evolved sufficiently in order to become explicitly or systematically methodological.

84. See Mary Ann Glendon et al., *Comparative Legal Traditions in a Nutshell,* 2d ed. (St. Paul, Minn.: West Group, 1999), 11 (drawing on Ernst Rabel, *Aufgabe und Notwendigkeit der Rechtsvergleichung* [1925], reprinted in Ernst Rabel, *Gesammelte Aufsätze,* vol. 3 [Tübingen: Mohr Siebeck, 1967], 1). See generally Max Rheinstein, *Einfuhrung in die Rechtsvergleichung* (Munich, 1974); Max Rheinstein, "Comparative Law— Its Functions, Methods, and Usages," *Ark. L. Rev.* 77 (1968): 415.

85. See Glendon et al., 9–12 (noting these two concepts as "key to Rabel's understanding" of comparative law).

86. See generally chapter 1, notes 8–16 (discussing the development of methodological discourse in other fields).

87. For a seminal treatment of the history of the philosophy of science, see Blaug, 1–46, and for a discussion of the "great" divide between the "methods of the physical and social sciences," see ibid., 46–52.

88. Munroe Smith crudely stated that comparison was "preeminently the scientific method." Munroe Smith, *A General View of European Legal History and Other Papers* (1927), 263, quoted in McDougal, 24.

89. See Mauro Cappelletti et al., "Integration through Law: Europe and the American Federal Experience: A General Introduction," in *Methods, Tools, and Institutions,* vol. 1 of

"Integration through Law" series, ed. Mauro Cappelletti, Monica Seccombe, and Joseph H. Weiler (Berlin: DeGruyter, 1986), 5 ("In political, legal, and economic analysis one does not have the benefit of the laboratory conditions available to the natural and some of the human sciences."). Cappelletti, Seccombe, and Weiler describe comparative and historical methods themselves as "laboratories," which are designed to provide "an empirical basis of concrete data upon which to found realistic, not merely abstract, speculation" and to "overcom[e] the dangers of sheer empiricism and value-free positivism." Ibid. These three prominent scholars identify a primarily social purpose of comparison: "to reveal actual societal problems and needs, developments and trends, shared by certain societies." Ibid. They recognized the problem of the absence of laboratory settings, but argued that this was not a fatal objection because some sciences, such as astronomy, are "obliged to dispense with experimentation." Ibid.; see also Pierre Lepaulle, "The Function of Comparative Law with a Critique of Social Jurisprudence," *Harv. L. Rev.* 35 (1922): 839 (criticizing sociological jurisprudence by stating that "while it is undoubtedly a school of jurisprudence, it is hardly a school of sociology").

90. See Blaug, 21 ("[A]ny statistical test of a hypothesis always depends in an essential way on an alternative hypothesis with which it is being compared [the null hypothesis], even if the comparison is only with an artifact.").

91. See generally infra chapter 2. B. 1.

92. Medawar, 116.

93. Blaug, 47.

94. See Merryman et al., *The Civil Law Tradition,* 1 ("Most comparative law teaching and scholarship could more accurately be called 'foreign law,' since its principal aim is to describe foreign legal systems.").

95. Ibid.

96. Ibid.

97. Ibid.

98. Ibid.

99. Merryman et al., *The Civil Law Tradition,* 2.

100. Ibid.

101. See Kozyris, 166 (defining comparative law as a method); Malavet, 392 (defining comparative law as a method); see also Reitz, 618–20, 633–34 (arguing for benefits of explicit comparison).

102. In other words, the contrast alone, which presupposes an initial comparison, does not encompass a full comparison. Without a full comparison, contrasts with "difference" do not automatically effectuate the objectives of comparative law applauded by these scholars.

103. These examples are drawn mainly from an earlier, second edition (1977) of their classic work, republished in 1998. See Zweigert and Kötz, *An Introduction to Comparative Law,* vol. 1, trans. Tony Weir (New York: Clarendon, 1977), 35 ("Separate reports . . . should be objective, that is, free from any critical evaluation, though containing all significant qualifications or modifications.") (hereinafter "Zweigert and Kötz 1977").

104. Ibid., 35.

105. Ibid.

106. Ibid.

107. Ibid.

108. Zweigert and Kötz 1977, 36.

109. For a discussion of function (as well as context), see Glendon et al., 11–13 (drawing on the work of Ernst Rabel, Otto Kahn-Freund, and Max Rheinstein).

110. Zweigert and Kötz 1977, 36. But see Watson, *Legal Transplants,* 4 (arguing that

"political, moral, social and economic values which exist between any two societies make it hard to believe that many legal problems are the same for both except on a technical level"). Watson draws a bright line between a comparison of these factors and more technical legal comparisons when he writes: "[W]hen the starting point is the problem the weight of investigation will always be primarily on the comparability of the problem, only secondarily on the comparability of the law; and any discipline founded on such a starting point will be sociology rather than law." Ibid., 5.

111. Zweigert and Kötz 1977, 37.

112. Ibid.

113. Ibid.

114. Ibid., 38.

115. See also Cappelletti et al., "Integration," 5 ("Comparative legal analysis will then be brought to 'evaluate' laws, institutions and techniques in relation to [a] particular problem and need.").

116. Zweigert and Kötz 1977, 41.

117. See generally Max Gluckman, *Politics, Law and Ritual in Tribal Society* (Oxford: Blackwell, 1965), 1–34 (discussing the problems social anthropologists encounter in comparing different societies); *Ideas and Procedures in African Customary Law: Studies Presented and Discussed at the Eighth International African Seminar at the Haile Selassie I University, Addis Ababa, January 1966,* ed. Max Gluckman (London: Oxford University Press, 1969), 16, 20 (noting differences in "imprecise, ambiguous, multivocal" legal terminology and attempting to address "problems of comparison . . . in creating an analytic system for comparative analysis"); *Law and the Social System,* ed. Michael Barkun (New York: Lieber-Atherton, 1973) (dealing with the law's relationship to the social systems of various cultures); *Law and Warfare: Studies in the Anthropology of Conflict,* ed. Paul Bohannan (New York: Natural History Press, 1967) (exploring conflict resolution through two models: administered rules and war); *Law in Culture and Society,* ed. Laura Nader (Chicago: Aldine, 1969) (including a part on comparative studies); *The Ethnography of Law,* ed. Laura Nader, *Am. Anthropologist* (Special Publication) 67 (1965): 141–212 (providing a collection of anthropological studies on methodological approaches to primitive law); J. F. Holleman, "Law and Anthropology: A Necessary Partnership for the Study of Legal Change in Plural Systems," *J. African L.* 23 (1979): 117 (focusing on judicial process); Sally Falk Moore, "Law and Anthropology," in *Biennial Review of Anthropology,* ed. Bernard J. Seigel (Stanford: Stanford University Press, 1969), 252 (discussing emphasis on dispute settlement in anthropological literature); Laura Nader and Barbara Yngvesson, "On Studying the Ethnography of Law and Its Consequences," in *Handbook of Social and Cultural Anthropology,* ed. John J. Honigmann (Chicago: Rand McNally, 1973), 883 (pointing out the slow beginning for the comparative anthropological study of law). See also Brian Z. Tamanaha, *Bibliography on Law and Developing Countries* (New York: Kluwer Law International, 1995), xv–xvii (noting the absence from law and development collections of work in legal anthropology, even while claiming that many insights of the latter are incorporated in the former literature).

118. See Moore, *Law as Process,* 135 (stating that "deeply imbedded into the two [papers from a conference group gathered under the rubric Comparative Studies] . . . are differences of opinion about what is being compared and to what end").

119. See Catherine A. Rogers, "Gulliver's Troubled Travels, or the Conundrum of Comparative Law," *Geo. Wash. L. Rev.* 67 (1998): 150–51, 163 (arguing for applying methodologies developed in social sciences to comparative legal studies).

120. Ibid., 137.

121. Ibid.

122. See Pospisil, 39–96 (defining law by reference to four attributes, "authority, intention of universal application, obligatio (not to be confused with obligation) and sanction").

123. See Richard L. Abel, "A Comparative Theory of Dispute Institutions in Society," *L. & Soc'y Rev.* 8 (1973): 218–19 (explaining superiority of "dispute" over "law" as unit of comparison).

124. See F. L. Morton, "Judicial Review in France: A Comparative Analysis," *Am. J. Comp. L.* 36 (1990): 89 (addressing the debate over whether the Conseil Constitutionnel is a court).

125. Attempts to develop comparative frameworks in which to appreciate a functional and institutional definition of judge have either used greater abstractions, such as intermediary or neutral, or have used contrasts with other functional and institutional prototypes, such as arbitrator or mediator. See Martin Shapiro, "Courts," in *Handbook of Political Science: Governmental Institutions and Processes,* vol. 5, ed. Fred I. Greenstein and Nelson W. Polsby (Reading, Mass.: Addison-Wesley, 1975), 321 (describing the comparative frameworks that have been used by political scientists in the study of courts); see also Martin Shapiro, *Courts: A Comparative and Political Analysis* (Chicago: University of Chicago Press, 1981) (hereinafter cited as Shapiro, *Analysis*) (examining features of the prototype of courts in comparative perspective).

126. See Donald C. Clarke, "Dispute Resolution in China," *J. Chinese L.* 5 (1991): 294–96 (pointing out that the English term of mediation only represents a part of the Chinese function of tiaojie, which includes a "coercive" strain in addition to a voluntarist emphasis).

127. See Moore, *Law as Process,* 139–40 (pointing out the disagreements over purpose and selection of variables). Bohannan believed that English was a poor medium for cross-cultural legal comparisons and favored the use of the object culture's folk language and secondarily the development of a folk-system-free international language. Gluckman, however, saw no dispositive objection to using English with certain qualifications to mitigate misunderstanding. Ibid., 140. Moore reconciles the disagreements between these two prominent anthropologists by noting that Gluckman viewed concepts as part of a legal system, whereas Bohannan was primarily interested in the study of the concepts themselves. Ibid., 143. These, too, are equally comparative questions because they relate to the role of concepts in law, legal process, and legal systems.

128. Ibid., 217–18.

129. See generally *Do Institutions Matter? Government Capabilities in the United States and Abroad,* ed. R. Kent Weaver and Bert A. Rockman (Washington, D.C.: Brookings Institution, 1993) (posing questions about the effects of differences in institutional arrangements for governmental effectiveness and how knowledge can be applied in systemic reform).

130. See Shapiro, *Analysis* (generally using comparative analysis to discuss the concept of courtness from a political science point of view); John R. Schmidhauser, "Alternative Conceptual Frameworks in Comparative Cross-National Legal and Judicial Research," in *Comparative Judicial Systems: Challenging Frontiers in Conceptual and Empirical Analysis,* ed. John R. Schmidhauser (Boston: Butterworths, 1987), 34–58 (applying empirical examinations and scientific testing to court systems of selected developed and undeveloped nations in two alternative conceptual frameworks); C. Neal Tate, "Judicial Institutions in Cross-National Perspective: Toward Integrating Courts into the Comparative Study of Politics," in *Comparative Judicial Systems,* 7–33 (suggesting that the integration of judicial politics and judicial law would be beneficial to both comparative and political scholars); see also Theodore L. Becker, *Comparative Judicial Politics: The Political Functioning of*

Courts (Chicago: Rand McNally, 1970) (arguing that the comparative study of court systems is indispensable to the study of politics); Jean Blondel, *Comparative Legislatures* (Englewood Cliffs, N.J.: Prentice Hall, 1973), 22–28 (addressing methodological difficulties in the examination of legislatures in a comparative framework); Robert C. Fried, *Comparative Political Institutions* (New York: Macmillan, 1966) (examining alternative allocations of shared powers among political institutions, including the courts, in comparative perspective).

131. Tate, 9:

[S]cholars of public law and judicial politics have often failed to put their research into the comparative political context which is essential for developing broad generalizations about courts, their operation, and political and policy significance in societies. . . . Judicial politics and behavior scholars who never get beyond comparing judges with themselves or, at best, with other judges within the same society, must inevitably face some constraints imposed by their inability to put judges into a comparative context including other political actors.

132. The five frameworks are developed respectively by Becker (see Becker, 140–68 (discussing the measure, conditions, and functions of judicial independence)); Blondel (analyzing the influence and functions of legislatures); Shapiro, "Courts," 321–73; Fried 44–59; Schmidhauser (see generally John R. Schmidhauser, "A Weberian Conceptual Framework for Comparative Judicial Research" (presentation at the Annual Meeting of the Southern Political Science Association, Atlanta, Georgia, 1978)); and Ehrmann (see generally Henry Ehrmann, *Comparative Legal Cultures* (Englewood Cliffs, N.J.: Prentice Hall, 1976) (discussing the comparability of law)).

133. Comparisons of dispute resolution must be sufficiently broad to encompass non-court dispute resolution, such as mediation, conciliation, and arbitration performed by professionals or laypeople who are not "judicial" actors. Tate, 8.

134. Ibid., 12–26.

135. Both concepts will be addressed below, respectively, in chapters 3. B. 2 and 3. C. 1–2.

136. Merryman et al., *The Civil Law Tradition*, 1.

137. Watson, *Legal Transplants*, 10.

138. See Lijphart's discussion of Sartori's notion of "unconscious thinkers" as "unaware of and not guided by the logic and methods of empirical science." Lijphart, 682. Lijphart explains: "One reason for this unconscious thinking is undoubtedly that the comparative method is such a basic, and basically simple, approach, that a methodology of comparative political analysis does not really exist." Ibid.

139. See Ellen Markman, "Constraints Children Place on Word Meanings," *Cognitive Sci.* 14 (1990): 64–66 (demonstrating the greater categorical sophistication of older children).

140. See Oscar Lewis, "Comparisons in Cultural Anthropology," in *Readings in Cross-Cultural Methodology,* ed. Frank. W. Moore (New Haven, Conn.: HRAF Press, 1961), 50–88, 51 (arguing that comparison is a "generic" rather than a "specific" method).

141. Many prominent scholars are now turning their attention to the intersection between law and the biological sciences. See "Neurobiology, Human Behavior, and the Law," (address at the Squaw Valley Conference of the Gruter Institute for Law and Behavioral Research, June 17–20, 1998) (on file with author) ("The goal of the Conference is to help bridge the gap between the brain sciences underlying human behavior and the teaching and practice of law."). The biological sciences hold much unexplored promise for legal scholars, particularly comparatists. See also *The Cognitive Neurosciences,* ed. Michael S. Gazzaniga (Cambridge: MIT Press, 1995) (providing a collection expanding a mechanistic

analysis to all areas of cognitive study); Michael S. Gazzaniga, *Nature's Mind: The Biological Roots of Thinking, Emotions, Sexuality, Language, and Intelligence* (New York: Basic Books, 1992) (arguing that the selection process governs more complex functions, like language); Steven Pinker, *How the Mind Works: The Surprising Science of Human Thought* (New York: W. W. Norton, 1997), 21 (examining the mind as a "system of organs of computation, designed by natural selection to solve the kinds of problems our ancestors faced in their foraging way of life, in particular, understanding and outmaneuvering objects, animals, plants, and other people" responsive to evolutionary pressures of natural selection). Research into the relationship between comparison as an intellectual process and contemporary understanding of neurological functions of the brain might offer insights to comparative legal studies on the biological basis for comparative thinking. Interdisciplinary legal scholars have begun to apply an understanding of biology to different areas of the law. See Owen D. Jones, "Evolutionary Analysis in Law: An Introduction and Application to Child Abuse," *N.C. L. Rev.* 75 (1997): 1126 ("[U]nderstanding the processes by which some of our diverse human behaviors evolved will inevitably further whatever social and legal goals we pursue that address those behaviors.").

142. See generally infra chapter 3.

143. Otto Kahn-Freund, "Comparative Law as an Academic Subject," *L. Q. Rev.* 82 (1966): 41 (discussing the study of comparative law); Florian Miedel, "Is West Germany's 1975 Abortion Decision A Solution to the American Abortion Debate: A Critique of Mary Ann Glendon and Donald Kommers," *N.Y.U. Rev. L. & Soc. Change* 20 (1994): 510 (pointing out that "what exactly the comparative method entails, of course, is interpreted differently by different people").

144. See Zekoll, 2736 ("Comparatists have long recognized that their discipline has many facets serving many purposes, and is one whose borders are difficult to define.").

145. For example, Mary Ann Glendon, in her comparative work on abortion and divorce, argues that comparative law analysis has moved beyond its nineteenth-century origins as a "variety of methods" to a more systematic study of the components of legal systems operating in practice. See Mary Ann Glendon, *Abortion and Divorce in Western Law* (Cambridge: Harvard University Press, 1987), 3–4 (discussing the origins of comparative law analysis); Fineman (critiquing Glendon's methodology and complaining that Glendon's book lacks the context that is so central to the methodology of her work).

146. This position is similar to that taken in Paul K. Feyerabend, *Against Method: Outline of an Anarchistic Theory of Knowledge* (Atlantic Highlands, N.J.: Humanities Press, 1975) (arguing that there are no canons of scientific methodology); see also Blaug, 43–44 (discussing the same position).

147. Steven Pinker and Paul Bloom, "Natural Language and Natural Selection," in *The Adapted Mind*, ed. Jerome H. Barkow, Leda Cosmides, and John Tooby (New York: Oxford University Press, 1992), 461–62 (discussing universals of major lexical categories, major phrasal categories, phrase structure rules, rules of linear order, case affixes, verb affixes, etc.).

148. See Watson, *Legal Transplants*, 1–2 (attempting to explain the comparative method).

149. See Geertz, 233 ("[I]t is through comparison, and of incomparables, that whatever heart [of the matter] we can actually get to is to be reached.").

150. The summer before I entered legal academics in 1993, a comparatist joked with me that I would spend my life comparing apples and oranges. Little did he contemplate that I would take his jest seriously. The apple-and-orange problem is hardly new to comparative legal studies. John Henry Merryman contends that

describing only one piece of a legal (or any other) system is impossible; [t]he peculiar national histories and traditions; the specific structures and processes of legal education, legal scholarship, lawmaking, executive, and administrative action; the different prevailing paradigms of the legal process; the different sources of law and methods of finding and applying it, all form part of a legal system's conception of what judges are and what they do.

Merryman, "How Others Do It," 1865. For a recent exposition of the apple/orange problem, see Rogers, 155 (focusing on problems of objectivity in making the comparison).

151. William Alford gave a thoughtful treatment of "comparability" in cross-national understanding of the Chinese criminal justice system, expressing concern that "grand" theoretical work may unwittingly lead us to believe that we are considering foreign legal cultures in universal or value-free terms when, in fact, we are examining them through conceptual frameworks that are products of our own values and traditions, and that are often applied merely to see what foreign societies have to tell us about ourselves. William P. Alford, "On the Limits of 'Grand Theory' in Comparative Law," *Wash. L. Rev.* 61 (1986): 945–46.

152. The conventional view that comparisons seek to identify only similarities and not also differences is reflected in the redundant phrase, "contrastive comparisons." See Vladimir Aleksandrovich Tumanov, "On Comparing Various Types of Legal Systems," in *Comparative Law and Legal Systems: Historical and Socio-Legal Perspectives*, ed. W. E. Butler and V. N. Kudriavtsev (Dobbs Ferry, N.Y.: Oceana, 1985), 73 ("[T]he concept of 'contrastive comparison' . . . is one of the most important when describing external, intertypal comparison at all levels. . . .").

153. This does not suggest that comparisons of legal processes are not analogous to comparisons of fruits, but only that the level of abstraction and the risks of incomparability are greater in the secondary analogy than in the primary analogy.

154. This is similar to what Blaug calls methodological monism, drawing a distinction between techniques and methodology: "No one denies that the social sciences frequently employ different techniques of investigation from those common in the natural sciences. . . . But methodological monism has nothing to do with techniques of inquiry but rather with 'the context of justification' of theories." Blaug, 46–47.

155. See Gustav Radbruch, *Einführung in die Rechtswissenschaft* (Stuttgart: K. F. Koehler, 1969), 253 (stating that "sciences which have to busy themselves with their own methodology are sick sciences"); see also Zweigert and Kötz, 23 (quoting Radbruch and arguing that there were no signs of this disease with regard to comparative law because "comparatists all over the world are perfectly unembarrassed about their methodology, and see themselves as being still at the experimental stage").

156. Huxley, 1924–25 (emphasis added); see also Rogers, 162 ("Inevitably, the process of picking and choosing the concepts for comparison, then plucking them out of their existing legal structure, affects the projects of comparative analysis.").

157. Many other comparisons are possible, even useful. The artist, the storekeeper, and the teacher each may have contrasting motivations (beauty, sales, instruction) in making such comparisons, and as the example illustrates, the motivation profoundly affects the comparison itself. As Huxley himself notes, after reading the books he reviews, "[o]ne can scarcely refrain from making comparisons." Huxley, 1591. Huxley implies that nothing in the materials dictates any specific comparison, when he invites those "who disagree with the comparative framework in this Review . . . to construct their own." Ibid., 1949–50.

158. In the comparison of apples and oranges, symbolic literary value is of little use to the botanist. The choice of color as a differentiating criterion is of little value to dieticians,

unless they are predisposed to consider presentation as an allure to healthy eating. The classification of the tree that bears the fruit is of minor interest to the chef. Martha Stewart includes oranges in her Mexican salad recipe, but not on the basis of origin, cost, or convenience. Martha Stewart, *The Martha Stewart Cookbook: Collected Recipes for Every Day* (New York: Clarkson Potter, 1995), 330.

159. Practically useful comparisons rarely can rest on a single variable. For example, the farmer will consider in addition to climate the potential risks of disease, available pesticides or other immunizing technologies, their related costs, and other factors.

160. For an explanation of threshold relativity and the relationship between tests of differentiation and the underlying purpose of distinction, see Hiram E. Chodosh, "The Distinction Between Treaty and Customary International Law: An Interpretive Theory," *Vand. J. Transnat'l L.* 28 (1995): 1007 (applying interpretive approach to the question of whether minivans are cars or trucks, and arguing that "[t]he selection of differentiating attributes should be justified by its connection to the policies achieved by treating cars and trucks differently").

NOTES TO CHAPTER 3

1. For a provocative attack on comparative law as an autonomous discipline, see Watson, *Legal Transplants,* 2 (concluding that comparative law is not an academic activity "worthy of pursuit in its own right," based on "the absence of discussion" on whether comparative law has "a method or technique" that needs to be "specifically learned").

2. Kahn-Freund identifies as distinct purposes: (1) international unification of law; (2) giving adequate legal effect to a social change shared by a foreign country; and (3) promoting social change that foreign law is designed either to express or produce. Otto Kahn-Freund, "On Uses and Misuses of Comparative Law," *Mod. L. Rev.* 37 (1974): 12. For a comparison and reconciliation of the views of Kahn-Freund and those of Alan Watson, see Stein.

3. Pierre Lepaulle, "The Function of Comparative Law with a Critique of Social Jurisprudence," *Harv. L. Rev.* 37 (1974): 12. 855–57 (discussing the role of comparative law in the international context); John Henry Wigmore, *A Panorama of the World's Legal Systems,* vol. 3 (St. Paul, Minn.: West Publishing Co., 1928), 1120 (advocating comparative nomothetics to address the comparative merits of different legal institutions).

4. Huxley, 1925 ("[T]he comparative method must be judged by whether it works to increase the reader's understanding.").

5. Merryman, *Comparative Law,* 86 (claiming that explanation provides a basis for prediction).

6. Zweigert and Kötz, 3 (identifying knowledge as objective of comparative law).

7. See Pound, "Space and Time," 72 (identifying legal history as important focus of comparative law). For a more recent discussion of the relationship between comparative law and legal history, see Mathias Reimann and Alain Levasseur, "Comparative Law and Legal History in the United States," *Am. J. Comp. L.* 46 (1998): 1.

8. See Ewald (arguing for comparative jurisprudence as integration of comparative law and legal philosophy).

9. See David and Brierley, *Major Legal Systems,* 4 ("It was in relation to legal history, the philosophy of law and general legal theory, that comparative law was first recognized [sic], in the nineteenth century, as having importance."); ibid., 6 ("Comparative law is useful in gaining a better understanding of one's own national law. . . ."); W. J. Wagner, "Comparative Law and Social Theory," *Colum. L. Rev.* 64 (1964): 992 (book review) (noting that Hall's "lofty standards" for transdisciplinary work "will not be easy to

meet"); and Rudolf B. Schlesinger, "Comparative Law and Social Theory," *Cornell L. Q.* 50 (1965): 570 (book review) (applauding Hall's plea for integration of comparative law and the social sciences but criticizing Hall's underestimation of preexisting achievements in such integration); Zweigert and Kötz, 12 ("The primary aim of comparative law, as of all sciences, is knowledge."); Rodolfo Sacco, "Legal Formants: A Dynamic Approach to Comparative Law (Installment 1)," *Am. J. Comp. L.* 39 (1991): 1 (stating "the use to which scientific ideas are put affects neither the definition of a science nor the validity of its conclusions," and arguing that a different standard has been applied to comparative law).

10. Basil S. Markesinis, *Foreign Law and Comparative Methodology: A Subject and a Thesis* (Oxford: Hart Publishing, 1997), 1–14 (arguing for the study of foreign legal decisions to resolve domestic legal problems).

11. David and Brierley, *Major Legal Systems,* 6–8 (noting the role of comparative law in the improvement of national law and the growth of "comparative legislation" in the past century); Zekoll, 2732:

> In Europe, this comparative method has long been a valuable instrument designed to measure the actual effects of a foreign rule both in its "natural environment" and in the adoptive system. Likewise, mixed jurisdictions such as Quebec and Louisiana, which are under constant pressure from different legal traditions, depend on comparative law as an instrument for law reform.

12. As Zweigert and Kötz have observed, the founding of the International Conference of Comparative Law in 1900 by Edouard Lambert and Raymond Saleilles was largely motivated by the view that "a world law must be created" and "comparative law must create it." Zweigert and Kötz, 2; ibid., 19–23 (discussing unification of law as a major use of comparative law). Stein, for example, pled:

> Any major business enterprise is bound to reach across national frontiers. In a world that has become so much more complex, the United States remains the most powerful nation, but it is no longer able—or willing—to "carry the burden" of freedom everywhere. Those who speak abroad on behalf of American interests— governmental and private—must now rely on their art of persuasion rather than one imperial voice from Washington. For this purpose, lawyers require better knowledge and deeper understanding of the international scene and particularly of the foreign legal systems within which their counterparts function. (Stein, 216)

See also Kozyris, 166 (stating that "the comparative method has played a major part in the growth of international law because it is mainly through the study of domestic law that a suitable international legal order is crafted"); Malavet, 392–93 (noting that "[t]he comparative method gives a national scholar a better understanding of his own law, assists in its improvement and . . . opens the door to working with those in other countries in establishing uniform conflict or substantive rules or at least their harmonization"). Kozyris further notes:

> [T]he utility of the comparative method is beyond dispute. Comparative law not only provides alternative solutions to be used in legal reform but also gives us a better understanding of our existing law. In short, it is an indispensable tool of legal science. In addition, the internationalization of transactions and the increasing applicability of foreign law make comparative law an indispensable tool of the legal practitioner. (Kozyris, 167)

George Winterton, "Comparative Law Teaching," *Am. J. Comp. L.* 23 (1975): 69 (outlining practical, sociological, and political objectives of comparative law).

13. In this connection, Glendon has emphasized the educational purpose of comparative legal studies. Glendon, *Abortion and Divorce,* 1 ("What [comparatists] are usually

looking for is, at a minimum, a deepened understanding of the problem and, if they are lucky, a source of inspiration.").

14. Lepaulle, 858.

15. Huxley, 1896: "A distinguished civil lawyer noted that the only way European legal culture can become intelligible as a cultural entity is in contrast to other, chiefly Asiatic high cultures, "among them, as the ones reaching farthest in time and space, those of the Islamic world, India, and China. These above all, present a challenge to Europeans to become conscious of the peculiar nature and the limitations of their own conception of law." Ibid. (citing Michael R. Anderson, "Classifications and Coercions: Themes in South Asian Legal Studies in the 1980s," *S. Asia Res.* 10 (1990): 162.

16. Arthur Sigismund Diamond, *The Comparative Study of Primitive Law* (University of London: Athlone, 1965); Arthur Sigismund Diamond, *The Evolution of Law and Order* (Westport, Conn.: Greenwood, 1973); Arthur Sigismund Diamond, *Primitive Law* (London and New York: Longmans, Green, and Co., 1935); Max Gluckman, *Politics, Law and Ritual in Tribal Society* (Chicago: Aldine, 1965), 209–13 (comparing different societies' legal concepts); E. Adamson Hoebel, *The Law of Primitive Man: A Study in Comparative Legal Dynamics* (Cambridge: Harvard University Press, 1954); Moore, *Law as Process,* 216 (discussing the work of Diamond and Hoebel); Richard. D. Schwartz and James C. Miller, "Legal Evolution and Societal Complexity," *Am. J. Soc.* 70 (1964): 159 (analyzing comparative cross-cultural data).

17. Zweigert and Kötz, 4 (including in the definition of comparative law the comparison of "solutions of comparable legal problems in different systems"); ibid., 9–10 (stating that "comparative law, though it has many different aims, is basically concerned with the question of how the law ought to be").

18. See David and Brierley, *Major Legal Systems,* 8 ("But the use of comparative law as a means of improving one's national law is open to courts and legal commentators as well as legislators. Legislation (loi) may well have a national character but law (droit) is never to be identified solely with legislation.").

19. See Susan Rose-Ackerman, "American Administrative Law under Siege: Is Germany a Model?" *Harv. L. Rev.* 107 (1994): 1279 (discussing the advantages of German administrative law).

20. Ibid.

21. Stein, 209–13; see also Winterton, 99–106 (outlining practical, sociological, and political objectives of comparative law).

22. See Zweigert and Kötz, 19–23 (noting the importance of comparative law in efforts to unify the laws of different national systems).

23. Ibid., 5–6 (evaluating the relationship between comparative law and private international law, or conflict of laws, in the examination of problems of characterization, ordre public, and renvoi).

24. Ibid., 6–7 (exploring the relationship between comparative and public international law, for example, in the determination of general principles or customary international law or in the interpretation of treaties). See also United Nations, "Statute of the International Court of Justice," Art. 38, *U.S. Statutes at Large* 59 (1945): 1060, *Treaty Series* no. 993 (1945). Article 38 contains the functional equivalent of rules of recognition recognized by Hart to be indispensable to any legal system. Hart, 210 (noting that certain rules are indispensable for any legal system to be effective). Article 38 provides that the International Court of Justice shall apply "(a) international conventions, whether general or particular, establishing rules expressly recognized by the contesting states"; (b) "international custom, as evidence of a general practice accepted as law"; and (c) "general principles of law recognized by civilized nations." What rules, practices, or principles that states (civilized or not)

have recognized or accepted often depends on not only a comparison of national rules, practices, and principles but also a comparison of not infrequently conflicting positions over what exactly has been recognized or accepted. Additionally, comparisons between these different sources of international law are equally frequent and significant. See Chodosh, *Interpretive Theory,* 1008–68 (identifying and evaluating the different ways in which the distinction between treaty and customary law may be, has been, and should be seen).

25. See Mark W. Janis, *Introduction to International Law,* 2d ed. (Boston: Little, Brown, 1995), 41–58 (discussing custom and general principles); Karol Wolfke, *Custom in Present International Law* (Boston: M. Nijhoff, 1993), xiv (examining "the universally accepted norms of international law, the most representative practice, to which the jurisprudence of the old and new international Court may be reckoned, and the opinions of contemporary doctrine, primarily those expressed in the records of the International Law Commission"); Anthony D'Amato, *The Concept of Custom in International Law* (Ithaca: Cornell University Press, 1971), 34 ("[W]riters on international law are constrained to describe the law as it exists in the consensus of nation-state officials.").

26. As in other areas of international regulation, such as trade and banking, international tribunals have developed significantly. Elihu Lauterpacht, *Aspects of the Administration of International Justice* (Cambridge, U.K.: Grotius, 1991), 9–23 (describing the range of international judicial and quasi-judicial machinery). For a recent discussion of the relationship between comparative and international law, see L. Amede Obiora, "Toward an Auspicious Reconciliation of International and Comparative Analyses," *Am. J. Comp. L.* 46 (1998): 671–72 (calling for "a reconciliation between comparative and international law for the benefit of human rights promulgations"). See also Ugo Mattei, "An Opportunity Not to Be Missed: The Future of Comparative Law in the United States," *Am. J. Comp. L.* 46 (1998): 718 (suggesting that the discipline's fortunes are not to be found in the context of globalization but, rather, in its linkage to other social sciences).

27. Sacco, 21–34.

28. See Chodosh and Mayo, "Palestinian Legal Study," 395:
[T]he purpose of the Palestinian Legal Study was to gain a contemporary appreciation of the actual operation of the legal systems in order to develop accuracy in assessment and practicability in the resulting recommendations. . . . Discoveries would not be made through traditional methods of legal research. If formal procedures were not consistently followed, basing assessments and recommendations on book learning attentive to code provisions would render poor results.

29. Anthropologists focus their attention on the practical limits of formal rulemaking. Moore, *Law as Process,* 4 (stating "[i]f partial rule by rules is all that can ever be managed, the fact has considerable import for planning and regulation"). They explore the causes of noncompliance and the inability to predict satisfactorily the social consequences of legal rules. Ibid., 6–7 (discussing problems of the "side-effects" of legislation). To explain the divergence between rules and practice, anthropologists look beyond the formal rules themselves to study the social context in which law is implemented and the personnel responsible for its implementation. Ibid., 7–8.

30. Volkmar Gessner, Armin Höland, and Csaba Varga, eds., *European Legal Cultures* (Aldershot, U.K.: Dartmouth, 1996) (discussing the historical and philosophical aspects of European law and the different roles they play in individual sectors).

31. See John H. Barton et al., *Law in Radically Different Cultures* (St. Paul, Minn.: West Publishing Co., 1983), 577–737 (comparing private orderings in different countries); Rudolf B. Schlesinger et al., *Formation of Contracts: A Study of the Common Core of Legal Systems* (Dobbs Ferry, N.Y.: Oceana, 1968). Comparisons of national and international contract law are not unprecedented. Hanokh Dagan, *Unjust Enrichment: A Study of*

Private Law and Public Values (New York: Cambridge University Press, 1997) (offering a comparative analysis of the doctrine of unjust enrichment in the North American and Jewish legal systems and in international law); Ewald, "Comparative Jurisprudence," 1896 (criticizing contemporary comparative legal scholarship for its inattention to the philosophical underpinnings of law in its unique contexts).

32. Moore, *Law as Process,* 137.

33. Chodosh and Mayo, "Palestinian Legal Study," 379:

The difficulties faced by those attempting to unify the two systems convinced experts in the Study that legislative efforts aimed at long-term unification had to be deferred. Prior to unification, legal opinion leaders had to determine which procedural mechanisms and institutional development measures would satisfy the aspirations of both Palestinians and the international community for the achievement of a just civil and criminal justice system.

34. See Ibrahim F. I. Shihata, Judicial Reform in Developing Countries and the Role of the World Bank, Paper submitted to the Seminar of Justice in Latin America and the Caribbean in the 1990s, organized by the Inter-American Development Bank, San Jose, Costa Rica (February 1993), 68 (on file with author) (noting the tendency to assume that once appropriate changes are made in substantive legal rules, "the legal system as a whole will be more responsive to the demands of modernization and development").

35. When one country adopts the mirror image of a foreign country's law, that country is implicitly comparing its own preexisting law to the new one and choosing the latter, without much critical attention or creative adaptation. This choice is based on an extremely crude comparison that attributes a special causal role to legislation in the development of a powerful or economically developed national community. For example, Boris Yeltsin's widely publicized impressions of a Houston supermarket were taken by many as Russian legislative reform, built on U.S. models. See Stefanie Asin, "Yeltsin Loves the Free Market," *Houston Chron.*, Sept. 17, 1989, A1 (reporting Yeltsin's comment that if the people saw U.S. supermarkets, "there would be a revolution"). The crude nature of the comparative enterprise should raise immediate doubts and skepticism toward the effectiveness of the reform efforts. Legislative reform may be necessary in the development of a powerful country, but a number of legal and nonlegal factors determine whether the Russian supermarkets are full or empty. Inattention to these other factors may lead to disappointments, which can have a negative feedback effect on confidence in a national marketplace.

36. Pound, "Space and Time," 75.

37. Stein, 199.

38. Kahn-Freund, "Uses," 7; Stein, 199.

39. Kahn-Freund, "Uses," 7; Stein, 199.

40. Kahn-Freund, "Uses," 11–12; Stein, 200.

41. Kahn-Freund, "Uses," 27; Stein, 201.

42. Stein, 202 (quoting Alan Watson, "Legal Transplants and Law Reform," *L. Q. Rev.* 92 (1972): 80).

43. Stein, 203; Watson, *Legal Transplants,* 95–96.

44. Stein, 203–4.

45. Ibid.

46. Ibid. The distinction between micro-analysis and macro-analysis has been frequently drawn and is discussed briefly below in Part B. 3. See also Zweigert and Kötz, 4 ("The comparative lawyer may operate on a large scale or on a smaller one."); Tumanov, 69. Glendon, Gordon and Osakwe discuss the shading of one into the other. Glendon et al., 12; see also Gessner et al., 254–66 (identifying macro- and microindicators of legal systems in Europe).

47. Stein, 204.

48. Ibid.

49. Heinz J. Klug, "The South African Judicial Order and the Future: A Comparative Analysis of the South African Judicial System and Judicial Transitions in Zimbabwe, Mozambique, and Nicaragua," *Hastings Int'l & Comp. L. Rev.* 12 (1988): 212–28 (identifying central factors in the judicial order and the transition to a new society).

50. Watson, *Legal Transplants,* 96; Stein, 202.

51. Kahn-Freund, "Uses."

52. Alan Watson, *The Evolution of Law,* 73–76 (1985) (arguing that borrowing is not dependent on the presence of the donor's corresponding social institutions, citing as evidence of this claim the widespread reception of Roman law).

53. Kahn-Freund, "Uses."

54. Watson, *Legal Transplants,* 95–101 (pointing out that borrowing does not depend on an understanding of what has been borrowed).

55. Ibid., 96–97.

56. John Henry Merryman, "Comparative Law and Social Change: On the Origins, Style, Decline and Revival of the Law and Development Movement," *Am. J. Comp. L.* 25 (1977): 481 (arguing that the failure of the law and development movement may be attributed to weak comparative foundations, including, inter alia, "unfamiliarity with the target culture and society (including its legal system)").

57. Harmonization is a frequently misapplied concept when it is equated with uniformity in law. *Harmony* denotes the simultaneous playing of two or more different musical notes; if the notes were the same, the term *harmony* would not apply. Instead it would be a uniformity of sound. *Webster's Collegiate Dictionary,* 11th ed., s.v. "harmony" (noting the combination of simultaneous musical notes in a chord).

58. The international legal process denotes interaction, the creation of norms, internalization, and compliance. See generally Koh, "Transnational Legal Process"; Koh, "Why Do Nations Obey International Law?"

59. First, unification is underinclusive in its connotation that two or more nations become a unity through supranational forms of political organization. Uniformity of law may exist without any such unification of political organization. Second, unification is overinclusive because supranational forms of political organization may exist without necessitating a uniformity of law. The United States doctrine of federalism or the European Union's principle of subsidiary suggests a condominium of suprastate and state powers, which may involve hierarchically separated adjudicative, legislative, and executive jurisdiction and competence. For example, federal diversity jurisdiction in the United States involves a federally unified interstate judicial function, but courts sitting in diversity jurisdiction apply state, not uniform federal law.

60. For a full explanation of this pattern and its application to the globalization of U.S. legal education, see Hiram E. Chodosh, "Globalizing the U.S. Law Curriculum: The Saja Paradigm," *U.C. Davis L. Rev.* 37 (2004): 843–68.

61. See also Helms-Burton Act (providing punishment for corporations which have purchased property that the Cuban government has expropriated from U.S. citizens); Anne Q. Connaughton, "Exporting to Special Destinations: Terrorist-Supporting and Embargoed Countries," in *Coping with U.S. Export Controls, 1997* (New York: Practicing Law Institute, 1997), 318 (noting that Libya, Iran, Iraq, Cuba, and North Korea are subject to a comprehensive embargo by the United States); "Europe Moves to Ban all Exports of Hazardous Waste to Third World," *World Env't Rep.,* Jan. 17, 1996, 22 (noting that the European Community's stringent export rules comply with the Basel Convention, which calls for an international ban on waste exportation); Patrick Smikle, "Caribbean-U.S.:

Immigrant Bashing Raises Concern," *Inter Press Service,* Apr. 29, 1997 (available on West-law electronic database at 1997 WL 7075076) (describing recent efforts to limit immigration to the United States and American sentiment toward immigrants).

62. Decisions on the extraterritorial application of U.S. law have been made in a wide variety of contexts. Note Hartford Fire Ins. Co. v California, 509 US 764, 794–99 (1993) (applying U.S. antitrust law overseas because it did not conflict with British law); E. E. O. C. v Arabian Am. Oil Co., 499 US 244, 248–59 (1991) (deciding not to apply Title VII of the Civil Rights Act of 1964 extraterritorially); Lauritzen v Larson, 345 US 571, 573–93 (1953) (refusing to apply U.S. labor standards statute against a Danish ship sailing in Cuban waters).

63. Anne Marie Burley, "Law among Liberal States: Liberal Internationalism and the Act of State Doctrine," *Colum. L. Rev.* 92 (1992): 1907 (arguing that the act of state doctrine helps to circumscribe a zone of "legitimate difference" among liberal states).

64. American Law Institute, *Restatement (Second) of Conflict of Laws* (1972), § 145 (directing the courts to apply the law of the state with the "most significant relationship to the occurrence"); see generally Griggs v Riley, 489 SW2d. 469, 472–74 (Mo Ct App 1972) (applying the "most significant relationship" test).

65. See Bernhard v Harrah's Club, 546 P2d 719, 722–25 (Cal 1976) (applying the comparative impairment doctrine); William Baxter, "Choice of Law and the Federal System," *Stan. L. Rev.* 16 (1983): 1 (arguing that courts should apply the law of the state whose policies would be most impaired by the rejection of its rules).

66. For an example of the domestic application of the lex fori rule, see Foster v Leggett, 484 SW2d. 827, 829 (Ky Ct App 1972) (stating "[t]he basic law is the law of the forum, which should not be displaced without valid reasons").

67. See, e.g., Babcock v Jackson, 191 NE2d 279 (NY Ct App 1963) (applying New York law to an accident that occurred in Ontario because the parties to the accident were citizens of New York); American Law Institute, *Restatement (Third) of Foreign Relations Law* (1986), § 402 cmts. d–g. (discussing principles based on the personality of the defendant (nationality) and the plaintiff (passive personality)); Brainerd Currie, *Selected Essays on the Conflict of Laws* (Durham, N.C.: Duke University Press, 1963) (discussing domestic legal theories that prioritize legal personality factors).

68. See, e.g., E. E. O. C. v Arabian Am. Oil Co. 499 US 244 (1991) (applying Saudi Arabian law to dispute regarding an employment contract); Alabama G. S. R. v Carroll, 11 So. 803 (Ala 1892) (applying Mississippi law to a dispute between an Alabama plaintiff and defendant because the dispute arose out of an accident that occurred in Mississippi); American Law Institute, *Restatement of Conflict of Laws* (1934), § 311 (describing law in contract disputes chosen by reference to place of contracting, or law in tort chosen by reference to place of wrong, which is place of last event necessary to make actor liable).

69. See, e.g., Wong v Tenneco Inc., 702 P2d. 570 (Cal 1985) (declaring California public policy allowed the application of Mexican Law to the dispute); Robert A. Leflar, "Conflicts Law: More on Choice Influencing Considerations," *Cal. L. Rev.* 54 (1966): 1586–88 (arguing that courts should apply the "better law" when making choice of law decisions); James Martin, "Constitutional Limitations on Choice of Law," *Cornell L. Rev.* 61 (1976): 221–23 (discussing the relevance of choice of law problems to the substantive and procedural components of statutes of limitation); Monrad G. Paulsen and Michael I. Sovern, "'Public Policy' in the Conflict of Laws," *Colum. L. Rev.* 56 (1956): 969 (describing the "public policy" exception in choice of law jurisprudence).

70. See generally William Alford, "Making the World Safe for What?" 136–40 (describing U.S. efforts to get the People's Republic of China to adopt and enforce laws protecting intellectual property); Kimberly Pace, "Recalibrating the Scales of Justice through

National Punitive Damages Reform," *Am. U. L. Rev.* 46 (1997): 1573 (arguing the United States should change its system of punitive damages so that it comports with standards found in other countries).

71. Uniform international standards have been promulgated in numerous fields. See World Trade Organization, "General Agreement on Tariffs and Trade 1994," 15 April 1994, 33 ILM 1125 (trade relations); United Nations, "Basel Convention on the Control of Transboundary Movements of Hazardous Wastes and Their Disposal," 22 March 1989, 28 ILM 649; United Nations, "International Covenant on Civil and Political Rights," 16 December 1966, 999 UNTS 171 (human rights).

72. Supranational organizations have been formed to attempt to resolve or prevent many different types of conflict. See generally United Nations, "United Nations Charter," arts. 9–22; ibid., Arts. 23–32 (laying down rules and functions of the Security Council); "General Agreement on Tariffs and Trade 1994" (establishing the World Trade Organization as a mechanism to govern the trade practices of member states); United Nations, "United Nations Convention on the Law of the Sea," U.N. Doc. A/CONF. 62/122 (opened for signature 10 December 1982), 21 ILM 1261 (1982) (establishing rules for the use of the ocean and its resources), *Statute of the ICJ*, Article 38 (stating that the purpose of the court is "to decide in accordance with international law such disputes that are submitted to it").

73. For example, many argue that engagement is superior to isolation in changing the policies of other countries. See "The Fading of Fidel," *Economist*, Jan. 17, 1998, 13 (arguing that engagement with Cuba will be more effective than isolating it); Julian Baum, "No Worries," *Far E. Econ. Rev.*, Oct. 30, 1997, 28 (noting Taiwan's support for the United States policy of engagement with China); Robin Wright and Shaul Bakhash, "The U.S. and Iran: An Offer They Can't Refuse?" *Foreign Policy*, Sept. 22, 1997, 124 (arguing that the United States needs to end its policy of isolating and containing Iran).

74. Most of these doctrines require weighing of more than one variable. American Law Institute, *Restatement (Second) of Conflict of Laws* (1971), § 6 (setting out seven factors courts need to consider when making a choice of law decision).

75. Trachtman, 351 (discussing financial institutions); Leila Sadat Wexler, "The Proposed Permanent International Criminal Court: An Appraisal," *Cornell Int'l L. J.* 29 (1997): 665 (providing similar commentary on permanent international criminal court); King and Theofrastous (discussing U.S. opposition to permanent court).

76. David Kennedy, "New Approaches to Comparative Law: Comparativism and International Governance," *Utah L. Rev.* 1997: 548 (exploring the difference between the internationalists' optic (governing above, outside, or below the state) and the comparatists' (understanding "us" and "them").

77. See chapter 3. B. (discussing classification and taxonomy).

78. Chodosh et al., "Egyptian Civil Justice," 879–90 (describing a functional and systemic approach to comparative legal process). For a recent series of comparative essays propounding a functional comparative legal problem-solving approach, see Markesinis, 4.

79. Another view of classification is that it is of little importance in comparative research. For a response to Hall's criticism of classification of entire systems and his call for a return to Weberian types, see Wagner, 990.

80. For example, one country may favor its method for handling the taking of evidence but decide to modify it in a transnational setting to avoid conflicts with other methods that are inferior in its view. This too will affect the choice of comparative criteria. Standards of role allocation and breadth of access to information may be alternatively emphasized. One criterion, such as breadth, may be chosen because it is identified as grasping the most important problem from a domestic perspective, whereas from an international perspective,

another feature of difference (such as a role allocation), in particular the one causing international conflict, will be chosen for comparative evaluation. David J. Gerber, "Extraterritorial Discovery and the Conflict of Procedural Systems: Germany and the United States," *Am. J. Comp. L.* 34 (1986): 745 (analyzing the difference between discovery methods in the United States and Germany); see also Societe Nationale v United States Dist. Ct., S. D. Iowa, 482 US 522, 529 (1987) (holding the Hague Evidence Convention to be a nonexclusive means for taking evidence abroad).

81. For a critical view of the place of comparative law in legal education, see Mathias Reimann, "The End of Comparative Law as an Autonomous Subject," *Tul. Eur. & Civ. L. F.* 11 (1996): 60 (arguing for the abandonment of comparative law as an autonomous discipline, and noting that "true comparison . . . hardly ever happens [because] [m]ost so-called comparative law teaching never gets that far").

82. Deborah L. Rhode, *Professional Responsibility: Ethics by the Pervasive Method,* 2d ed. (Boston: Little, Brown, 1998), xxix ("By limiting discussion of bar regulatory and ethical questions to a single course, many institutions have risked marginalizing, and ultimately subverting, their intended goal" of teaching ethics through the "pervasive method.").

83. See David W. Barnes and Lynn A. Stout, *The Economic Analysis of Tort Law* (Belmont, Calif.: West/Wadsworth, 1992), iii (one of a series providing "cases and materials to supplement law school courses in which economic analysis is particularly relevant"). For work at the intersection of comparative law and law and economics, see Ugo Mattei, *Comparative Law and Economics* (Ann Arbor: University of Michigan Press, 1997).

84. Zweigert and Kötz, 2.

85. Merryman notes that the convention of restricting comparative law to nations or societies is arbitrary, but convenient because legal systems tend to be organized on that level. This allows him to view "the use of legal systems as the basic unit of comparison as an easy one." Merryman, *Comparative Law and Social Explanation,* 87. This may answer why nations or societies are compared, but it does not answer why entire legal systems should provide the basic unit of comparison. This statement is relaxed as Merryman turns to consider the components of legal systems to be compared and observes that primary rules are the "basic matter of comparison." Ibid.

86. As F. H. Lawson tellingly wrote:
[A] comparative lawyer is bound to be superficial; he would soon lose himself in the sands of scholarship. It is hard enough to comprehend even the master subjects of a single modern system of private law. . . . Anything like the same intimate sense of a second system must seem almost impossible to acquire; and if one extends one's studies to other laws of other different families, one is indeed in danger of knowing very little of a great many things.
F. H. Lawson, *Selected Essays* (New York: North Holland Publishing Co., 1977), 2.

87. Zweigert and Kötz, 2.

88. Ibid.

89. For example, Zweigert and Kötz confine their discussion of interpretation to situations in which national law provides no clear answer and reference to foreign solutions is justified. Ibid., 14.

90. As Henry Abraham observed in drawing lessons from comparative studies in judicial systems: "No longer conceptually or linguistically confined to a study of diverse states or nations and their cultures, [comparative government] is a concept that may well be profitably applied vertically as well as horizontally: or to put it differently, intra as well as inter state, country or division." Henry Abraham, Foreword to *Comparative Judicial Systems: Challenging Frontiers in Conceptual and Empirical Analysis,* ed. John R. Schmid-

hauser (Boston: Butterworths, 1987), iv. Many other fields of social research come at this point from a different angle. They may already recognize the comparative dimensions of their research within a cultural setting and wonder more critically about the expansion of that research across cultures. Else Øyen, "The Imperfection of Comparisons," in *Comparative Methodology: Theory and Practice in International Social Research* (Newbury Park, Calif.: Sage Publications, 1990), 3–4:

> [F]or most sociologists the very nature of sociological research is considered comparative, and thinking in comparative terms is inherent in sociology. . . . One of the main questions in the present context is whether comparisons across national boundaries represent a new or a different set of theoretical, methodological and epistemological challenges.

91. See Zweigert and Kötz, 7 (recognizing that "all legal history uses the comparative method").

92. See Catherine A. Rogers, "Gulliver's Troubled Travels, or the Conundrum of Comparative Law," *Geo. Wash. L. Rev.* 67 (1998): 150–51 (describing comparative law in the United States as in a state of "disarray" and reflecting a "zealousness of self-flagellation," and applauding Ugo Mattei in his recent book on law and economics); Mattei, *Comparative Law and Economics*; see generally Yves Dezalay and Bryant Garth, *Dealing in Virtue: International Commercial Arbitration and the Construction of a Transnational Legal Order* (Chicago: University of Chicago Press, 1996) (exploring social scientific models for empirical testing in international arbitration); Rogers, 167 (concluding that the Dezalay/Garth "methodology bears only a faint resemblance to social science").

93. Langbein, "Influence," 547 (making the claim that "the study of comparative procedure in the United States has little following in academia, and virtually no audience in the courts or in legal policy circles."); Stiefel and Maxeiner, "Isolation," 147 (reporting on present and past efforts at criminal justice reform in the United States and for learning from conventional models).

94. Langbein, "Influence," 547; see also Ugo Mattei, "Why the Wind Has Changed: Intellectual Leadership in Western Law," *Am. J. Comp. L.* 42 (1994): 218 ("American academia is becoming more and more turned upon itself.") (quoted in Langbein, "Influence," 547).

95. Langbein, "Influence," 554.

96. For example, Langbein explores more briefly a complacency factor, the view that whatever is to be taught has already been accomplished. This view, Langbein notes, is evident in European legal circles as well: "Once René David has written, once you have Zweigert and Kötz on the shelf, there seems to be less reason to keep doing it." Ibid., 547 (citations omitted). One may counter complacency by questioning the methods of comparison employed in these concededly great works of accomplishment. See chapter 3. B. 1 (examining the use of classification by prominent comparative legal scholars).

97. Langbein's commentary is similar to Inga Markovits's criticism of those who focus only on doctrine and thus neglect the actors responsible for its practical operation. Inga Markovits, "Hedgehogs or Foxes? A Review of Westen's and Schleider's *Zivilrecht im Systemvergleich*," *Am. J. Comp. L.* 34 (1986): 132 (noting the "most serious shortcoming" as "confinement to doctrine" applied and executed by courts who "have no life of their own").

98. Langbein, "Influence," 551–52.

99. Ibid., 551.

100. Ibid., 552.

101. Ibid., 551.

102. Richard S. Frase, "Comparative Criminal Justice as a Guide to American Law

Reform: How the French Do It, How Can We Find Out, and Why Should We Care?" *Cal. L. Rev.* 78 (1990): 547–48 (noting that much comparative literature, in a self-defeating manner, focuses on large, rather than small, reforms).

103. Langbein, "Influence," 552; for a contrary view, see Chodosh et al., "Egyptian Civil Justice," 884 (arguing that such classifications do not pose any real obstacle to reform based on cross-national comparative study).

104. Zweigert and Kötz uniquely discuss the potential role of comparative law in the interpretation of national laws. See Zweigert and Kötz, 14 (noting "[o]n this matter, the standard textbooks say nothing"). For a more recent explanation of how comparative law can be used in interpretation, see Peter Häberle, "Grundrechtsgeltung und Grundrechtsinterpretation im Verfassungsstaat—Zugleich zur Rechstvergleichung als Funfter Auslegungsmethode," *Juristin Zeitung* 1989: 918 (advocating comparative law as a fifth method of statutory construction in civil law systems). For two recent articles on comparative literary analysis of French and U.S. judicial discourse, see Mitchel de S.-O.-l'E. Lasser, "Judicial (Self-)Portraits: Judicial Discourse in the French Legal System," *Yale L. J.* 104 (1995): 1325; Mitchel de S.-O.-l'E. Lasser, "'Lit. Theory' Put to the Test: A Comparative Literary Analysis of American Judicial Tests and French Judicial Discourse," *Harv. L. Rev.* 111 (1998): 689.

105. For a methodological critique of studies expressing support for or resistance to alternative dispute resolution in the United States, see Carrie Menkel-Meadow, "For and Against Settlement: Uses and Abuses of the Mandatory Settlement Conference," *UCLA L. Rev.* 33 (1985): 485.

106. For purposes of illustration, consider the problems involved in comparing legal processes. The processes might be compared for one or more reasons: (1) to understand the nature of the process falling under one or the other rubric; (2) to reform one or the other process; or (3) to unify processes because of conflicts caused by interactions among different systems in transnational litigation. Even within each general purpose, greater specification would be necessary: the question of what exactly should be understood, reformed, or unified would be an important question to answer. If reform is the objective, for example, on the basis of what evaluation is the system in need of reform? Does the process frustrate, instead of promote, truth? Is it too slow or corrupt? Answers to these questions will affect the focus of the inquiry, e.g., the method of taking, hearing, and determining factual evidence or the terms of employment of different procedural actors such as judges, administrators, lawyers, and others.

107. If comparisons differ depending on the underlying motivations of those engaged in them, what can be done to avoid confusion of one set of values for another? The only way to illuminate disagreements over comparisons that result from purpose conflicts is to explicate the values at the core of the comparative motivations. This requires one to question the linkages drawn between the features under the comparative views and the values to be promoted or demoted by such features. This is easier to articulate than to achieve. The abstract nature of "values," the difficulties involved in articulating them, and the frequent discrepancy between stated and practiced values will all tend to frustrate this objective. However, failure to attempt such clarification leaves societies vulnerable to two types of mistaken cross-national attitudes: false disagreements, where value clarification can expose common objectives or their functional equivalents; and false agreements, where societies appear to agree upon ambiguous language but actually fail to appreciate the profound conflicts hidden by common rhetorical usage.

108. An article by John H. Langbein, "The German Advantage in Civil Procedure," *U. Chi. L. Rev.* 52 (1985): 823, spurred an interesting discourse on the merits of examining foreign procedural systems, which has been recently renewed. Ronald J. Allen et al., "The

German Advantage in Civil Procedure: A Plea for More Details and Fewer Generalities in Comparative Scholarship," *Nw. U. L. Rev.* 82 (1988): 705; Ronald J. Allen, "Idealization and Caricature in Comparative Scholarship," *Nw. U. L. Rev.* 82 (1988): 785; Samuel R. Gross, "The American Advantage: The Value of Inefficient Litigation," *Mich. L. Rev.* 85 (1987): 734; John H. Langbein, "Trashing the German Advantage," *Nw. U. L. Rev.* 82 (1988): 763; John C. Reitz, "Why We Probably Cannot Adopt the German Advantage in Civil Procedure," *Iowa L. Rev.* 75 (1990): 987; see also Chase, "Legal Processes and National Culture"; Langbein, "Chauvinism" (responding to Chase).

109. Fiss, "Against Settlement," 1075 (arguing that settlement may include disadvantages for some parties).

110. For example, although no attempt to do so is ventured here, it might be possible to reconcile conflicting views on degrees of compliance by reference to deeper seated beliefs about the desirability of compliance with international law. It is an understandable tendency to base an argument for what should be on a representation of what already is. Query how many law review articles have invoked Moliere's *Le Bourgeois Gentilhomme* for the proposition that one has already been doing what should have been done. Koh, "Transnational Legal Process," 207 (arguing that idea of international legal process not only should be, but already has been, accepted as an approach to international legal studies); Curran, "Cultural Immersion," 52–53 (describing the émigré community of comparatists as interdisciplinary *avant la lettre*).

111. Berman complained, for example, that "[w]e are still stuck with a separation of international law from comparative law and of both of these from the customary law of communities that transcend national boundaries." Harold Berman, "World Law," *Fordham Int'l L. J.* 18 (1995): 1621–22.

112. Another set of purpose-related justification requires additional explanation, however. Purposes may be accepted or rejected in terms of their practicability. That is, one might agree with the purpose of understanding, reform, or unification, yet disagree that comparison itself can advance the objective. Therefore, to agree or disagree with an articulated purpose may depend on one's view of how well the comparison proceeds from beginning to end.

113. On the level of methodology, a comparison of purposes would carry an obvious risk that many comparisons could be rejected on the basis of the underlying motivations of the comparatist. Illuminating this as a point of disagreement is to be encouraged; however, transforming this into a universally applicable rationale for rejecting comparisons would be very undesirable. Developing rules that would proscribe comparisons motivated by some purposes and not others would severely limit the scope of permissible comparative inquiry.

114. Sally Falk Moore, "Legal Systems of the World: An Introductory Guide to Classifications, Typological Interpretations, and Bibliographical Resources," in Leon Lipson and Stanton Wheeler, eds., *Law and the Social Sciences* (New York: Russell Sage Foundation, 1986), 11.

115. For an example of a multifeature classification system, see Adam Podgórecki, "Social Systems and Legal Systems—Criteria for Classification," in Adam Podgórecki et al., eds., *Legal Systems and Social Systems* (Dover, N.H.: Croom Helm, 1985), 1 (specifying ten factors but failing to apply them to specific legal systems).

116. Gessner et al., 258 (following a critique of Podgórecki and suggesting "there are no simple formulae for classifying legal cultures and perhaps, given the complexity of the matter, we would be better off not trying to come up with one").

117. Indeed, Lijphart argues for a theoretically parsimonious selection of variables in comparative political science. Lijphart, 690 (arguing that one of the strategies for dealing

with the comparative problem of too many variables is to focus on the "key" variables rather than Lasswell's plea for the study of more variables in a more configurative approach).

118. This insufficiently explored problem is a critical issue in the explanation of social systems. Coleman, 3–15 (recognizing the failure to shift between levels in work of Weber and others in the social sciences).

119. Even political scientists pay deference to categories that are based on facially inconsistent differentiating criteria. Ehrmann, 13 (classifying legal culture families into Roman-Germanic, common law, socialist law, and non-Western law). Other scholars have been critical of this form of scholarship. Watson, *Legal Transplants,* 4 ("[A]n elementary account of various legal systems or of various families of systems cannot be decently regarded as the proper pursuit of Comparative Law as an academic activity. The description lacks the necessary intellectual content."). For a recent and more sophisticated attempt at updating comparative legal taxonomies, see Ugo Mattei, "Three Patterns of Law: Taxonomy and Change in the World's Legal Systems," *Am. J. Comp. L.* 45 (1997): 5 ("Taxonomy is as important in the law as in any other discipline.").

120. An additional flaw is addressed in Part C. 1. That is, classifications tend to rely on primarily polar contrasts, e.g., black and white without gray, of the existence or nonexistence of differentiating variables.

121. Schlesinger et al., *Comparative Law,* 284–85 ("[C]lassification is a beginning rather than an end, a preliminary step 'designed to facilitate study of otherwise unwieldy bodies of information.' It is a prerequisite to thinking and speaking about the underlying differences and similarities among various objects."). Ibid. (citation omitted).

122. Rodolpho Sacco, "Legal Formants: A Dynamic Approach to Comparative Law," *Am. J. Comp. L.* 39 (1991) (Installment II of II): 344 (elaborating on the concept of legal formant in sources of law: "No one who wishes to describe the law realistically can ignore the existence of sources other than those formerly recognized in the Constitution.").

123. See David S. Clark, "The Selection and Accountability of Judges in West Germany: Implementation of a Rechtsstaat," *S. Cal. L. Rev.* 61 (1988): 1847 (commenting on German judges' responsibility). Clark argues:

> [T]he role of judges in filling in gaps that the legislature has left or in giving specificity to general clauses is part of the responsibility that judges share for the evolution and modernization of law. Judge made law in Germany occupies large areas in the corpus of legal rules. In some ways German judges are just as bold and innovative as their common law colleagues. (Ibid.)

After having stressed the comparability of German and common law judicial powers, Clark notes, "[B]ut the range of choice available to [German] judges is limited." Ibid.

124. Source differentiation has focused alternatively on the power of the judge to create a rule of decision in the absence of a controlling legislative act and the role of precedent. The identification of civil law counterparts to common law judicial powers is not difficult. For example, the Swiss civil code provides that if no statutory provisions can be found, the judge must apply customary law. If there is no customary law, the judge must create the rule she believes the legislature would have adopted. In so doing, the judge must follow accepted doctrine and tradition, Switzerland, *Civil Code of Switzerland,* 10 December 1907, Art. 1, Paras. 2, 3. The "binding" effect in practice in French Court of Cassation decisions (together, the "jurisprudence") has also been frequently noted. See also Merryman et al., *The Civil Law Tradition.*

125. Langbein, "German Advantage," 824 (noting the overdrawn quality of the dichotomy—"the familiar contrast between our adversarial procedure and the supposedly nonadversarial procedure of the Continental tradition has been grossly overdrawn"—yet

identifying the greater responsibility for fact-gathering in the latter tradition as a distinguishing attribute).

126. See Damaska, 16–46 (tracing the history of the hierarchical and coordinate ideals).

127. Ehrmann, 12.

128. For an explanation of polythetic classification, see Rodney Needham, "Polythetic Classification: Convergence and Consequences," *Man* 10 (1975): 355 (describing polythetic classifications of groups with overall similarity but in which no single feature is either essential to group membership or sufficient to qualify as a member of that group). Such classifications are not mutually exclusive, ibid., 336, and are "a recognized taxonomic principle in a wide range of natural sciences," ibid., 357.

129. David and Brierley, *Major Legal Systems,* 21 (discussing the application of the two criteria of technique and ideology as "whether someone educated in the study and practice of one law will then be capable, without much difficulty, of handling another" and whether two laws are "founded on opposed philosophical, political or economic principles").

130. Zweigert and Kötz, 57–67 (reducing five criteria to one coined style).

131. Lawrence M. Friedman, "Some Thoughts on Comparative Legal Culture," in John Henry Merryman and David S. Clark, eds., *Comparative and Private International Law: Essays in Honor of John Henry Merryman on his Seventieth Birthday* (Berlin: Duncker and Humblot, 1990), 49–55 (discussing comparative legal culture).

132. See text accompanying notes 148–52 for discussion on Ugo Mattei's recent attempt at classificatory revision.

133. The discipline in which one is trained affects the criteria chosen for comparison. As Moore has noted:

> One's approach to classifying legal systems may thus depend on whether one sees the problem in terms of the kinds of society in which law operates, or in terms of the distribution of specific procedures or concepts or rules. The first, the attention to social context, is very much the anthropologist's approach, the second very much more the approach of the scholar-lawyer who specializes in comparative law.

Moore, "Law and Anthropology," 253. Moore notes three common classificatory dichotomies in law and anthropology: (1) technologically simple and technologically complex societies (Maine, Durkheim and Gluckman); (2) decentralized and centralized political and legal systems (Diamond and Hoebel); and (3) direct dispute settlement and third-party dispute settlement (Gulliver, Bohannan, Gluckman). Ibid., 3–55 (describing the different classifications).

134. Henri Levy-Ullmann, "Observations Générales sur les Communications Relative au Droit Privé dans les Pays Étrangers," in *Les Transformations du Droit Dans les Principaux Pays Depuis Cinquante Ans* (1869–1919) (Paris: Librairie Générale de Droit et de Jurisprudence, 1923), 81–108; Hart, 209–10 (exploring the question of whether international law is "really" law).

135. See Damaska, 3 (noting the distinction between adversarial and inquisitorial processes "came to be used by comparativists on a broader scale, mainly to express the contrast between Continental and Anglo-American administration of justice").

136. Ibid.

137. These classificatory typologies bear resemblance to racial classifications based on shifting criteria and poor applications. Enrique Martinez Paz, *Introducción al estudio del derecho civil comparado* (Córdoba (R.A.): Imprenta de la Universidad, 1934) (introducing genetic classification system on the basis of how much the system had been affected by Roman law). The relationship between comparative law and physical anthropology is

closest in the work of Sauser-Hall, who used race as the differentiating factor in his classification. See Georges Sauser-Hall, *Fonction et méthode du droit comparé* (Geneva: Imp. A. Kündig, 1913).

138. See generally David, *Grands Systèmes*, 21 (discussing the purpose of the law in achieving different types of societies); A. Saidov, "O Sravnimosti Sovremennykh Raznotip-nykh Provovykh Sistem," *Sov. Gos I Pravo* (1984): 126–30.

139. Arthur Spiethoff, "Die Allgemeine Volkswirtschaftslehre als geschictliche Theorie: die Wirtschaftsstile," in *Festgabe für Werner Sombart zur Siebenzigsten* Wiederkehr Seines Geburtstages, ed. Arthur Spiethoff (Munich: Duncker and Humblot, 1933), 51–84.

140. Tumanov, 76 (applying a macrocomparison to comparative law); Sacco, 6–7 (discussing comparability of socialist and nonsocialist legal systems).

141. Tumanov, 76.

142. Ibid. ("The basic typology of modern legal systems is the capitalist type of law on one hand, and the socialist type on the other."). This typology would place the Chinese legal system in the same category as the Soviet legal system, without any basis for further differentiation, and would distinguish between the People's Republic of China and Taiwan without any means of comparison based on a common Chinese heritage.

143. Ewald, 1891 (criticizing contemporary comparative legal scholarship).

144. Damaska, 98 (focusing on structure of authority and function of government); David, 96 (identifying ideology and sources of law as primary comparative criteria).

145. Zweigert and Kötz, 62 (collapsing several criteria into the notion of "style").

146. See Glendon, *Abortion and Divorce,* 3 (commenting on the comparative methods developed in the late nineteenth century). Glendon notes:

> [They] have not proved fully adequate to the analysis of contemporary legal problems . . It concentrated on formal rules, institutions, and procedures; it took the primacy of private law for granted, largely ignoring public law; and its sources-of-law theory assumes the centrality of case law in the Anglo American systems and of civil codes in the Romano-Germanic systems. (Ibid.)

In contrast, Glendon applauds the achievements of Ernst Rabel in Germany and Edouard Lambert in France for their work between the two world wars focused on an inquiry of "how legal rules and institutions actually operate in practice and of seeing them in their full social and economic context." Ibid., 4; Mark Andrew Sherman, "Book Review, Transfer of Prisoners under International Instruments and Domestic Legislation: A Comparative Study," *Geo. Wash. J. Int'l L. & Econ.* 28 (1995): 531.

147. Merryman et al., *The Civil Law Tradition,* 2 (detailing "the fact that different legal systems are grouped together under such a rubric as 'civil law,' for example, indicates that they have something that distinguishes them from legal systems classified as 'common law.' . . . It is this uniquely shared something that is here spoken of as a legal tradition.") Merryman defines a legal tradition as "a set of deeply rooted, historically conditioned attitudes about the nature of law, about the role of law in the society and the polity, about the proper organization and operation of a legal system, and about the way law is or should be made, applied, studied, perfected, and taught." Ibid., 3–4. For a contrary view, see David S. Clark, "The Idea of the Civil Law Tradition," in Clark, *Comparative and Private International Law,* 11–23. David Clark, Merryman's former student and now coauthor, notes that scholars within the tradition Merryman describes seldom refer to their own tradition as "civil law" because the *ius civile* developed in Roman law applied to actions between citizens, and the term *civil law* identifies the core of private law norms, rather than the entire system. Instead of *civil law,* Clark notes that Zweigert and Kötz and David and Brierley employ the term "Romano-Germanic" or "Romanistic" and "Germanic." Ibid., 13, footnotes 13 and 14 (citing

Zweigert and Kötz, 68–186, and David and Brierley, *Major Legal Systems*, 22–24, 33–154).

148. Mattei, "Taxonomy," 12.

149. Ibid., 12–13 (explaining the relationship between social control and the law).

150. Ibid., 12.

151. Ibid.

152. Ibid., 23–40. The families resemble prior classifications of (1) Western, (2) socialist, and (3) primitive law.

153. See Moore, *Law as Process*, 215 (pointing out that her classifications are based on societal factors). The societal emphasis of anthropology appears to be inconsistent with that of legal historians who focus on Western, state-centered, political receptions of foreign law. For example, in a 1993 afterword to his book on legal transplants, Watson asserted his belief "that even in theory there was no simple correlation between a society and its law." Watson, *Legal Transplants*, 107. This view bluntly contradicts much of the anthropological work on classifications of legal systems, which frequently focuses attention on societal, rather than autonomous legal, factors. This apparent inconsistency becomes partially reconcilable when one considers that law in the Western legal tradition is traditionally considered to be a more autonomous social realm than it is in most of the societies studied by anthropologists. Ibid.

154. For an interesting integration of broad, nonlegal sphere comparisons, see Vivian Grosswald Curran, "Romantic Common Law, Enlightened Civil Law: Legal Uniformity and the Homogenization of the European Union," *Colum. J. Eur. L.* 7 (2001): 63–64 (observing "defining characteristics of civil-law legal culture" as "prominently and pervasively present in *non-legal* spheres of common-law European Union Member States.").

155. Moore, *Law as Process*, 215–17 (explaining the Maine-Durkheim-Gluckman tradition, the Diamond and Hoebel tradition, and the procedural dichotomy).

156. Ibid., 215–16.

157. H. S. Maine, *Ancient Law: Its Connection with the Early History of Society and Its Relation to Modern Ideas* (London: John Murray, 1861); Moore, *Law as Process*, 216 (discussing how Maine divides cultures).

158. Emile Durkheim, *De la Division du Travail Social,* trans. George Simpson (New York: Free Press, 1947); Moore, *Law as Process*, 216 (describing how Durkheim distinguishes societies).

159. Max Gluckman, *The Judicial Process among the Barotse of Northern Rhodesia* [Zambia]. 2d ed. (Manchester, U.K.: Manchester University Press, 1967); Max Gluckman, *The Ideas in Barotse Jurisprudence* (Manchester, U.K.: Manchester University Press, 1965); Max Gluckman, introduction to *The Craft of Social Anthropology,* ed. A. L. Epstein (London: Tavistock Publications, 1967), xi–xx; Moore, *Law as Process*, 216 (describing Gluckman's theory).

160. In his discussion of social-legal comparisons posited by Maine, Marx, and Weber, Andrew Huxley wrote that "[n]o one now seriously believes that law moves inexorably from status to contract, or that cultures with the same means of production must share the same legal culture, or that Buddhism is an essentially otherworldly and antisocial religion." Huxley, 1950.

161. Moore, *Law as Process*, 216 (discussing how Diamond and Hoebel classify legal systems); William L. F. Felstiner, "Influences of Social Organization on Dispute Processing," *Law & Soc'y Rev.* 9 (1974): 65, 69 (differentiating technologically complex rich society and technologically simple poor society and exploring "whether the consequences of, and the availability of resources required by, any form of dispute processing vary with social organization").

162. Moore, *Law as Process,* 20 (noting informal usages elevated to status of law in modern societies). Diamond, *Comparative Study;* Diamond, *Evolution,* vii; Diamond, *Primitive Law,* 173–331; Moore, *Law as Process,* 216 (describing Diamond's framework).

163. Hoebel, *The Law of Primitive Man,* 288–333 (discussing trends in the development of law); Moore, *Law as Process,* 216–17 (describing Hoebel's framework); see also Max Gluckman, *Politics, Law and Ritual in Tribal Society* (Chicago: Aldine, 1965), 123–68 (identifying stages from stateless societies through chiefdoms to kingdoms); R. D. Schwartz and J. C. Miller, "Legal Evolution and Social Complexity," *Am. J. Soc.* 70 (1964): 159 (using comparative cross-cultural studies to argue that legal characteristics occur on a continuum).

164. Tate, 24–25 (raising questions about the ability to "operationalize," that is, compare Shapiro's functions effectively); Moore, *Law as Process,* 217 (describing the classification of dispute resolution systems); Shapiro, *Analysis,* 1–64 (categorizing the activities of third parties in conflict resolving triads, and placing types on a mediative continuum measured by the degree of consent and seeking of mediative solutions that characterize the roles).

165. P. H. Gulliver, *Social Control in an African Society: A Study of the Trisha: Agricultural Masai of Northern Tanganyika* (London: Routledge and Kegan Paul, 1963), 173 (describing public assembly and conclave); Moore, *Law as Process,* 217 (describing Gulliver's use of classifications); P. H. Gulliver, "Dispute Settlement without Courts: The Ndendeuli of Southern Tanzania," in *Law in Culture and Society,* ed. Laura Nader (Chicago: Aldine, 1969), 24 (describing a society where disputes are settled without an arbitrator or judge).

166. For an example, see Felstiner, 69 (differentiating adjudication and mediation on the one hand and negotiation and self-help on the other by the presence or absence of a third and independent party).

167. Gulliver, *Social Control,* 173–274 (discussing the methods of dispute resolution of Arusha); ibid., 217 (noting the differences between the dispute resolution classification and other legal system classifications).

168. See Gulliver, *Social Control,* 173; ibid., 217 (describing Gulliver's framework).

169. Paul J. Bohannan, "The Differing Realms of the Law," in *The Ethnography of Law,* ed. Laura Nader, *Am. Anthropologist* (Special Publication) 67 (1965): 33 (exploring judicial definitions, norms, and customs, and their usefulness to the anthropological study of law); Paul J. Bohannan, *Justice and Judgment among the Tiv of Nigeria* (London: Oxford University Press, 1957) (discussing the judicial system of the Tiv tribe of Nigeria); *Law and Warfare: Studies in the Anthropology of Conflict,* ed. Paul Bohannan (New York: Natural History Press, 1967) (examining resolution of conflict through two forms—administered rules and war); Moore, *Law as Process,* 217 (comparing Bohannan's framework to Gulliver's).

170. Moore, *Law as Process,* 217 (describing Gluckman's framework in comparison to Bohannan's and Gulliver's).

171. David, *Grand Systèmes,* 21.

172. William T. Pizzi, "Essay: Soccer, Football and Trial Systems," *Colum. J. Eur. L.* 1 (1995): 369 (contrasting the American and European trial systems based on their emphases on rules, by analogy to popularity of American football and European soccer). Pizzi wrote:
> To the extent that soccer differs conceptually from football in its concept of the need for rules, in its view of the way rules should be enforced, and in its concept of what the game should emphasize on the playing field, it should not be surprising to find that some of these same basic conceptual differences exist in the respective trial systems as well. (Ibid., 370)

Pizzi does not include common law trial systems similar to that of the United States functioning in cultures that prefer soccer to football, e.g., Britain and India, in his comparison and does not address the effect of the jury system on the features of concern to him, but focuses on a comparison between the two sports as reflective of deeper cultural values that underlie the different trial systems. Ibid., 369.

173. Huxley, 1912 ("[O]n the vexed question of law and the state, Buddhism provides arguments to both sides of the debate.").

174. *Corporate Counsel's Guide to International Alternative Dispute Resolution,* ed. William A. Hancock (Chesterland, Ohio: Business Laws, 1997) §§ 21.01–37.001 (dealing with the rules of international, regional, and national arbitration centers).

175. Chodosh et al., "Egyptian Civil Justice"; Hiram E. Chodosh et al., *Indian Civil Justice System Reform,* 41–45 (discussing alternative means of dispute resolution); Chodosh and Mayo, *Palestinian Legal Study,* 407 (discussing arbitration); Joseph J. Derma, "Dispute Resolution and China," in *International Alternative Dispute Resolution* § 13.00.

176. See Felstiner, 84–85 ("Where adjudication and mediation are feasible, avoidance is costly: where avoidance has tolerable costs, adjudication and mediation are difficult to institutionalize. This complementarity has a logical base. The same set of social circumstances which makes one set of processes available frustrates the other and vice-versa.").

177. Karen Halverson, "Resolving Economic Disputes in Russia's Market Economy," *Mich. J. Int'l L.* 18 (1996): 59 (discussing the utility of economic courts and commercial arbitration in Russia for resolving disputes in its evolving market economy).

178. I heard many anecdotal reports of such activity during my summer stay in St. Petersburg in June and July of 1996.

179. Pospisil, 97–106 (devoting a chapter to the discussions of how different legal systems operate within the same culture).

180. The search for causes may be traced back to the so-called founder of comparative law, Montesquieu, who emphasized the unique qualities of the law of different nations by reference to "causes," such as religion or environment (climate). See Baron de Montesquieu, *The Spirit of the Laws,* trans. Thomas Nugent (Cincinnati: Clarke, 1873). More universalist approaches, contradicting the relativist emphasis of Montesquieu, focused on the common nature of legal problems or a common ideology of economic development. W. E. Moore, "Global Sociology: The World as a Singular System," *Am. J. Soc.* 72 (1966): 475 (arguing that sociology should have methodological systems that "cut across national frontiers").

181. Lasser, "Comparative Law and Comparative Literature," 520. Lasser states:
[T]he project has . . . consisted of collapsing the common law/civil law distinction as it has been traditionally used in the American/French context. This required stressing the deep similarities between the two systems. Both deploy the rigid application of existing legal norms (including judicial ones); and both deploy policy analysis (of assorted kinds). They just do so in historically and culturally contingent ways (bifurcated French vs. integrated American judicial discourse). (Ibid.)

182. Abraham Goldstein, "Reflections on Two Models: Inquisitorial Themes in American Criminal Procedure," *Stan. L. Rev.* 26 (1974): 1009 (arguing that the accusitional and inquisitorial procedural models are secondary to the common substantive principal of legality).

183. Mattei, too, recognizes that his categories are not strictly applicable. However, to preserve them, he argues in favor of a standard of hegemony for determining which pattern dominates the others. Mattei, "Taxonomy," 21. He also recognizes the existence of subfamilies and hybrids. Ibid., 40–43. Notwithstanding these differences, Mattei utilizes an age-old method of taxonomy of dubious value and application. He identifies a single feature (source of social norms) for differentiating purposes and applies it crudely, with

judgment-based differentiations based on his identification of primary or hegemonic characteristics.

184. See David and Brierley, *Major Legal Systems,* 20–22.

185. Ibid., 21.

186. Ibid.

187. Ibid.

188. Chad Hansen, "Chinese Language, Chinese Philosophy, and 'Truth,'" *J. Asian Stud.* 44 (1985): 500 (discussing the Chinese language's lack of grammatical inflections).

189. See David and Brierley, *Major Legal Systems,* 12 (stating that "if [legal systems] are founded on opposed philosophical, political or economic principles, and if they seek to achieve two entirely different types of society," they belong to different families).

190. Ibid., 22–26 (discussing the Romano-Germanic and common law families); see Franz Wieacker, "Foundations of European Legal Culture," *Am. J. Comp. L.* 38 (1990): 1 (discussing the basis, scope, and history of European legal culture).

191. David and Brierley, *Major Legal Systems,* 26–27.

192. Ibid. (finding that the socialist family of law is different because of its revolutionary nature).

193. Ibid., 27–28 (stating that all systems of law draw from at least one of the three families of law but not discussing the two criteria).

194. Ibid., 28–29.

195. Ibid., 29–30; see Huxley, (reflecting on the merits of postulating a Buddhist legal tradition).

196. David and Brierley, *Major Legal Systems,* 30–31.

197. Zweigert and Kötz, 61.

198. Adhemar Esmein, "Le Droit compare et l'enseignement du Droit," in *Congres Internationale de Droit Compare, Proces-Verbaux des Seances et Document,* vol. 1 (1905), 445, 451, noted in Zweigert and Kötz, 57–58.

199. Levy-Ullmann, 81, noted in Zweigert and Kötz, 58.

200. See Sauser-Hall, 324, noted in Zweigert and Kötz, 58 (finding that race is the essential factor in Sauser-Hall's division).

201. Martinez Paz, 149–60, noted in Zweigert and Kötz, 58.

202. Pierre Arminjon et al., *Traité de Droit Comparé,* vol. 1 (Paris: Librairie Générale de Droit et de Jurisprudence, 1950), noted in Zweigert and Kötz, 58–59 (pointing out the limitations of their classification to private law).

203. Zweigert and Kötz, 62–67.

204. Ibid., 61.

205. Schlesinger, "Comparative Law," 284. Schlesinger suggests that classification itself is a primary objective rather than a means of comparative law: "Classification involves relating one object to others and specifying how those objectives are similar and how they differ. In a sense, classification is the ultimate purpose of any kind of comparative scholarship." Ibid.

206. Myres S. McDougal, "Comparative Study of Law for Policy Purposes: Value Clarification as an Instrument of Democratic World Order," *Am. J. Comp. L.* 1 (1952): 29 (describing a "literature that is voluminous, obsessively repetitive, and sterile—a literature that feeds and grows, like a psychic cancer, upon logical classification and reclassification and technical refinement and sub-refinement, without limit and with a minimum of external reference and relevance").

207. Watson, *Legal Transplants,* 7 (stating that "where there is no relationship there is no comparative law"). For Alan Watson, a relationship may include a direct or common derivation or influence. Ibid.

208. Ibid. Watson argues that the net of comparative legal studies has been cast too widely and should be concerned with "similarities and differences in the context of a historical relationship," similar to comparative linguistics. Ibid. His view of comparative linguistics is too narrow. Useful comparisons are made in comparative linguistics between languages, e.g., English and Chinese, that have had no such historical relationship. Hansen, 498–500 (comparing English speakers who distinguish word groups and Chinese speakers who do not).

209. In the second edition of *Legal Transplants,* Watson conceded that "knowledge of a number of systems, related or unrelated, may enable us to draw a few general conclusions." Watson, *Legal Transplants,* 117. However, the conclusions he draws are still limited to the Western legal history of primary interest to him, and the primary role of legislation in that history. He writes:

> [G]overnments often are little interested in making law; . . . massive legislation, such as codification, frequently—as with Ataturk's code for Turkey—contains no specific social message fitted to legislating society; . . . much lawmaking is left to a subordinate legal elite such as judges and jurists; and . . . such subordinate lawmakers tend to make law according to a legal culture that they create for themselves.

Ibid., 117–18.

210. As Needham points out, one of the consequences of polythetic classification is that "comparative studies . . . are rendered more daunting and perhaps even unfeasible." Needham, 358; Schlesinger, "Comparative Law," 313–24 (discussing alternative groupings).

211. Lijphart, 690.

212. Zweigert and Kötz answer the question of "which legal systems" should be chosen "to compare in the first place." Zweigert and Kötz, 33. They advise "self-restraint" because "it is hard to take account of everything" and "as soon as one tries to cover a wide range of legal systems the law of diminishing returns applies." Ibid. Zweigert and Kötz see this choice as a function of the topic and purpose of the research. Ibid.

213. Even short of classifications of entire systems, social typologies, espoused by Weber and later advocated by Hart, also require comparative thinking in advance of identifying the type itself. Hart, 13–17 (addressing the comparative dimensions of defining law). Wagner noted the necessity of engaging in comparison prior to the establishment of social types. Wagner, 990 (reviewing Hall by stating that "[i]t does not seem possible to reach any conclusion as to the social type of a particular body of law without engaging in some comparison beforehand, and at times a rather thorough comparative study may be required").

214. Needham concluded that "[c]omparative studies are likely to be defective and unproductive so long as they continue to be carried out within conventional, i.e., monothetic, taxonomies and by reliance on substantive paradigms." Needham, 365.

215. For example, Dan Fenno Henderson once argued for the substitution of Japan for France and Germany as "the model for the civil law system," in part because "Japanese law is . . . more important . . . than French or German law because Japan has a much greater economic and business impact on the United States." Dan Fenno Henderson, "The Japanese Law in English: Some Thoughts on Scope and Method," *Vand. J. Transnat'l L.* 16 (1983): 605–6 (emphasis added).

216. Becker's definition of a court has been criticized by Shapiro for this failure. Shapiro, *Analysis,* 1 (stating that "such a tactic [the use of prototype] is unconvincing because, if we examine what we generally call courts across the full range of contemporary and historical societies, the prototype fits almost none of them"). Becker's definition incorporates notions of norm-based adjudication, impartiality, objectivity, detachment, and

independence. Becker, 13; Tate, 12–13 (pointing out the strengths and weaknesses of Becker's definition).

217. Shapiro, *Analysis,* 1–64.

218. Ibid., 1.

219. Ibid.

220. Ibid.

221. See ABA Report, (quoting on the cover of the Judicial Conference of the United States that "if the federal courts alienate the public and lose its support and participation, they cannot carry out their appropriate role"); ibid., 43 ("Maintaining the Appropriate Balance Between Independence and Accountability is of Critical Importance to Our Democracy."). A fully politically accountable judiciary is not an entirely independent one; and an entirely independent judiciary is not necessarily accountable.

222. Ibid., 65 (incorporating relativity, probability, and qualification into the conclusion, stating, "[w]hile the current state of federal judicial independence remains essentially sound, a number of potentially serious problems exist that, if left unremedied, could degenerate into real threats to judicial independence").

223. Shapiro, *Analysis,* 1–64.

224. Ibid., 63.

225. Laura Nader, "A Comparative Perspective on Legal Evolution, Revolution, and Devolution," *Mich. L. Rev.* 81 (1983): 993 (reviewing Martin Shapiro, *Courts: A Comparative and Political Analysis* (1981)). Nader discusses the method of controlled variables, and critiques Shapiro's work as vulnerable to the criticisms he himself wages.

226. Harold J. Berman, "Courts and the Comparative Historical Method," *Yale L. J.* 91 (1981): 385 (book review) (observing that "Professor Shapiro's alternative to the conventional prototype of courts . . . is also framed so broadly that almost any model—even the one he attacks—can be fitted within it").

227. Shapiro, *Analysis,* 20 (stating that "[t]o make independence [as separation of courts from the remainder of the political system] the touchstone of courtness is to measure from the most deviant case").

228. For example, India does not employ out-of-court discovery, as in the United States. Chodosh et al., *India,* 20–46 (assessing the civil justice system).

229. For example, the judicial management of the early stages of litigation in the United States is frequently considered incomparable to that in Egypt based on the lack of a pretrial/trial distinction in the Egyptian courts. Because the Egyptian trial is a discontinuous process that begins with the filing of the claim, everything following initiation is considered part of the trial. However, regardless of when a system deems "trial" to begin by reference to public hearings in court, many of the U.S. pretrial functions of judicial management are comparable to the intended design of judicially controlled Egyptian trial functions. See Chodosh et al., "Egyptian Civil Justice," 887–90 (comparing U.S. and Egyptian legal processes).

230. Pound, "Expect," 56 (emphasis added).

231. See generally Tumanov.

232. Zweigert and Kötz, 4.

233. Article 3b of the Treaty of Rome provides:

> The Community shall act within the limits of the powers conferred upon it by this Treaty and of the objectives assigned to it therein. In areas which do not fall within its exclusive competence, the Community shall take action, in accordance with the principle of subsidiarity, only if and in so far as the objectives of the proposed action cannot be sufficiently achieved by the Member States and can therefore, by rea-

son of the scale or effects of the proposed action, be better achieved by the Community. Any action by the Community shall not go beyond what is necessary to achieve the objectives of this Treaty.
European Community, *Treaty Establishing the European Economic Community,* 25 March 1957, 298 UNTS 11 (renamed *Treaty Establishing the European Community* by the Maastricht Treaty of 1992), art. 3b (hereinafter Treaty of Rome).

234. Sampson v Channell, 110 F2d 754 (1st Cir 1940) (holding burden of proof to be substantive for Erie purposes (resulting in application of state not federal law) but procedural for state choice of law purposes (resulting in application of forum, not foreign, state law)).

235. Moore, *Law as Process,* 4 ("A central concern of any rule maker should be the identification of those social processes which operate outside the rules, or which cause people to uses rules, or abandon them, bend them, reinterpret them, side-step them, or replace them.").

236. Langbein, "German Advantage," 824 (stating that "the greater responsibility of the bench for fact-gathering is what distinguishes the Continental tradition").

237. Damaska, 17 (focusing on two composite structures of procedural authority and noting that "variables from each dimension [of authority] could be assembled in a great number of ways, and their implications for procedural form examined in a complex classificatory scheme").

238. Each of these stages may be broken down further. Entry may include initiation, submission, filing, notice, service, and appearance. Preparation may include the taking of evidence, the development of legal authorities or other argumentation. Decision may include consensual resolution, evaluation, or judgment. Outcome may include the behavioral response to a decision, such as satisfaction, enforcement, or compliance.

239. Langbein, "German Advantage," 824.

240. See note 108 for discussion of Langbein's article, "The German Advantage in Civil Procedure," and responses to that article.

241. Fiss, "Against Settlement" (arguing that ADR proponents bear the burden of differentiating the public from the private dispute).

242. Koh, "Why Do Nations Obey International Law?" 2599–2600 and fn. 2 (citing studies that "tend to confirm not only that most nations obey international law most of the time, but also that, to a surprising extent, even non-complying nations gradually come back into compliance over time with previously violated international legal norms").

243. Merryman argues that comparison should seek to explain, based on his view, that all explanation involves comparison. Merryman, "Comparative Law and Scientific Explanation," 92.

244. By "cross-referential," I mean the understanding of two expressions in terms of each other. This term is used instead of many alternatives, such as "opposite," "opposed," "polar," or "antithetical." See Needham, 27. Each of these alternatives assumes a significant contrast, indeed a mutual exclusivity. "Cross-reference" may include an equivalent relationship between two terms and is intended to be neutral as to whether the existence of two terms denotes contrast or similarity. "Cross-referential" is also used in lieu of several Aristotelian typologies of distinctions as developed in Aristotle, *Categories and De Interpretatione,* trans. J. L. Ackrill, ed. J. L. Hudson (Oxford: Clarendon Press, 1963) and Aristotle, *Metaphysics,* trans. John Warrington (London: Dent, 1956). "Cross-reference" includes (i) correlative terms such as "senior"/"junior," i.e., terms defined in relation to each other, e.g., "the double and the half," (ii) contraries, of which there are two types, i.e., the first includes a pair of terms with no intermediate between them, e.g., a number must

be odd or even but may not be both; the second encompasses pairs of terms that denote maximum difference and have intermediates between them, such as black and white, between which there are hues of gray; (iii) privation and possession, i.e., opposites that are connected with the same thing, e.g., blindness and sight of the eye; and (iv) affirmation and negation, in which it is necessary as a matter of logic for one to be true and the other false, e.g., a contradiction. G. E. R. Lloyd, *Polarity and Analogy: Two Types of Argumentation in Early Greek Thought* (Cambridge: Cambridge University Press, 1966), discussed in Needham, 44–49 (describing the use of opposition as a spatial metaphor for contrasted terms). Needham correctly questions Aristotle's treatment of each of these pairs of distinctions as merely oppositional. Ibid., 50–52.

245. Chodosh, "Interpretive Theory," 979 (defining the six architectonic types).

246. See Levy-Ullmann (providing examples of common and civil law distinctions).

247. Damaska, 3 (noting that the distinction between adversarial and inquisitorial processes "came to be used on a broader scale, mainly to express the contrast between Continental and Anglo-American administration of justice").

248. Ibid., 16–70 (describing ideals of hierarchical and coordinate authority and the process before officialdom organized according to these two ideals).

249. Koh, *Transnational Legal Process,* 183–84 (explaining how transnational law is formed and enforced); Koh, "Why Do Nations Obey International Law?" 2645 (examining the necessary enforcement of global rules).

250. W. Michael Reisman, "Law from the Policy Perspective," in Myres S. McDougal and W. Michael Reisman, eds., *International Law Essays: A Supplement to International Law in Contemporary Perspective* (Mineola, N.Y.: Foundation Press, 1981), 6 (discussing the distinction of "law" and "politics" in international law).

251. Walter Wheeler Cook, ""Substance" and "Procedure" in the Conflict of Laws," *Yale L. J.* 42 (1933): 334 (analogizing the split between substance and procedure to "face" and "background"); John H. Ely, "The Irrepressible Myth of Erie," *Harv. L. Rev.* 87 (1974): 724 (noting that "[w]e were all brought up on sophisticated talk about the fluidity of the line between substance and procedure").

252. Huxley, 1927; Mattei, "Taxonomy," 35–39 (addressing the alternative ways of distinguishing Eastern and Western law).

253. Chodosh, "Interpretive Theory," 996, fn. 110 (explaining interrelationships between these structural principles).

254. However, the conventions of classification do not easily accommodate "hybrids." Ehrmann, 12 ("Classifications of legal systems are hampered by the fact that law, like nature, does not submit to sharply divided and mutually exclusive categorization."). Indeed, he emphasizes that a "hybrid system . . . defies classification." Ibid.

255. Chodosh, "Interpretive Theory," 995–96 (defining principles).

256. Basil Markesinis characterizes the divergent comparative theories on the distinction between French cause and British consideration in contract law by stating "the study of the two notions has led some to argue that they are, in reality, the same; others to insist that they are totally different; while yet another school of thought could be taken to doubt whether there is "any point in comparing cause and consideration, even to contrast the two." Markesinis, 47–48 (citations omitted).

257. Huxley, 1896 (describing the challenge to the French of European dualisms, including primitive/modern, public/private, which "permeate the investigation, modeling, and presentation of Western material on legal systems"). The uniqueness of this kind of dualism does not rest in the use of groupings of two but in the separation between the two distinct concepts. The Chinese yin/yang is equally contingent on a typology of two; however, the model treats opposites as interdependent.

258. Felstiner, 347 (formulating and applying the dichotomous typology of technologically rich, complex societies and technologically poor, simple societies in order to examine the social conditions for varying types of dispute settlement).

259. Abel, 221. Abel employs both relativity (continuity) and interdependence (complementarity) to evaluate the dichotomous positions taken by Radcliffe-Brown and Malinowski ("Indeed the positions of the two antagonists are really complementary. This can be suggested by the . . . list of dichotomous qualities which indicate the opposing emphases. . . . All societies, of course, fall somewhere between the poles."). Ibid., 222–24, 305, and fn. 18.

260. Markesinis's provocative examination of litigation rates in the United States, Britain, and Germany harps on what he describes as the leitmotif of much of his work, "namely that common lawyers and civil lawyers though different are *not as different* as common mythology considers them to be." Markesinis, 479.

261. Merryman, "On the Convergence," 359–71 (commenting on philosophies and strategies of convergence).

262. Ibid., 371–75.

263. Ibid., 359–60.

264. Ibid., 372–73.

265. Ibid. ("The Scots and Welsh in Britain, the Bretons in France, the Basques and Catalans in Spain, the Quebecois in Canada, these and other current manifestations of the demand for ethnic recognition in political terms are only one kind of example [of divergence]."). These convergent forces of divergence are even stronger today than they were in 1981, when Merryman contributed these useful insights.

266. Moore, *Law as Process* (describing lack of disagreement among anthropologists on the establishment of poles and the series of differences between them).

267. Abel, 251–84.

268. Stein, 208.

269. Ibid.

270. For a seminal treatment of the comparative method in comparative political science, see Lijphart, 685–91 (explaining the weaknesses and strengths of the comparative method).

271. Schmidhauser, 46–47 (stating that such scales were employed to describe spectrums of functional separation, tenure, salary guarantees, compliance with judicial decision, and prohibitions on corrupt practices).

272. Rogers, 190 (discussing the advantages of independent baselines offered by social sciences as some promise of relief from subjective cultural perspectives).

273. By maintaining the coherence of the distinction by reference to conceptual polarities, one may guard against what I have criticized as the equivalent view of legal distinctions. Chodosh, "Interpretive Theory," 1036–44, 1053; Herbert Marcuse, *One-Dimensional Man: Studies in the Ideology of Advanced Industrial Society* (Boston: Beacon Press, 1964), 84–120. Marcuse addressed discourse in which opposites are reconciled or unified (e.g., "peace is really the brink of war"), as a means to eliminate the expression of ""protest and refusal." Ibid., 89–90.

274. Becker, 13–20; Tate, 12–16.

275. Tate, 21 (discussing Schmidhauser and noting the problem peculiar to judgment-based scales) (citing Arthur Banks and Robert B. Textor, *A Cross Polity Survey* (1963)).

276. Felstiner, at 81.

277. See Donald P. Warwick and Samuel Osherson, "Comparative Analysis in the Social Sciences," in D. P. Warwick and Samuel Osherson, eds., *Comparative Research*

Methods (Englewood Cliffs, N.J.: Prentice Hall, 1973), 11–40 (addressing different aspects of equivalence as a core issue in comparative analysis).

278. Gutteridge, 73.

279. Ibid.

280. Zweigert and Kötz, 25 (stressing the importance of the similarity of functionality).

281. Ibid.

282. Ibid. (claiming that "in law the only things which are comparable are those which fulfill the same function").

283. See also Curran, 67 (noting the danger of viewing similarity as confirmation of the validity of the comparative act).

284. Cappelletti et al., "Integration," 9; Curran, "Dealing in Difference," 666 ("Comparative law's habitual focus on identifying commonalities may also endanger the field's receptivity to human distinctiveness.").

285. Chodosh, "Interpretive Theory," 1044–50 (demonstrating the underlying objective/subjective dichotomy at the root of a critical legal studies approach to international law).

286. Huxley, 1927 fn. 288.

287. See chapter 3. C. (dealing with comparative methods of differentiation).

288. This point is evident of Huxley's writing about Hansen. Huxley, 1932 (citing Hansen, 498–500).

289. Ibid.

290. Ibid.

291. Peter Waldman, "Jurists' Prudence: India's Supreme Court Makes the Rule of Law a Way of Governing," *Wall Street J.*, May 6, 1996, A1 (noting that the Indian Supreme Court is riding a wave of positive public sentiment based on its role in fighting political corruption).

292. Joseph W. Singer, "The Player and the Cards: Nihilism and Legal Theory," *Yale L. J.* 94 (1984): 14 (arguing that if one takes determinacy as a necessary feature of rule of law, the rule of law "has never existed anywhere").

293. Lijphart, 687–88 (describing what John Stuart Mill described as the method of concomitant variation: "instead of observing merely the presence or absence of the operative variables, it observes and measures the quantitative variations of the operative variables and relates these to each other").

NOTES TO CHAPTER 4

1. Amartya Sen, *Development as Freedom* (Oxford: Oxford University Press, 1999), 142.

2. Hernando de Soto, *The Mystery of Capital: Why Capitalism Triumphs in the West and Fails Everywhere Else* (New York: Basic Books, 2000), 179.

3. See Linn A. Hammergren, *The Politics of Justice and Justice Reform in Latin America: The Peruvian Case in Comparative Perspective* (Boulder, Colo.: Westview Press, 1998), 3.

4. Part II of the book synthesizes and advances previous writings, inter alia, on globalization, e.g., Hiram E. Chodosh, "Globalizing the U.S. Law Curriculum: The Saja Paradigm," *U.C. Davis L. Rev.* 37 (2004): 843–68; and reform, e.g., Hiram. E. Chodosh, "Local Mediation in Advance of Armed Conflict," *Ohio St. J. on Disp. Resol.* 19 (2003): 213–27; Hiram E. Chodosh, "Emergence from the Dilemmas of Justice Reform," *Tex. J. Int'l L.* 38 (2003): 587–620; Hiram E. Chodosh, "Reforming Judicial Reform Inspired by U.S. Models," *DePaul L. Rev.* (2002): 351–81; Hiram E. Chodosh, "Indonesia," in *Legal*

Systems of the World: A Political, Social, and Cultural Encyclopedia, edited by Herbert Kritzer, vol. 2, 705–9 (Santa Barbara, Calif.: ABC-Clio, 2002); Hiram E. Chodosh, *Mediation in India: A Toolkit* (New Delhi: United States Education Foundation in India, 2004); Hiram E. Chodosh, "Indian Civil Justice System Reform: Limitation and Preservation of the Adversarial Process." *N.Y.U. J. Int'l L. & Pol.* 30 (1998): 1–76; Hiram E. Chodosh, "Reflections on Reform: Considering Legal Foundations for Peace and Prosperity in the Middle East," *Case W. Res. J. Int'l L.* (1999): 427–53; and Hiram E. Chodosh, "Judicial Mediation and Legal Culture," *Issues of Democracy* 4, no. 3 (1999): 6–12.

5. In the past dozen years, emerging democracies include the Republic of Angola (Angola), the Russian Federation (Russia), and the Republic of South Africa (South Africa), all of whom have stated in their respective constitutions the intention to be democratic states by way of regular elections. See Angola Constitution, Part I, Art 2 ("The Republic of Angola shall be a democratic State based on the rule of law, national unity, the dignity of the individual, pluralism of expression and political organizations, respecting and guaranteeing the basic rights and freedoms of persons, both as individuals and as members of organized social groups."); ibid., Part I, Art 3, § 2 ("The Angolan people shall exercise political power through periodic universal suffrage to choose their representatives, by means of referendums and other forms of democratic participation in national life."); Russia Const, Part I, Chap. 1, Art 1 ("The Russian Federation—Russia is a democratic federal rule-of-law state with the republican form of government."); id., Art 3(3) ("The referendum and free elections are the supreme direct manifestation of the power of the people."); South Africa Constitution, Chap. I, § 1 ("The Republic of South Africa is one sovereign democratic state founded on the following values: . . . Universal adult suffrage, a national common voters roll, regular elections and a multi-party system of democratic government, to ensure accountability, responsiveness and openness.").

6. See GATT (establishing the World Trade Organization as a mechanism to govern the trade practices of member states); see also Beth A. Simmons, "The Legalization of International Monetary Affairs," in *Legalization and World Politics,* ed. Judith Goldstein et al. (Cambridge: MIT Press, 2001), 189–218.

7. See Sachs, "Globalization and the Rule of Law"; Larry Diamond et al., introduction to *The Self-Restraining State: Power and Accountability in New Democracies,* ed. Andreas Schedler, Larry Diamond, and Mark F. Plattner (Boulder, Colo.: Lynne Rienner, 1999), 1–12 ("Modern democratic constitutionalism requires elected political leaders, the state, and even the sovereign citizenry to agree to a complex series of "self-binding" mechanisms.").

8. See Alexander M. Bickel, *The Least Dangerous Branch: The Supreme Court at the Bar of Politics,* 2d ed. (New Haven: Yale University Press, 1986).

9. Pilar Domingo, "Judicial Independence and Judicial Reform in Latin America," in *The Self-Restraining State: Power and Accountability in New Democracies,* ed. Andreas Schedler et al. (Boulder, Colo.: Lynne Rienner, 1999), 151–76, 151 ("The judiciary is a key institution in the tasks of legal accountability and constitutional control.").

10. See William C. Prillaman, "Towards a Theory of Judicial Reform in Latin America," in *The Judiciary and Democratic Decay in Latin America: Declining Confidence in the Rule of Law* (Westport, Conn.: Praeger, 2000), 1–14 ("a strong judiciary is essential for checking potential executive and legislative breaches of the constitutional order, laying the foundations for sustainable economic development, and building popular support for the democratic regime").

11. See, e.g., Edgardo Buscaglia, Maria Dakolias, and William Ratliff, *Judicial Reform in Latin America: A Framework for National Development* (Stanford: Stanford University Press, 1995), 1 ("Even the best legislation is meaningless without an effective judicial system to enforce it."); Edmundo Jarquin and Fernando Carrillo, eds., *Justice Delayed:*

Judicial Reform in Latin America (Inter-American Development Bank; for sale by Johns Hopkins University Press, 1998), chaps. 8–11 (relating the importance of judicial institutions to economic performance, property rights, civil society, and democratization).

12. See Sen, 142.

13. See "Universal Declaration of Human Rights," Art 10 ("Everyone is entitled in full equality to a fair and public hearing by an independent and impartial tribunal, in the determination of his rights and obligations and of any criminal charge against him"); see also [European] Convention for Protection of Human Rights and Fundamental Freedoms, 4 Nov. 1950, 213 UNTS 222, Art 6(1) ("everyone is entitled to a fair and public hearing within a reasonable time by an independent and impartial tribunal"). See, e.g., Capuano v Italy, 13 EHRR 271 (1991); Santilli v Italy, 14 EHRR 421 (1992); Massa v Italy, 18 EHRR 266 (1994); Paccione v Italy, 20 EHRR 396 (1995).

14. Hiram Chodosh, Indonesia Notes, Entry of January 9, 2001.

15. See Convention on Combating Bribery of Foreign Officials in International Business Transactions, Dec. 18, 1997, 37 I.L.M. 1 (hereinafter OECD Anti-Bribery Convention) (adopted by OECD to address problems that raise serious moral and political concerns, undermine good governance and economic development, and distort international competitive conditions); International Anti-Bribery and Fair Competition Act of 1998, Pub. L. No. 105-366, 112 Stat 3302 (1998) (amending Securities Exchange Act of 1934 and Foreign Corrupt Practices Act of 1977 to improve competitiveness of American business, promote foreign commerce, and implement OECD Anti-Bribery convention); Foreign Corrupt Practices Act of 1977, Pub. L. No. 95-213, 91 Stat. 1494 (1977) (codified as amended in 15 U.S.C. § 78 (2000)) (amending Securities Exchange Act of 1934 to make it unlawful for an issuer of securities to make payments to foreign officials and other foreign persons and to require such issuers to maintain accurate records).

16. See Takeshi Kojima, "Civil Procedure Reform in Japan," *Mich. J. Int'l L.* 11, (Summer 1990): 1218, 1220–34 (noting that a "speedy hearing is guaranteed by constitutional provisions in Spain, Turkey, and South American countries. Such guarantees can also be read through the interpretation of constitutional law in Japan, West Germany, the United States and Greece."). See also, e.g., "Federal Rules of Civil Procedure, Rule 1; Mauro Cappelletti, Fundamental Guarantees of the Parties in Civil Litigation: Comparative Constitutional, International and Social Trends," *Stan. L. Rev.* 25 (1973): 651.

17. See also Office of Democracy and Governance, *Guidance for Promoting Judicial Independence and Impartiality* (Washington, D.C.: U.S. Agency for International Development, 2002), preface ("Judicial independence lies at the heart of a well-functioning judiciary and is the cornerstone of a democratic, market based society based on the rule of law.").

18. Rachel L. Swarns, "The World; An Election, Yes. But Free and Fair?" *New York Times*, Mar. 17, 2002, § 4, 6 (reporting that in Zimbabwe's recent presidential campaign, leading to the contested victory of President Robert Mugabe, "more than 20 opposition party supporters were killed while the authorities looked the other way; officials eliminated polling stations in opposition strongholds, effectively disenfranchising thousands of voters, and the police fired choking clouds of tear gas to disperse hundreds more who were waiting to cast their ballots").

19. For an incisive treatment of these problems in Peru and Latin America more generally, see Hammergren, *Politics of Justice,* 6 ("It is conventional wisdom among Latin Americans that their judiciaries and indeed their entire justice systems are the orphan branch of government, underfinanced, bypassed by modernization, and politically dominated by the executive and legislature or by various governmental and nongovernmental elites.").

20. See, e.g., Mark Ungar, "Independent Judicial Functioning," in *Elusive Reform: Democracy and the Rule of Law in Latin America* (Boulder, Colo.: Lynne Rienner, 2002), 119–68 (discussing the absence of judicial independence in Latin America); Juan E. Mendez, Guillermo O'Donnell, and Paulo Sergio Pinheiro, eds., *The (Un)rule of Law and the Underprivileged in Latin America* (Notre Dame: University of Notre Dame Press, 1999), Part 3, Institutional Reform, Including Access to Justice, 227–337; Suzanne Daley, "French Judge Investigating Chirac Quits Bench," *New York Times,* Jan. 15, 2002, A6 (reporting that French Magistrate Eric Halphen, who led main corruption investigations of President Jacques Chirac (and was then removed from the case), resigned from the bench, charging his work has been sabotaged at every turn, and that efforts to get truth were undermined by procedural tricks, manipulation of media against him, and a lack of cooperation by the police).

21. Robert E. Klitgaard, "International Cooperation Against Corruption," *Finance and Development,* March 1998, 3, available online at http://www.imf.org/external/pubs/ft/fandd/1998/03/pdf/klitgaar.pdf; Robert E. Klitgaard, *Controlling Corruption* (Berkeley: University of California Press, 1988), available online at http://emedia.netlibrary.com/reader/reader.asp?product_id=5800; Susan Rose-Ackerman, "Redesigning the State to Fight Corruption: Transparency, Competition, and Privatization," *Public Policy for the Private Sector,* Note No. 75, April 1996, available online at http://www.worldbank.org/html/fpd/notes/75/75ackerm.pdf; Susan Rose-Ackerman, *Corruption and Government: Causes, Consequences and Reform* (New York: Cambridge University Press, 1999). See also John T. Noonan, Jr., *Bribes: An Intellectual History of a Moral Idea* (Collingdale, Penn.: Diane Publishing Co., 1984); Kimberly Ann Elliot, ed., *Corruption and the Global Economy* (Washington, D.C.: Institute for International Economics, 1996); Mark Robinson, ed., *Corruption and Development* (Portland, Ore.: Frank Cass and Co., 1998).

22. See, e.g., Edmundo Jarquin and Fernando Carrillo, eds., *Justice Delayed: Judicial Reform in Latin America* (Inter-American Development Bank; for sale by Johns Hopkins University Press, 1998).

23. See, e.g., Domingo, 156 (the courts of Latin America "reproduce an image of corruption, clientelism, and inefficiency" and are not viewed as impartial administrators of justice or autonomous agents of constitutional and legal control). See, e.g., Maria Dakolias, *The Judicial Sector in Latin America and the Caribbean: Elements of Reform,* World Bank Technical Paper No.319 (Washington, D.C.: World Bank, 1996), v (documenting the extent to which public institutions in the region have not been able to respond effectively to the challenges of markets, with the courts "experiencing lengthy case delays, extensive case backlogs, limited access by the population, a lack of transparency and predictability in court decisions and weak public confidence in the judicial system.").

24. Edgardo Buscaglia, *Judicial Corruption in Developing Countries: Its Causes and Economic Consequences,* Berkeley Olin Program in Law and Economics Working Paper No. 28 (1999), available online at http://repositories.cdlib.org/blewp/28/, 8.

25. The United States–led international war on terrorism may place additional burdens on courts as the last word on core democratic and human rights principles. As one example, the Supreme Court of Pakistan recently affirmed the arguable legality of General Musharraf's self-styled referendum to prolong his term for another five years, holding that the referendum fell within the constitutional provision for such votes on "important national issues." See "Pakistan Top Court Backs Musharraf," CNN, Apr. 27, 2002, available online at http://www.cnn.com/2002/WORLD/asiapcf/south/04/27/pakistan.supreme/index.html.

26. See, e.g., Buscaglia, *Judicial Corruption.*

27. See Tanzania, Presidential Commission of Inquiry Against Corruption: *Report on*

the Commission of Corruption, vol. 1 (1996) 51 ("Magistrates accept bribes from advocates so that they may give preferential judgements. . . . Court Assessors accept bribes in order to give favourable verdicts to those who corrupt them."); and Hiram E. Chodosh and Stephen A. Mayo, *Combating Judicial Corruption in Tanzania* (San Francisco: Institute for the Study and Development of Legal Systems (ISDLS), 2001) (on file with author).

28. Manzoor Hasan, "Corruption in Bangladesh Surveys: An Overview," available online at http://www.ti-bangladesh.org/survey/overview.htm. See also Maria Dakolias and Kim Thachuk, "Attacking Corruption in the Judiciary: A Critical Process in Judicial Reform," *Wis. Int'l L. J.* 18, no. 2 (Spring 2000): 366–67 (reporting that polls in Latin American indicate comparably high perceptions of corruption: in Argentina, 57 percent see corruption as a main problem; in Honduras, three out of every four polled see the judiciary as corrupt; in Costa Rica, 54 percent believe that external pressures affect judicial decisions).

29. See Transparency International, "Transparency International Releases New Bribe Payers Index (BPI) 2002," May 14, 2002, available online at http://www.transparency .org/pressreleases_archive/2002/2002.05.14.bpi.en.html (stressing the ineffectuality of domestic and international law: "The BPI shows that US multinational corporations, which have faced the risk of criminal prosecution since 1977 under the Foreign Corrupt Practices Act, have a high propensity to pay bribes to foreign government officials," and "[t]he BPI results signal the rejection by multinational firms of the spirit of international anti-bribery conventions. . . .").

30. See generally Peter H. Schuck, *The Limits of Law: Essays on Democratic Governance* (Boulder, Colo.: Westview Press, 2000), 434–44 (discussing interaction between law, social norms, and markets).

31. See Maria Dakolias, *Court Performance around the World: A Comparative Perspective* (Washington, D.C.: World Bank, 1999), 1 ("Many developing countries . . . find that their judiciaries advance inconsistent case law and carry a large backlog of cases, thus eroding individual and property rights, stifling private sector growth, and even violating human rights.").

32. Buscaglia, *Judicial Corruption,* 10 ("the frustrations of backlogs . . . as well as litigants' desires to get their cases heard and won, provide the opportunities for the courts to extract rents."). See also Irwin P. Stotsky, ed., *Transition to Democracy in Latin America: The Role of the Judiciary* (Boulder, Colo.: Westview Press, 1993).

33. Peter H. Solomon, Jr., and Todd S. Foglesong, "The Administration of Justice: Simplification and Efficiency," in *Courts and Transition in Russia: The Challenge of Judicial Reform* (Boulder, Colo.: Westview Press, 2000), 114–15.

34. See Adrian A. S. Zuckerman, "Justice in Crisis: Comparative Dimensions of Civil Procedure," in *Civil Justice in Crisis: Comparative Perspectives of Civil Procedure,* ed. Adrian A. S. Zuckerman (Oxford; New York: Oxford University Press, 1999), 3–52, 23 (in Italy, for example, "[I]t is not uncommon for plaintiffs to be forced to wait 10 years for final judgment.")

35. Amnesty International, *Take a Step to Stamp Out Torture* (New York: Amnesty International, 2000) (reporting that "common criminals and criminal suspects are the most frequent victims of torture by state agents" and that they "have reportedly been subjected to torture or ill-treatment in over 130 countries since 1997").

36. See John Conroy, *Unspeakable Acts; Ordinary People: The Dynamics of Torture* (New York: Knopf, 2001).

37. See, e.g., Charles J. Ogletree, Jr., "From Mandela to Mthwana: Providing Counsel to the Unrepresented Accused in South Africa," *B.U. L. Rev.* 75 (Jan. 1995): 1–56; Hiram E. Chodosh and Stephen A. Mayo, "The Palestinian Legal Study: Consensus and Assess-

ment of the New Palestinian Legal System," *Harv. Int'l L. J.* 38 (Spring 1997): 275, 421–24 (detailing related problems in the Palestinian criminal justice process).

38. International Legal Assistance Consortium, "Report from an ILAC Mission to Iraq," 10, 13–14 (2003) (noting the large numbers of suspects and the limited "resources to process these cases," including the lack of appointed counsel and financial compensation for defense lawyers" and recommending programs that focus on "Judging in a Democratic Society" with an emphasis on judicial independence).

39. The following discussion and notes in part C. 1. draw from Hiram E. Chodosh, "Indonesia," in *Legal Systems of the World: A Political, Social, and Cultural Encyclopedia,* ed. Herbert Kritzer, vol. 2 (Santa Barbara, Calif.: ABC-Clio, 2002), 705–9. The assessments are derived heavily from Ali, Budiardjo, Nugroho, and Reksodiputro, *Diagnostic Assessment of Legal Development in Indonesia* (Jakarta, Indonesia: Cyberconsult, 1997), vols. I–V [hereinafter "Diagnostic"] and notes from several exchanges with Indonesian legal experts in Jakarta and in the United States, see Chodosh, Indonesia Notes.

40. The following discussion and notes in part C. 2. draw from previous writings cited in note 67, below.

41. See Timothy Lindsey, "An Overview of Indonesian Law," 1–10, in Timothy Lindsey, ed., *Indonesia: Law and Society* (Leichardt, New South Wales: Federation, 1999); Daniel S. Lev, "Judicial Institutions and Legal Culture in Indonesia," in *Culture and Politics in Indonesia,* ed. Claire Holt, 246–318 (Ithaca: Cornell University Press, 1972); and Chodosh, "Indonesia," 705–6:

> Until the early nineteenth century, Indonesian law was as diverse as the society itself. Village communities and developing urban centers largely determined their own local legal norms. Early attempts at codification were influenced heavily by Hindu and Buddhist cultures. Islamic influence through the sharia (Islamic law) began in the fourteenth century and continues to play a significant role today.

42. See Chodosh, "Indonesia," 705–6 (drawing on Lindsay, "Overview"):

> Animism, spirit and ancestor worship, Hindu and Buddhist concepts of universalism, and Islamic principles of sacred authority were received with varying success in different regions of the archipelago—from Hindu-Buddhist influences in Bali to Islamic impacts in northern Sumatra. Europe began to assert economic control over the region in the mid-seventeenth century.

43. Ibid., 706:

> By the time of Napoleon's defeat, European control over most of the archipelago was turned over to the Netherlands, who consolidated their power over Sumatra and many other islands in the course of several decades. Not until 1854 did the Dutch create a divided constitutional structure, whereby the population was divided into three groups—Europeans, [native Indonesians], and non-Christian natives—with laws, courts, and procedures varying widely in terms of their application to the different groups and subject matter. All criminal and most commercial law applied to the three groups. Local Indonesian adat (customary) law applied to the land, and contract law allowed for customary Indonesian law or the civil code to apply at the discretion of the parties; however, the determination of family law depended on the imposed sociological divisions. Furthermore, Indonesian litigants, even in serious cases, did not come before the European courts (unless on appeal) and thus did not enjoy the procedural protections afforded European litigants.

44. Ibid.
45. Ibid.
46. Ibid.

47. Ibid., 708–9:

There is no unified body of legal professionals in Indonesia. The functions and self-regulatory bodies of lawyers are diverse. *Advokat* (advocates) and *pengacara* (attorneys) take a professional oath and represent clients in court, whereas *konsultan hukum* (legal advisers) do neither. Additionally, *notaris* (notaries), similar to the notaries of the continental European systems, specialize in the drafting and execution of legal documents. Generally, admission into the legal profession is relatively easy. The quality of legal education is considered low, and the best students tend to enter the private sector, thus leaving the public sector with a deficit in adequately trained professionals. To become a legal professional, only graduation from a recognized law school is required. To become an advokat, applicants must complete on-the-job training; however, the supervision and standards of this practical requirement are minimal. Konsultan hukum do not even need to obtain a license to provide legal advice on commercial matters. Additionally, several competing organizations for the legal profession have their own charters and rules of conduct, and efforts are under way to unify the legal profession under a common set of self-regulatory norms and procedures.

48. See The Supreme Court of the Republic of Indonesia, *The Judicial System in Indonesia (General View)* (Jakarta: The Supreme Court of Indonesia, May 10, 1993) (noting that Articles 24 and 25 provided that the judicial power shall be executed by one Supreme Court and other judicial bodies as established by law, and quoting from the Elucidation to these articles: "the judicial power is an independent power, which means free from the influence of the government. In this connection the status of Judges must be guaranteed by Law."); Republic of Indonesia, Law No. 14 of 1970 Concerning Basic Principles of Judicial Power; Republic of Indonesia, Law No. 14 of 1985 on the Supreme Court.

49. See Daniel S. Lev, "Between State and Society: Professional Lawyers and Reform in Indonesia," in Lindsey, ed., 227–46.

50. Chodosh, Indonesia, 707:

According to Law No. 14/1970 (the basic legal provision on the contours of judicial power), the judicial system is divided into four substantive jurisdictions: (1) the Courts of General Jurisdiction, which handle all cases not designated for the three other jurisdictions; (2) the Administrative Courts; (3) the Military Courts; and (4) the Religious (Islamic) Courts. The jurisdiction of the Military Courts covers only military criminal law involving military personnel. The Religious Courts' jurisdiction is limited to Islamic family law (issues of polygamous marriage, divorce, and inheritance). The general courts handle civil and criminal matters, and the Administrative Courts adjudicate disputes between private persons or corporations and administrative bodies or organs of the state. The general and Religious Courts are the most numerous, with Religious Courts in nearly each of the 280 districts.

51. Ibid., 707–8:

Beneath the Supreme Court, the High Courts sit in the capitals of all the provinces. The High Court's territorial jurisdiction is coterminous with that of the province in which it sits. The High Court is an appellate court of general jurisdiction that handles appeals from the districts under its territorial jurisdiction, including jurisdictional disputes between the District Courts. The High Court hears cases in panels of three judges. A chief judge, vice chief judge, and several High Court judges sit on each High Court. Selection to the High Court is made by the Department of Justice on the recommendation of the Supreme Court, which chooses names from a list of senior judges. The District Courts sit at the second level of regional government below the province. The District Court has general jurisdiction over civil and criminal matters. A chief judge, vice chief judge, and other District Court judges hear cases either in panels of three or as single judges, depending on the nature of the case. These courts are said to dispose of approximately 1.7 million cases each year. The Religious Courts are parallel to the general courts, with a High Court in each provincial capital and Courts of First Instance in the second level of provincial government. Judges have expertise in Islamic law. In contrast, there are only six Military High Courts in the country, and they administer law drawn from the General Criminal Code, the Military Criminal Code, and the Military Disciplinary Code.

52. The court currently has many vacancies. Ibid.

53. Within each chamber, the court hears cases primarily in panels of three judges. Ibid.

54. Ibid.

55. The current count is 2,670. Supreme Court of Indonesia, "Judicial Personnel Management Reform" (2003), 46.

56. Chodosh, Indonesia, 708.

57. Ibid., 707.

58. Ibid., 709:
The president appoints justices of the Supreme Court from a list of nominees submitted by Parliament. In contrast to the process before the reformasi, candidates in the fall of 2000 submitted to a "fit and proper" test applied publicly by the Parliament. The nominees, who included legal experts from outside the career judiciary, gave public presentations and subjected themselves to integrity reviews by new nongovernmental organizations dedicated to establishing judicial integrity.

59. Ibid.

60. Ibid.

61. Ibid.

62. See Indonesia, Law No. 35/1999.

63. See Third Amendment to the 1945 Constitution of the Republic of Indonesia, Art 24B(1) (vesting authority in a Judicial Commission to make nominations for judicial appointments to the Supreme Court and for "guarding and upholding the honor, noble prestige, and behavior of the judge"); Draft Bills Concerning Judicial Commission, Art 5 (defining the commission's function as "(1) Proposing the appointment of the Supreme Court Judge to the House of Representatives (DPR) to attain approval and subsequently to be appointed by the President; (2) Maintaining and ensuring the honor, dignity and behavior of judges.") The Third Amendment also reconfirms the normative principle for judicial independence (see Art 24 (1) ("The power of the judiciary is the power of freedom to implement justice in order to enforce law and justice") and establishes the framework for a constitutional court with broad powers (see Art 24 C (2): "The Constitutional Court has the authority to issue a decision over the opinion of the House of Representatives concerning suspicious violations of the President and/or Vice-President according to the Constitution.")

64. Indonesian Supreme Court, "The Academic Draft and Bill on Judicial Commission" (2003) (hereinafter, the "Blueprint").

65. Article 24B provides in full:
(1) The Judicial Commission that is characterized as independent has the authority to propose the promotion of the supreme judge and has other authorities in the framework of guarding and upholding the honor, noble prestige, and behavior of the judge.
(2) The members of the Judicial Commission must possess the knowledge and experience in the legal aspect and must possess integrity and a personality that is not disgraceful.

(3) The members of the Judicial Commission is [*sic*] promoted and dismissed by the President with the approval of the House of Representatives.

(4) The structure, status, and membership of the Judicial Commission is [*sic*] regulated by law. (Third Amendment to the 1945 Constitution of the Republic of Indonesia.)

66. Ibid., 708:

Specialized jurisdictions are beginning to emerge within and around the general courts. To handle the acute problem of widespread insolvencies in the wake of the Asian financial crisis, Indonesia established the special Commercial Court as a District Court chamber in Jakarta, with direct appeals to the Supreme Court. The Commercial Court introduced many significant reforms to the general court system, including the appointment of ad hoc (noncareer) judges, the use of dissents, strict deadlines in the process (including appeals), public hearings, and the prompt publication of and full access to court decisions. The Commercial Court is in the process of expanding to other major commercial centers and subject matter jurisdiction beyond bankruptcy cases, for example, intellectual property and insurance matters. Reformers are currently working on plans for other specialized tribunals to handle tax, human rights, and corruption issues.

67. The following discussion in C. 2. draws heavily on Hiram E. Chodosh et al., "Indian Civil Justice System Reform," *N.Y.U. J. Int'l L. & Pol.* 30 (1998), 4–5, 22–50 (assessing the practical operation of the civil justice system), and Hiram Chodosh et al., *Mediation in India: A Toolkit* (New Delhi: United States Education Foundation in India, 2004).

68. British-style courts were established in India by the East India Company in 1775. See Bernard C. Cohn, "Some Notes on Law and Change in North India," *Econ. Dev. & Cultural Change* 8 (1959): 90.

69. See Raj Kumari Agrawala, "History of Courts and Legislatures," in *The Indian Legal System,* ed. Joseph Minattur (Dobbs Ferry, N.Y.: Oceana, 1978), 103, stressing discontinuity in Indian legal history:

Present legal mechanics has virtually no link with the Hindu and Muslim periods to which its source may be traced. Hindu law and its jurisprudence got stifled and had waned, giving way to Islamic law, except in certain pockets, since the Muslim conquest of the country. . . . [T]he original Indian law is much more alien to Indians today than the imported alien forms of the English common law system. It is therefore futile to go beyond the seventeenth century for any appreciation or understanding of the existing Indian legal institutions or concepts.

See also Cohn. For a brief summary of the history of the Indian legal system, see Chun-Chi Young, "The Legal System of India," in *Modern Legal Systems Cyclopedia,* ed. Kenneth Robert Redden (Buffalo: William S. Hein, 1990), ch. 5, 9.80.7–.9 (describing Ancient, Mogul, British, and Modern periods).

70. See Mirjan R. Damaska, "Organization of Authority: The Hierarchical and the Coordinate Ideas," in *The Faces of Justice and State Authority: A Comparative Approach to the Legal Process* (New Haven: Yale University Press, 1986), 16–28, 38–46 (distinguishing coordinate and hierarchical ideals in comparative legal systems and processes and relating coordinate ideals to the Anglo-American machinery of justice). The structure of the Indian judiciary has both vertical and horizontal dimensions and is more accurately described as a pyramid, arguably a comparatively flat one. See also Raj Kumari Agrawala, "History of Courts and Legislatures," in *The Indian Legal System,* ed. Joseph Minattur (Dobbs Ferry, N.Y.: Oceana, 1978), 115–16 (describing the judicial structure as a "correlated hierarchy resulting in a pyramid with the Supreme Court at the apex," the High Courts in each state, and districts within the states).

71. Party control over evidentiary development of litigation has traditionally been a significant distinguishing feature of the British, American, and Indian systems, compared to the Continental European systems of Germany and France, and former colonies influenced by models of greater judicial control. See, e.g., Langbein, "The German Advantage."

72. The outcome of a legal judgment in favor of one party or the other, rather than a compromise or conciliated settlement, is a feature common to formal legal systems of Roman origin, not only those based on European or more specifically British models. The traditionally separate British procedures for equitable remedies to a significant extent qualified the win-lose feature of these formal justice systems. See George E. Palmer, *The Law of Restitution* (Boston: Little, Brown, 1978). Cohn emphasizes the conflict between the British value, which requires a clear-cut decision, and the Indian value, which encourages the parties "to compromise their differences in some way." Cohn, 91.

73. The British Raj is the major historical cause of limited alternatives to the formal court system. The British "ignored local indigenous adjudication procedures and modeled the process of adjudication in the courts on that of the British law courts of the period." Cohn, 90. Britain itself is reported to suffer from an antiquated court system. See "Britain's Antiquated Courts" (discussing the proposal of a government-appointed judge to streamline court procedures and encourage mediations and arbitration).

74. See Cohn, 91.

75. For a historical account of the trial court under the Anglo-American system, see Robert Winess Millar, *Civil Procedure of the Trial Court in Historical Perspective* (New York: Law Center of NYU, 1952).

76. For a description of the institutional indicia of judicial independence in India, see S. N. Jain, "Judicial System and Legal Remedies," in *The Indian Legal System,* ed. Joseph Minattur (Dobbs Ferry, N.Y.: Oceana, 1978), 133–47.

77. In this respect, the Indian judiciary differs from the dual federal/state system in the United States.

78. For a fundamental description of the courts, their jurisdiction and procedures, see D. C. Singhania, "INDIA—Courts: Their Jurisdiction and Procedures," in *World Reports 1989–1996,* Lex Mundi Doing Business Guides, vol. 9 (Houston: Lex Mundi, 1997), 1447.

79. See Agrawala, 116.

80. See Agrawala, 115–16; Chun-Chi Young, "The Legal System of India," in *Modern Legal Systems Cyclopedia,* ed. Kenneth Robert Redden (Buffalo: William S. Hein, 1990), ch. 5, 9.80.25–27.

81. See generally Sudipto Sarkar and V. R. Manohar, et al., *Sarkar Code of Civil Procedure,* 10th ed. (Nagpur, India: Wadhwa and Company, 2004); Alan Gledhill, "Laws Relating to Contract: The Indian Contract Act" in *The Republic of India: The Development of Its Laws and Constitution* (Westport, Conn.: Greenwood Press, 1970), 237–38.

82. See generally India Code of Civil Procedure (Act No. V of 1908) (hereinafter CPC). For a brief description of these stages, see V. S. Deshpande, "Civil Procedure," in *The Indian Legal System,* ed. Joseph Minattur (Dobbs Ferry, N.Y.: Oceana, 1978), 177–209; Gledhill, "Laws," 238–41.

83. Cohn sees many features of British procedural justice as incompatible with the values of Indian rural jurisprudence. See Cohn, 91. See also Robert L. Kidder, "Courts and Conflict in an Indian City: A Study in Legal Impact," *J. Commonwealth Pol. Stud.* 11 (1973): 121; Oliver Mendelsohn, "The Pathology of the Indian Legal System," *Mod. Asian Stud.* 15 (1981): 823. Cf. Law Commission of India," Seventy-Seventh Report on Delay and Arrears in Trial Courts" (1978), 7 [hereinafter "Seventy-Seventh Report"] (stating:

[I]t seems hardly correct to say that the present judicial system is a foreign trans-plant on Indian soil, or that it is based on alien concepts unintelligible to our peo-ple. . . . The criticism that the present system of administration of justice is not suited to the genius of our people is based on the ground that our society is basically an agrarian society, not sophisticated enough to understand the technical and cum-bersome procedure followed by our courts).

84. See Peter Waldman, "Jurists' Prudence," *Wall St. J.,* May 6, 1996, A1.

85. See Cohn, 90 (stating that there were serious faults in the courts "almost from the[ir] establishment." It took "years for disputes to be resolved, and there were too many appeals from lower courts. . . . The courts did not settle disputes, but were used either as a form of gambling on the part of legal speculators . . . or as a threat in a dispute.").

86. See Sonali Verma, Reuters, New Delhi, July 1, 1997 (stating that "[I]ndia an-nounced sweeping measures . . . to overhaul the judiciary which is wrestling with a backlog of more than 30 million cases," and quoting Law Minister Ramakant Khalap: "We consid-ered the heavy backlog of cases and have resolved that the 50th year of our independence be observed as the docket clearance year.").

87. Similar arguments in relation to the United States adversarial system have begun to emerge. See Carrie Menkel-Meadow, "The Trouble with the Adversary System in a Post-modern, Multicultural World," *Wm. & Mary L. Rev.* 38 (Oct. 1996): 5–44.

88. See Hiram E. Chodosh et al., "Egyptian Civil Justice Process Modernization: A Functional and Systemic Approach," *Mich. J. Int'l L.* 17 (Summer 1996): 865–917. See also Peider Konz (Rapporteur), introduction and summary to "World Association of Judges & International Legal Center," in *Court Congestion: Some Remedial Approaches* (Buffalo: William S. Hein, 1971), 1–19 (stating that "[c]ongestion and delay in the admin-istration of justice are matters of major concern in a variety of countries, both developed and developing").

89. For example, the first Civil Justice Committee (Justice Rankin, Chairman) was ap-pointed in 1925 to deal with the problem of delay among other matters. See Justice K. N. Saikia, "Report on Modernisation, Court Management and Alternative Dispute Resolu-tion in Civil Judicial Process" (Dec. 1996), 2 (revealing that even seventy years ago, the problem of delay appeared so daunting that the Civil Justice Committee, headed by Justice Rankin, concluded that "improvement in methods alone cannot be expected in such cir-cumstances to produce a satisfactory result even in a decade" and described the outlook as "gloomy"). The High Court Arrears Committee in 1949 was appointed to look into ways that would curtail delay. As Saikia reports, "The Committee made few concrete propos-als." Ibid., 4. Again, in August 1955, the Indian government appointed a Law Commission (Attorney General Shri M. C. Setalvad) to improve the ways and means of judicial admin-istration to make it "speedy and less expensive." Ibid., 5. The commission rejected the sug-gestion that the India Civil Procedure Code (CPC) was the cause of delay: "The delay re-sults not from the procedure laid down by [the code] but by reason of nonobservance of its important provisions, particularly those intended to expedite the disposal of proceedings." Instead, the 1955 Commission cited "[i]nsufficient numbers of judicial officers, an incom-petent and corrupt ministerial and process serving agency, the diverse delaying tactics adopted by the litigants and their lawyers, the unmethodical arrangement of work by the presiding judge and the heavy file of arrears." Ibid., 6–7. A High Court Arrears Committee would reconvene in 1969 and complete its report in 1972, followed by a Law Commission (chaired by Justice H. R. Khanna) and its "Seventy-Seventh Report." Again, the report ex-pressed the same despair articulated by Justice Rankin fifty years earlier: "As long as courts remain burdened with arrears, the other suggestions for expediting the disposal of cases would be nothing more than palliatives and would not provide any effective relief." Ibid.,

2. Any suggestion of a revival of pre-British legal processes was summarily put to rest: "The real need appears to be to further improve the existing system to meet modern requirements in the context of our national ethos and not to replace it by an inadequate system which was left behind long ago." Ibid., 7–10. The Seventy-Ninth Report, also written by Justice Khanna, stressed the human factor, arguing that the delays could not be dealt with adequately through "statutory reforms" and citing the procedure for service of process as presupposing a prompt and effective postal service. See Law Commission of India, "Seventy-Ninth Report on Delay and Arrears in High Courts and other Appellate Courts" (1979), 5. In 1988, Justice D. A. Desai chaired the Law Commission of India and wrote the one hundred twenty-fourth report. This commission endeavored to make several recommendations, including limiting argument time, reducing the judge's workload, and modernizing the courts, including computerization and classification. See Law Commission of India, "One Hundred Twenty-Fourth Report on the High Court Arrears—A Fresh Look" (1988), 23–26, 29. Finally, in 1989–90, three prominent High Court justices, Justice V. S. Malimath (Chief Justice of the High Court of Kerala) Justice P. D. Desai (Chief Justice of the High Court of Calcutta), and Justice A. S. Anand (Chief Justice of the High Court of Madras, who is currently on the Supreme Court and will eventually become Chief Justice of the Supreme Court), issued Report of the Arrears Committee 1989–1990. This most recent report provides an outstanding assessment of the Indian civil justice system; its findings are completely consistent with the conclusions of the Indo-U.S. team. Specifically, it addresses managerial issues in the regulation of the courts generally and court proceedings in particular (see, e.g., vol. I, sections 8.21, 8.37) and envisions a heavy reliance on conciliation (vol. II, sections 8.71–.91, at 112–17). All of the above reports are on file with the author.

90. The backlog and delay problem has reached profound dimensions in India. In the High Court of Bombay, for example, there are more than three thousand matters docketed for each judge, current hearings of interim (not final) appeals are proceeding with appeals filed in 1984, and statistics indicate that caseloads are increasing significantly with each year's new matter/disposition rate. See "Statement Showing the Main Cases Instituted and Disposed of by Bombay High Court for the Period Ending July 30, 1996" (Sept. 23, 1996) (reflecting 13,038 initiated and 8,713 disposed during this period) (on file with author). See also Dr. Dhananyaya Y. Chandarachud, "Note on Dimensions and Causes of Delay in the Courts in the City of Bombay and in the State of Maharashtra" (Sept. 27, 1992) (unpublished manuscript, on file with the author) (noting that the "disposal of suits [in the Bombay High Court] is approximately 50% of fresh filings every year") (hereinafter Chandarachud, "Note on Bombay & Maharashtra"). The Lok Sabha gathered statistics on the numbers of cases instituted, disposed, and pending in the High Courts for the years 1992, 1993, and 1994. These data show that during this time the High Courts were falling further behind, disposing of roughly 78–79 percent of the number of cases instituted in a year's time. Thus, in each of the three years, on a nationwide basis, the High Courts added a little more than 20 percent of the total yearly cases to the total backlog. Saikia, 19–22. Unlike backlog, delays are more difficult to quantify empirically because the court registrars do not have the case-tracking capability in order to determine rates of disposition.

91. See "India Sets Changes to Tackle Mounting Court Cases," Reuters, Oct. 6, 1995, available in LEXIS, News Library, Wires File (arguing that the economic liberalization program initiated in 1991 brought in a fresh need for speedy justice). Suits brought against the government of India because of its role in the economy and legal limits on its powers are reportedly one of the greatest sources of new cases, and ones to which the responsiveness of the defense is slowest.

92. See Sh. S.B. Sinha, "Alternative Dispute Resolution with Special Reference to Civil

Procedure (Amendment) Act, 1999," *Nyaya Kiran* (Delhi Legal Services Authority, 2003), 7.

93. Ibid.

94. A broad range of rights, from protections against discrimination, to creditors' rights, to collateral, to compensation for acts of negligence, are all rendered nearly meaningless by the extent of the delay. Many injured persons lack the time and/or money to pursue their claims. Defendants (or plaintiffs granted preliminary injunctive relief) systematically benefit from the courts' inability to function effectively within a reasonable amount of time. Civil claimants are left without timely remedies. For example, long delays and no recovery for prejudgment interest can easily transform bank loans into open-ended credit facilities, and this risk increases market interest rates. Thus, the problem of backlog and delay blocks access to justice, exacerbates resource disparities between contesting parties, frequently forces claimants to bear the cost of their legal injuries, and increases the costs of doing business. These problems must be addressed in order to deliver civil justice to the Indian population and to effectively implement substantive legal reforms aimed at economic growth. The impact of the problem of backlog and delay is both profound and disturbing; it effectively eliminates the rights of citizens to obtain effective remedies. This is particularly critical in light of India's recent efforts (since 1991) to liberalize its economic system. See "India's Economy: Work in Progress; India's Economy Survey," *Economist,* Feb. 22, 1997, 3, 4 (noting that in 1991 an "insanely repressive system of domestic planning and regulation" was "virtually dismantled").

95. See Robert Moog, "Delays in the Indian Courts: Why the Judges Don't Take Control," *Just. Sys. J.* 16 (1992): 19, 22–30. Moog cites various structural constraints, including a three-year judicial rotation system and an imbalance of power between judges and attorneys in favor of the attorneys, as the major impediments to case-management approaches in India.

96. See Chandarachud, "Note on Bombay and Maharashtra," 3 (point 4, citing the availability of multiple venues for legal challenges; point 5, citing exercise of appellate and revisional powers causing functional stays of main actions; point 6, citing remands as additional cause; and point 7, citing overlapping jurisdiction preventing final disposition of matters simultaneously litigated on more than one level).

97. Chodosh et al., "Indian Civil Justice Reform," 4–5, 22–50 (assessing the practical operation of the civil justice system).

98. Consequently, many helpful provisions of the Code of Civil Procedure (India Code Civ. Proc. [CPC]) remain underutilized.

99. See India, CPC, Section 89.

100. Ibid.

101. Ibid.

102. Cf. Arbitration and Conciliation Act, 1996, The Gazette of India, New Delhi, the 16th January, 1996/Pausa 26, 1917 (Saka), Part III, Section 73 (using language nearly identical to Section 89).

103. Salem Advocate Bar Ass'n v. Union of India, 35 S.C.R. 146–52 (2002). Former Supreme Court Justice Rao, who is also chairman of the Law Commission, chairs this committee, on which Law Minister Arun Jetley also serves. The Supreme Court gave the Rao committee four months to seek comments and to report back. Chairman Rao drafted consultation papers, including rules on mediation and case management, and circulated them to the High Courts for comments; however, these papers did not reach the High Courts until late January, thus leaving insufficient time for adequate study and commentary. Chairman Rao asked for an extension of time until July, and organized a national conference on mediation and case management. The national conference involved chief

justices of each of the High Courts, and two lower court judges, as well as prominent lawyers from the bar.

104. These goals include the attraction of foreign investment. Despite the disadvantages imposed by the backlog and delay problem, many multinational investors frequently point to the Indian legal system as a distinctive advantage in attracting foreign investment. See "U.S. Businessmen Enthused by Legal System in India," Reuters, Dec. 8, 1995 (quoting Paul Griesse, U.S. Chairman of the Indo-U.S. Joint Business Council: "[A] legal remedy is available to [multinational corporations] in India, a well-defined legal system to protect their investment.").

105. Many others have made similar observations. See, e.g., Prillaman, 2 (noting a "deep and widening gap between the role that institutions theoretically serve in a democracy and that which they actually perform.").

106. For example, a recent World Bank study in Argentina and Mexico found far less backlog and delay than previously estimated, due to a great number of cases eventually "abandoned." However, the study does not express any evaluation of the merits of those dropped cases, any diagnosis of why they were dropped (e.g., an early failure at obtaining injunctive relief; an internalization of the likelihood of an endless delay; the litigants ran out of money used to pay off the registrar to keep the case moving) and the social or economic effect of their abandonment (noncompliance with contract and property rights, increase in the risk—and thus cost—of doing business, etc.). World Bank, "Reforming Courts: The Role of Empirical Research," *PREMNotes* 65 (Washington, D.C.: World Bank, 2002), 1, available online at http://www1.worldbank.org/publicsector/legal/PREMnote65.pdf.

107. See Douglass C. North, *Institutions, Institutional Change and Economic Performance* (Cambridge: Cambridge University Press, 1991), 7.

NOTES TO CHAPTER 5

1. See Mary L. Volcansek and Jacqueline Lucienne Lafon, *Judicial Selection: The Cross-Evolution of French and American Practices* (Westport, Conn.: Greenwood Press, 1988).

2. Sergio Rinaldi et al., "Corruption Dynamics in Democratic Societies," *Complexity* (May/June 1998), 53 (corruption "may help to mitigate the abuse of state authorities").

3. See Chodosh et al., "Indian Civil Justice Reform," 37–38.

4. Sally Falk Moore, "Treating Law as Knowledge: Telling Colonial Officers What to Say to Africans about Running "Their Own" Native Courts," *L. & Soc'y Rev.* 26 (1992): 29.

5. Ibid.

6. Ibid.

7. Ibid.

8. See Hernando de Soto, "The Mystery of Legal Failure," *The Mystery of Capital: Why Capitalism Triumphs in the West and Fails Everywhere Else* (New York: Basic Books, 2000), 198–206, 198 (noting that "most lawyers in developing and former communist countries have been trained not to expand the rule of law but to defend it as they found it.")

9. Dakolias, *Court Performance*, 6 ("[E]fficiency is a promising starting point for the study and design of judicial reform because of its relatively apolitical nature.").

10. See Linn A. Hammergren, *The Politics of Justice and Justice Reform in Latin America: The Peruvian Case in Comparative Perspective* (Boulder, Colo.: Westview Press, 1998), 297.

11. See, e.g., Simeon Djankov et al., *Courts: The Lex Mundi Project,* Working Paper

No. w8890 (Cambridge, Mass.: National Bureau of Economic Research, 2002) (implicitly treating efficiency as the absence of delay).

12. In addition to the Blueprint, see also Supreme Court of Indonesia, "Permanent Judicial Education System Reform," 2003; Supreme Court of Indonesia, "Judicial Personnel Management Reform," 2003; Supreme Court of Indonesia, "Court's Financial Management Reform" 2003.

13. Even if objectives had not been articulated, the helpful identification of underlying problems provides useful guidance absent here.

14. The separation of documents prepared by the Supreme Court on the judicial commission (the Blueprint), judicial education, judicial personnel management, and court financial management results in the absence of (1) an overarching description of these initiatives and their interrelationships, and (2) an articulation of the underlying problems that currently need attention.

15. Ironies abound. Take, for example, the continued primary interest of Indonesians in Dutch reforms, or the disturbing realization that a group of reformers from Pakistan have to rely on U.S. expertise in India to answer questions about the structure, process, and impacts of the *lok adalat* (People's Court) system in neighboring India.

16. India, Civil Procedure Code (CPC), Section 89.

17. Ibid.

18. Ibid.

19. This may be seen by some to mean that a judge might refer parties to binding arbitration without their consent. Surely, the statute can be read to allow for that understanding; however, it would be inconsistent with the principle of consent and self-determination to compel parties to binding arbitration without their consent. The control of the parties over the outcome in each of the other proceedings reduces concern about compelling a constrained choice of an ADR technique.

20. See India, CPC, Section 89.

21. Cf. Arbitration and Conciliation Act, 1996.

22. Order X (1a) may solve this and other problems raised in the context of Section 89, including the question of timing: "After recording the admissions and denials, the court shall direct the parties to the suit to opt either mode of the settlement outside the court as specified in subsection (1) of section 89."

23. Indeed, based on arguable assessments that Order X (Rule 1–a) is more expansive than Section 89, suggestions have been made to alter this provision to mirror the Section 89 procedures. See, e.g., Justice R. P. Sethi, *Code of Civil Procedure* (New Delhi: Professional Book Publishers, 2002), 480 ("On the general principle that rules should not go beyond the sections, it would be a point worth considering if Order 10, rule 1–A would not require some change ").

24. Deprived and demoralized constituencies also have an understandable propensity to make purely self-interested proposals rather than to justify or reject reforms based on what benefits they provide to the broader society. Rigorous facilitation to redirect their thinking toward the functional goals of the judicial system is therefore frequently required.

25. Watson, for example, took the position that "many legal rules make little impact on individuals, and that very often . . . it is important that there be a rule; but what rule actually is adopted is of restricted significance for general human happiness." Alan Watson, *Legal Transplants: An Approach to Comparative Law,* 2d ed. (Athens: University of Georgia Press), 95–96.

26. See generally Linn A. Hammergren, *Do Judicial Councils Further Judicial Reform? Lessons from Latin America,* Working Paper No. 28 (Washington, D.C.: Carnegie Endow-

ment for International Peace, 2002), available online at http://www.ceip.org/files/pdf/wp28.pdf.

27. For a typology of different European models of judicial commissions, see Wim Voermans, *Councils for the Judiciary in EU Countries* (European Commission/TAIEX, Tilburg University Schoordijk Institute, 1999) (available at http:://cadmos.carlbro.be/Library/Councils/Councils.html#_toc4592267097).

28. Chodosh, Indonesia Notes, Entry of November 6, 2002.

29. This is the nearly universally articulated view of U.S. mediation experts in India.

30. Donald L. Horowitz, "Constitutional Design: Proposals Versus Processes," in *The Architecture of Democracy: Constitutional Design, Conflict Management, and Democracy,* ed. Andrew Reynolds (Oxford; New York: Oxford University Press, 2002), 17 ("Despite international consultations that are more or less impervious to whatever international wisdom has purveyed or, for that matter, to what a careful examination of comparative experience might reveal.").

31. The paper on education and training speaks of *"ensuring a domino effect"* without much specification of exactly how to do that. Supreme Court of Indonesia, "Permanent Judicial Education System Reform" (2003), 30; Supreme Court of Indonesia, "Judicial Personnel Management Reform" (2003); Supreme Court of Indonesia, "Court's Financial Management Reform" (2003).

32. The Blueprint addresses the need to develop a short-term strategy, placing priority on the supervision and discipline of leaders within the courts. Supreme Court of Indonesia, "Academic Draft and Bill on Judicial Commission" (2003), 67.

33. Supreme Court of Indonesia, "Policy Paper on Judicial Personnel Management Reform" (2003), Appendices 1–10; Supreme Court of Indonesia, "Policy Paper on Court's Financial Management Reform" (2003), Appendices 1–2; Supreme Court of Indonesia, "Policy Paper on Permanent Judicial Education System Reform" (2003), Appendices 1–2.

34. Supreme Court of Indonesia, "Court's Financial Management Reform" (2003), 56.

35. Sinha, "Alternative Dispute Resolution with Special Reference to Civil Procedure (Amendment) Act, 1999," *Nyaya Kiran* (New Delhi: Delhi Legal Services Authority, 2003), 9.

36. The following explanation borrows from Hiram E. Chodosh, "Mediating Mediation in India," in Chodosh et al., *Mediation in India: A Toolkit* (New Delhi: United States Education Foundation in India, 2004), 101–29, 107–9.

37. This paradox, however, is not necessarily a negative one; nor is it as relevant to the question of access to justice. More cars on the road or more legally cognizable claims coming into the court system is not necessarily a bad development; (aside from the negative externalities (e.g., pollution, noise, overcrowding) it may be actually quite positive). Greater traffic may mean that more people are getting to their destination. More case filings may mean that more legal conflicts are being redressed (rather than just lumped or forgotten). Even so, the metaphor requires an additional qualification. The law is unlike getting from one place to another in at least one critical respect: access to justice does not mean merely gaining access to courts. If the legal system works well, people internalize the norms (and possibly the conflict resolution techniques employed) in their daily lives. In that way the legal system brings the destination to the people (rather than the people to their destination). Mediation thus may enhance access by helping to bring justice to the society.

38. For a domestic illustration of the difference local participation can make in the effectiveness of judicial reform, see, e.g., Tony A. Freyer and Paul M. Pruitt, Jr., "Reaction and Reform: Transforming the Judiciary under Alabama's Constitution, 1901–1975," *Ala. L. Rev.* 53, no. 1 (Fall 2001): 77–133 (contrasting the frustrations of the federally forced

changes of the 1950s to the reforms led by Chief Justice Howell Heflin between 1970 and 1975, which drew on newer demands of the market legal services and "undermined the political and social inertia the constitution had reinforced").

39. An interactive civil justice conference in Egypt in 1996, involving more than 250 opinion leaders, was the first participatory process on reform in the country's recent legal history. See Hiram E. Chodosh et al., "Egyptian Civil Justice Process Modernization: A Functional and Systemic Approach," *Mich. J. Int'l L.* 17 (Summer 1996): 893–94.

40. Stuart Kauffman, *At Home in the Universe: The Search for Laws of Self-Organization and Complexity* (Oxford: Oxford University Press, 1995), 28 ("Democracy may be far and away the best process to solve the complex problems of a complex evolving society. . . ."); ibid., 29 ("[W]e must give up the pretense of long-term prediction. We cannot know the true consequences of our best actions. All we players can do is be locally wise, not globally wise.").

41. See Hammergren, *Politics of Justice*, 3.

42. For a superb collection of essays on transplants, adaptation, and legal culture, see generally David Nelken and Johannes Feest, eds., *Adapting Legal Cultures* (Oxford; Portland, Ore.: Hart Publishing, 2001). For an excellent body of essays on American legal culture in global perspective, see Lawrence M. Friedman and Harry N. Scheiber, eds., *Legal Culture and the Legal Profession* (Boulder, Colo.: Westview Press, 1996).

43. See, e.g., Stacey Steele, "The New Law on Bankruptcy in Indonesia: Towards a Modern Corporate Bankruptcy Regime," *Melb. U. L. Rev.* 23, no. 1 (April 1999): 144, 152–60 (arguing that the reform of Indonesia's bankruptcy legislation will have little influence on the economic stability of the nation in the absence of substantive changes to the country's legal culture).

44. *See* India, CPC, Order X, Rule 1(a)–(c) (as amended by Code of Civil Procedure (Amendment) Act (1999), at 90) (directing court to utilize dispute resolution mechanisms, including arbitration, conciliation, judicial settlement, judicial settlement through lok adalat, or mediation).

45. See generally Adrian A. S. Zuckerman, "Justice in Crisis: Comparative Dimensions of Civil Procedure," in Zukerman, ed., *Civil Justice in Crisis: Comparative Perspectives of Civil Procedures* (Oxford; New York: Oxford University Press, 1999).

46. Douglass C. North, *Institutions, Institutional Change and Economic Performance* (Cambridge: Cambridge University Press, 1991), 61 ("It takes resources to define and protect property rights and to enforce agreements.").

47. In Indonesia, for example, the Chair of the National Law Commission once described judicial recruits as what's left over in the "garbage bin." Foreign training experts in Jakarta report that, among all the professionals in the legal system, including the police, judges score the lowest as a group on standard examinations. What draws people into police work is the money (not from their salary) but from the rents they can extract. A young police recruit may spend up to his first two years' of salary as an "entrance fee," which he makes back through bribes in about four to six months. Chodosh, Indonesia Notes, Entry of November 15, 2000.

48. See, e.g., "Bayelsa CJ Wants National Judicial Council Scrapped," *Africa News Service,* May 14, 2001 (noting handpicking of members of judicial council in Nigeria as "absolutely wrong"); see also Mark Ungar, "Independent Judicial Functioning," *Elusive Reform: Democracy and the Rule of Law in Latin America* (Boulder, Colo.: Lynne Rienner, 2002), 169 ("Latin America's judicial councils have already been caught up in party politics, institutional rivalries, and counteraccusations from the officials being investigated."); Hammergren, *Judicial Councils,* 5 (noting that, in many Latin American countries, the judiciary would literally be replaced at the change of a national administration and, as a re-

sult, "[they] came to be staffed by politically compliant judges of dubious substantive competence and still more questionable ethical proclivities.").

49. See generally James S. Kakalik et al., "Discovery Management: Further Analysis of the Civil Justice Reform Act Evaluation Data," *B.C. L. Rev.* 39, no. 3 (May 1998): 613–82; see also Kakalik et al., "Just, Speedy and Inexpensive? An Evaluation of Judicial Case Management under the Civil Justice Reform Act," *Judicature* 80 (Jan./Feb. 1997): 184–89.

50. Under a recently passed law, the entire administration of the courts will shift from the Ministry of Justice to the Supreme Court by 2004. See Indonesia, Law No. 35/1999.

51. For the most influential essay pointing out these weaknesses, see Owen M. Fiss, "Against Settlement," *Yale L. J.* 93 (May 1984): 1073–90.

52. See Supreme Court Advocates on Record Association v. Union of India (1993); V. Vemlatesan, "Judiciary and Social Justice," *Frontline,* Oct. 14–27, 2000 ("As the judiciary becomes over-protective of its powers vis-a-vis the executive, the nature of its social base causes concern.").

53. See "China Defends Corruption Claims," CNN, Mar. 9, 2002, available online at http://www.cnn.com (reporting that China's top graft-buster disputes claim that "the more one fights corruption, the worse it gets").

54. See George Priest, "Private Litigants and the Court Congestion Problem," *B.U. L. Rev.* 69 (May 1989): 527–59.

55. See Hammergren, *Judicial Councils,* 15–25.

56. No attempt here is made to synthesize the vast literature on independence and accountability. *See* Amy B. Atchison, Lawrence Tobe Liebert, and Denise K. Russell, "Judicial Independence and Judicial Accountability: A Selected Bibliography," *S. Cal. L. Rev.* 72, no. 2–3 (Jan.–Mar. 1999): 723–810.

57. Charles Gardner Geyh, "Customary Independence," in *Judicial Independence at the Crossroads: An Interdisciplinary Approach,* ed. Stephen B. Burbank and Barry Friedman (Thousand Oaks, Calif.: Sage Publications, 2002): 161 ("The problem is that independence and accountability are, at least in absolute terms, incompatible.).

58. See, e.g., John D. Fabian, "The Paradox of Elected Judges: Tension in the American Judicial System," *Geo. J. Legal Ethics* 15, no. 1 (Fall 2001): 155, 159–63 (discussing "ongoing controversy over whether judges should be independent arbiters of legal principles, isolated from political life, or whether judges should be held accountable to the electorate for their decisions").

59. Under the Wahid government, a Joint Anti-Corruption Team (TGPTPK) was established in Indonesia, and in April 2001, it began to prosecute three retired and serving Supreme Court judges on corruption charges. However, on March 23, 2001, the Supreme Court annulled as unconstitutional the legislation on which TGPTPK was based. See *Human Rights Violations through Judicial Corruption,* available online at http://www .thinkcentre.org/article.cfm?ArticleID=739 (May 13, 2001).

60. Ibid. (After Georgia's break from the Soviet Union, for example, the government removed large numbers of judges through the establishment of an independent council charged with authority to review the performance of incumbent judges and create a new transparent process for recruitment of new judges).

61. *See* Report by the Commission for Examining the Structure of a Case Management Department, Jerusalem (March 1999) (on file with author).

62. *See* Mauro Cappelletti, "Who Watches the Watchmen? A Comparative Study on Judicial Responsibility," *Am. J. Comp. L.* 31 (Winter 1983): 1–62.

63. Private interviews I conducted in May 2000 with a chief first instance court judge in Istanbul who is in charge of forwarding private complaints charging unethical behavior

indicated that the judicial commission in charge of enforcing judicial ethics was completely ineffectual.

64. *See generally* Mary L. Volcansek, Maria Elisabetta de Franciscis, and Jacqueline Lucienne Lafon, *Judicial Misconduct: A Cross-National Comparison* (Gainesville: University Press of Florida, 1996) (comparing the system of discipline and removal of errant judges in France, Italy, England, and the United States in an examination of the tension between judicial independence and political accountability).

65. Stephan O. Kline, "Judicial Independence: Rebuffing Congressional Attacks on the Third Branch," *Ky. L. J.* 87, no. 3 (Spring 1999): 679, 687–91 (quoting L. Ralph Mecham, Director of the Administrative Office of United States Courts, on whether judicial independence is dependent on more than life tenure and salary protection: judicial independence extends "to encompass those conditions in which and under which a judge decides the cases. These ancillary elements of individual judicial independence, including security, facilities, support, workload, rules of procedure, and case management, normally do not impact upon judicial independence but under extreme circumstances may do so" (citation omitted)).

66. In the United States and Australia, for example, some see the delay problem to be sufficiently serious to raise constitutional concerns. See David Hittner and Kathleen Weisz Osman, "Federal Civil Trial Delays: A Constitutional Dilemma?" *S. Tex. L. Rev.* 31 (May 1990): 341–60 (exploring several theories to be advanced in support of an argument that backlog and delay have deprived litigants of their constitutional rights). See also R. E. McGarvie, "Judicial Responsibility for the Operation of the Court System," *Austl. L. J.* 63 (Feb. 1989): 79–97 (noting that "[a] system, . . . which keeps people waiting for years before recovering money due to them, is not providing applied justice"). Backlog and delay at least equally affect the criminal justice system. The consequences of delay to those accused of crime who await trial are extremely grave. See, e.g., Lewis R. Katz, Lawrence Litwin, and Richard Bamberger, *Justice Is the Crime: Pretrial Delay in Felony Cases* (Cleveland: Press of Case Western Reserve University, 1972).

67. See "Schweiz: Neuer Anlauf fur die Verfassungsreform," *Neue Zuericher Zeitung,* May 5, 1995 (pointing out the chronic problems of work overload); Takeshi Kojima, "Civil Procedure Reform in Japan," *Mich. J. Int'l L.* 11 (1990): 1218 (reporting that the "average delay between filing and judgment for cases that require at least a minimum level of proof-taking or an evidentiary hearing is 27 months").

68. See Richard B. Cappalli, "Comparative South American Civil Procedure: A Chilean Perspective," *Univ. Miami Inter-Am. L. Rev.* 21 (Winter 1990): 240, 306–10.

69. See *Bulletin of the European Union,* Commission Opinion on the Czech Republic's Application for Membership of the European Union, at 17 (1997) (noting that "[t]he courts are overloaded, numerous cases do not receive a judgment and the average length of commercial law proceedings, for example, exceeds 3 years").

70. See Oscar G. Chase, "Civil Litigation Delay in Italy and the United States", *Am. J. Comp. L.* 36 (Winter 1988): 41, 55–56; Maria Rosaria Ferrarese, "Civil Justice and Judicial Role in Italy," *Just. Sys. J.* 13 (1988–1989): 168–85. Both Ferrarese and Chase cite lack of judicial control as a major factor in causing backlog and delay in the Italian courts. For a discussion of Italian criminal justice reforms responsive to long delays, see Jeffrey J. Miller, "Plea bargaining and Its Analogues under the New Italian Criminal Procedure Code and in the United States: Towards a New Understanding of Comparative Criminal Procedure," *N.Y.U. J. Int'l L. & Pol.* 22 (Winter 1990): 215, 225–26.

71. Chodosh et al., "Egyptian," 870–87.

72. See *Bulletin of the European Union,* Commission Opinion on Hungary's Application for Membership of the European Union, at 15 (1997) (noting that "[t]he courts are

overloaded; the number of cases put to them has increased greatly in recent years and it takes longer for rulings to be given").

73. See Zhang Huanwen, Excerpts of Address Before the Third Session of the Eight Provincial People's Congress, in Liaoning Ribao, Mar. 7, 1995, at 3, translated and reprinted in Liaoning Provincial Higher People's Court Work Report (BBC Summary of World Broadcasts, June 30, 1995) (quoting statistics delivered by the President of the Provincial Higher People's Court indicating an 18.6 percent increase in the number of cases overall, including a 58.6 percent increase in economic criminal cases and a 27 percent increase in economic dispute cases, and noting complications and difficulties in handling the newly increased caseload).

74. See "Britain's Antiquated Courts," *Economist,* Sept. 16, 1995, 20; Lord Harry Woolf, *Access to Justice* (London: Law Society, 1997).

75. See North, 6 ("institutions typically change incrementally rather than in discontinuous fashion"). Ibid. at 89 (institutional change is "overwhelmingly incremental"). Incrementalism is itself often seen as a political strategy in the face of strong opposition. See e.g., Buscaglia et al., *Judicial Reform in Latin America* (Stanford, Calif.: Hoover Institution Press, 1995), 21 ("Reforms that seem threatening to those in power should be undertaken in stages."). See also Solomon and Foglesong, "The Administration of Justice," 177 ("advocating a moderate reform agenda," differing from more radical and minimal approaches to reform, that focuses on "building and improvement of courts and legal practices rather than their transformation."). See also Maria Dakolias and Javier Said, *The World Bank, Judicial Reform: A Process of Change through Pilot Courts* (1999), 2–3, available online at http://www4.worldbank.org/legal/publications/JudicialReform-72.pdf (arguing that pilot projects alleviate barriers of inexperience in reform, allow for more focused testing, and help to build consensus).

76. See Prillaman, *The Judiciary and Democratic Decay,* 137–61 (discussing that in Chile's encouraging (though tentative) success, the pace of reform was gradual but the scope and breadth were comprehensive).

77. For an excellent commentary on the U.S.-based critique of the law and development movement, see Brian Z. Tamanaha and Richard Bilder, "Law and Development" (book review), *Am. J. Int'l L.* 89, no. 2 (Apr. 1995): 470–86.

78. See generally Beverly M. Carl, "Peanuts, Law Professors and Third World Lawyers," *Third World Legal Stud.* 1 (Annual 1986), 13; James A. Gardner, *Legal Imperialism: American Lawyers and Foreign Aid in Latin America* (Madison: University of Wisconsin, 1980); David F. Greenberg, "Law and Development in Light of Dependency Theory," *Res. L. & Soc.* 3 (1980): 129–59; Gridley Hall and Burton Fretz, "Legal Services in the Third World," *Clearinghouse Rev.* 24 (Dec. 1990): 783–96; David M. Trubek and Marc Galanter, "Scholars in Self-Estrangement: Some Reflections on the Crisis in Law and Development Studies in the United States," *Wis. L. Rev.* 4 (1974): 1062.

79. Thomas M. Franck, "The New Development: Can American Law and Legal Institutions Help Developing Countries?" *Wis. L. Rev.* (1972): 767, 770.

80. See John Henry Merryman, "Comparative Law and Social Change: On the Origins, Style, Decline and Revival of the Law and Development Movement," *Am. J. Comp. L.* 25 (1977): 457, 481.

81. See Jose E. Alvarez, "Promoting the 'Rule of Law' in Latin America: Problems and Prospects," *Geo. Wash. J. Int'l L. & Econ.* 25 (1991): 281–331.

82. Thomas Carothers, *Aiding Democracy Abroad: The Learning Curve* (Washington, D.C.: Carnegie Endowment for International Peace, 1999).

83. Carothers criticizes the lack of self-criticism and expressed awareness of weaknesses in the U.S. system. He admonishes: "Democracy promoters, however, need to be more

conscious of and more explicit about the flaws of American democracy, and pay more attention to them in aid programs." Ibid. at 63. "These issues should be built into . . . programs . . . so that others can anticipate the problems that arise in democratic systems and learn from American efforts, successful or not, to address them." Ibid. at 64.

84. Carothers observes that the external model often inculcates superficial views of problems, with the tendency of focusing on symptoms instead of deeper pathologies. For example, he claims that there is a tendency to focus on judicial reform as a purely institutional problem without addressing deeper power structures that are important determinants. In his discussion of judicial reform, he notes that the aid community has underestimated several inhibiting factors, including the economic incentives of corruption; the decentralized nature of judicial institutions; the independent-mindedness of judicial officials; the limited will to reform; the vulnerability of a small group of reformers to removal from positions of power; and resistance to reform by vested interests of judges and lawyers who may benefit from a dysfunctional system through their ability to manipulate and get compensated for manipulation of the system. In order to address these problems, Carothers encourages a more direct confrontation of power and incentive structures that lie beneath the appearances of formal institutional structures. Ibid. at 163–74.

85. Carothers criticizes the uniformity, U.S.-centricity, and inflexibility of the core model and strategy for building democracy abroad, including the assumed sequencing of change. He also observes that there is little borrowing from academic literature. In response, he suggests a broadening of models to be studied, the use of non-American, regional experts, creativity in the design of programs, and study of multiple alternatives of reform sequencing. For example, he advocates greater use of local or regional expertise with more common grounding in the national context, e.g., Latin American or European experts used in Latin American judicial reform projects. Ibid. at 104.

86. Carothers notes the tendency to focus on "endpoints rather than process." Ibid.

87. Ibid. at 93.

88. Carothers points out that many experts are (1) reluctant to publish and share information, (2) resistant to deep self-evaluations; and (3) inclined to zealous action rather than self-critical reflection. Ibid. at 8–9. This leads to insufficient learning, the frustration of wheel reinvention, and no middle ground between avid proponents and cynical detractors. Ibid. at 10.

89. Carothers identifies problems in the evaluation of success and the extent to which aid enhanced reform, including the specification of criteria, the measurement of satisfaction by qualitative and quantitative means, and the identification of key causes. He distinguishes three different kinds of evaluation and argued for their specialization: first, the provision of material to convince others of merits of program; second, the provision of information on effects, weak spots, room for improvement, and other issues of implementation and development; and finally, critical engagement in deep learning about aid that questions assumptions, finds new approaches, and understands how aid projects are perceived and valued. Carothers stresses the need for beginning with modest expectations. Ibid. at 281–313

90. For a recent critique of the role of foreign experts in local mediation reform, see Hiram E. Chodosh, "Local Mediation in Advance of Armed Conflict," Ohio St. J. on Disp. Resol. 19 (2003): 213–27.

91. World Bank, "Reforming Courts: The Role of Empirical Research," PREMNotes 65 (2002), 1, available online at http://www1.worldbank.org/publicsector/legal/PREM-note65.pdf ("judicial reform must be built on a solid empirical basis").

92. Ibid. ("In both countries a large portion of cases were considered 'abandoned' (un-resolved). Such cases are technically open, but their files indicate that the parties are no

longer pursuing them, whether because of an unrecorded settlement, frustration, or some other reason.")

NOTES TO CHAPTER 6

1. For the first application of the emergence metaphor to justice reform, and the first exposition upon which this chapter is based, see Hiram E. Chodosh, "Emergence from the Dilemmas of Justice Reform," *Tex. J. Int'l L.* 38 (2003): 569, 571–77.

2. See Steven Johnson, *Emergence: The Connected Lives of Ants, Brains, Cities, and Software* (New York: Scribner, 2001), 11–23. A similar process is the subject of a brilliant book by Malcolm Gladwell. Gladwell identifies three common elements in both social and biological contagions: a few people become infected with a sticky idea and spread it through peer-to-peer interaction. Malcolm Gladwell, "The Law of the Few: Connectors, Mavens, and Salesmen," in *The Tipping Point: How Little Things Can Make a Big Difference* (Boston: Little, Brown, 2000), 15–29.

3. Scott Camazine et al., eds., *Self Organization in Biological Systems* (2001), 8 ("Self-organization is a process in which pattern at the global level of a system emerges solely from numerous interactions among the lower-level components of the system. Moreover, the rules specifying interactions among the system's components are executed using only local information, without reference to the global pattern.").

4. Ibid.:

In a school of fish, for instance, each individual bases its behavior on its perception of the position and velocity of its nearest neighbors, rather than knowledge of the global behavior of the whole school. Similarly, an army any within a raiding column bases its activity on local concentrations of pheromone laid down by other ants rather than on a global overview of the pattern of the raid.

5. See Ian Beeson and Chris Davis, "Emergence and Accomplishment in Organizational Change," *J. Orgn'l Change Mgmt.* 13 (2000): 178, 181 (admonishing that "organizations are not organisms . . . weather systems or whirlpools. . . . Change is produced not by the complex interaction of effectively structureless atoms, but by the meaningful and value-laden interaction of already complex individual human beings.").

6. Subpart 1 of this chapter draws heavily on Johnson, *Emergence,* 11–23. For an early application of insights from emergence to law and society dynamics, see, e.g., J. B. Ruhl, "Complexity Theory as a Paradigm for the Dynamical Law-and-Society System: A Wake-Up Call for Legal Reductionism and the Modern Administrative State," *Duke L. J.* 45 (1996): 849, 856 ("The lesson for the law-and-society system is that the rules of any nonlinear dynamical system . . . even when followed deterministically . . . are capable of producing these unexpected behaviors that move the system off of its expected trajectory in unpredictable ways"). See also Harold Morowitz, "Emergence and the Law," *Complexity* (Mar./Apr. 2000): 11, 12 ("Hierarchies of deterministic rules don't form our aspirations and those things for which we pledge our life and honor. Those must come from a different source. . . .").

7. Toshiyuki Nakagaki, Hiroyasu Yamada and Ágota Tóth, "Maze-Solving by an Amoeboid Organism," *Nature* 407 (2000): 470 ("This remarkable process of cellular computation implies that cellular materials can show a primitive intelligence.").

8. Johnson, *Emergence,* 12–13.

9. Ibid. at 14.

10. *See* Evelyn Fox Keller and Lee A. Segel, "On the Aggregation of Acrasiales," *Biophysical Soc'y: Abstracts of the Annual Meeting* 13 (1969): A-69; Evelyn Fox Keller and Lee A. Segel, "Initiation of Slime Mold Aggregation Viewed as an Instability," *J.*

Theoretical Biology 26 (1970): 399–415; Evelyn Fox Keller and Lee A. Segel, "Conflict between Positive and Negative Feedback as an Explanation for the Initiation of Aggregation in Slime Mold Amoebae," *Nature* 227 (1970): 1365–66.

11. Johnson, *Emergence,* 18–21. For a recent (and gripping) literary account of emergence, see Michael Crichton, *Prey* (2002).

12. For an interactive essay illustrating these properties, visit Mitchel Resnick and Brian Silverman's website, *Exploring Emergence,* at http://el.www.media.mit.edu/groups/el/projects/emergence/ (visited May 7, 2000). See also http://emergence.org/ for the journal *Emergence.* See also John H. Holland, *Emergence: From Chaos to Order* (1998); Stuart Kaufman, *At Home in the Universe: The Search for Laws of Self-Organization and Complexity* (1995).

13. For an illustrative study of emergent ant behavior, see, e.g., Deborah M. Gordon and A. Kulig, "The Effect of Neighbors on the Mortality of Harvester Ant Colonies," *J. Animal Ecol.* 67 (1998): 141.

14. See, e.g., Jane Jacobs, *The Death and Life of Great American Cities* (1992).

15. Johnson, *Emergence,* 17–23.

16. See Indonesia Notes, Entry of Nov. 9, 2001.

17. See CyberConsult et al., "Law Reform in Indonesia" (1997), 160 ("The legal situation is indeed 'desperate but not hopeless'") (emphasis omitted).

18. Sh. S. B. Sinha, "Alternative Dispute Resolution," 7.

19. See, e.g., Chodosh, Indonesia Notes, Entry of January 10, 2000.

20. Ibid.

21. Ian Beeson and Chris Davis, "Emergence and Accomplishment in Organizational Change," *J. Organ'l Change Mgmt.* 13 (2000): 178 (criticizing a model of organizational behavior that "attributes too central a role to management and overestimates management's power to control events and actions. Direction of operations comes not from an integrated control centre but from a multiplicity of actors whose behavior is not merely adaptive but also creative and contentious.").

22. See, e.g., David S. Clark, "Judicial Protection of the Constitution in Latin America," *Hastings Const. L. Q.* 2 (1975): 405–42 (attempting to measure judicial effectiveness by quantitative reference to terms of employment, including tenure guarantees, appointment and removal methods, and salary guarantees). Cf. Christopher M. Larkins, "Judicial Independence and Democratization: A Theoretical and Conceptual Analysis," *Am. J. Comp. L.* 44 (1996): 605, 615 (noting the problem that "these formal indicators of judicial independence often did not conform to reality" and "revealed little about how independent the judiciaries of Latin America really were"); Pilar Domingo, "Judicial Independence and Judicial Reform in Latin America," in *The Self-Restraining State: Power and Accountability in New Democracies,* ed. Andreas Schedler et al. (Boulder, Colo.: Lynne Rienner, 1999), 151, 158 (observing that judicial "independence and impartiality are . . . to a large extent defined by constitutional formulas regarding appointment mechanisms, tenure, and budgetary provision for the judiciary"; however, noting that these defining attributes in Latin American systems are "not necessarily more politicized than, say, the U.S. method of Supreme Court appointments.").

23. See generally Judge J. Clifford Wallace, "Resolving Judicial Corruption While Preserving Judicial Independence: Comparative Perspectives," *Cal. W. Int'l L. J.* 28 (1998): 341, 347 (discussing the diversity of approaches used in Asian judicial systems to discipline judges, noting the low number of six claims for corruption or bribery in twenty-one countries in 1996, and yet concluding in part that "the breadth of approaches reinforces the understanding that there is not just one way to combat judicial corruption successfully").

24. See Maria Dakolias, *Court Performance around the World: A Comparative Perspective* 5 (World Bank Technical Paper No. 430, 1999).

25. Adrian A. S. Zuckerman, "Reforming Civil Justice Systems: Trends in Industrial Countries," *PREMNotes* 46 (2000), available online at http://www1.worldbank .org/publicsector/legal/PREMnote_46.pdf (last visited, December 17, 2002) (noting new theory of civil procedure that "resources devoted to resolving a dispute should be proportionate to the interests involved and that systemwide resources should be allocated fairly across all disputes." (Hereinafter, Zuckerman, "Reforming.")

26. *See generally* Adrian A. S. Zuckerman, "Justice in Crisis: Comparative Dimensions of Civil Procedure," in *Civil Justice in Crisis*, ed. Adrian A. S. Zuckerman (1999), 22–23 (noting, for example, that in France "fresh proposals" have been "resisted by the legal profession, whose self-interested objections proved a stumbling block to past reforms."); See also Zuckerman, "Reforming" ("[T]he economic interests of the legal profession explain many of the costs and delays in litigation and . . . overcoming these interests is difficult.").

27. See Hernando de Soto, *The Mystery of Capital* (2000), 179 (For the government "to find out what these extralegal arrangements are and then . . . find ways to integrate them into the formal property system . . . , [t]hey will have to go out in to the streets and roads and listen to the barking dogs.").

28. See generally Amartya Sen, *Development as Freedom* (New York: Knopf, 1999).

29. See generally Deborah L. Rhode, *In the Interests of Justice: Reforming the Legal Profession* (Oxford: Oxford University Press, 2000), 84–85 (arguing generally for more public oversight of the profession's self-regulation).

30. See Chodosh et al., *Indian Civil Justice System Reform,* 49–50. I once complained that notwithstanding these positive features the system tended to function as a whole less than the sum of its parts. My characterization was quickly contradicted by an Indian businessman: "No, the whole is the negative of the sum of its parts!"

31. J. K. Rowling, *Harry Potter and the Goblet of Fire* (London: Bloomsbury, 2000), 620–35.

32. See, e.g., Jack H. Knott and Gary J. Miller, *Reforming Bureaucracy: The Politics of Institutional Choice* (1987), 174 (noting that "*it generally is very difficult to structure an organization so that individuals, in pursuing their own self-interest, are always working for the institution's best interest at the same time.*") (emphasis in text); Thomas Romer and Barry R. Weingast, "Political Foundations of the Thrift Debacle," chap. 6 in *Politics and Economics in the Eighties,* ed. Alberto Alesina and Geoffrey Carliner (Chicago: University of Chicago Press, 1991), 175–214 (relating poor handling of thrift crisis to individual incentives of congressmen within the structure of congressional decision making).

33. Paul H. Brietzke and Teresa L. Kline, "The Law and Economics of the Native American Casinos," *Neb. L. Rev.* 78 (1999) 263, 333–43 (suggesting reforms in the face of sovereign dilemmas facing Native American tribes).

34. Stanley Lubman, "Bird in a Cage: Chinese Law Reform after Twenty Years," *Nw. J. Int'l L. & Bus.* 20 (Spring 2000): 383, 417–23 (noting dilemma facing the United States in Chinese accession to WTO of negotiating further guarantees pre-accession or relying on WTO dispute settlement postaccession).

35. Chodosh, Indonesia Notes, Entry of July 9, 1999.

36. See, e.g., Hiram E. Chodosh, "Judicial Mediation and Legal Culture," *Issues of Democracy* 4, no. 3 (1999): 6–12, 6:

> From the conventional perspective of most modern legal cultures, judicial mediation is a contradiction in terms. Judges are supposed to judge (not mediate), to apply law (not interests), to evaluate (not facilitate), to order (not accommodate),

and to decide (not settle). This view of judicial mediation as oxymoron falsely assumes that the functions of judging and mediation are mutually exclusive.

37. See *Buddha's First Sermon* (Sanderson Beck, trans.), at http://www.san .beck.org/Buddha.html (last visited Feb. 20, 2002).

These two extremes, monks, are not to be practiced by one who has gone forth from the world. What are the two?

That joined with the passions and luxury—low, vulgar, common, ignoble, and useless, and that joined with self-torture—painful, ignoble, and useless.

Avoiding these two extremes the one who has thus come has gained the enlightenment of the middle path, which produces insight and knowledge, and leads to peace, wisdom, enlightenment, and nirvana.

38. Tony Blair, *The Third Way: New Politics for the New Century* (1998); Tony Blair et al., eds., *Third Way . . . Where To?* (Nottingham, U.K.: Spokesman Books, 2002).

39. Indeed, the first chapter in the seminal book *Getting to Yes* begins with the mandate "Don't Bargain over Positions." See Roger Fisher and William Ury, *Getting to Yes* (New York: Penguin Books, 1983), 3–8.

40. See, e.g., Christopher M. Larkins, "Judicial Independence and Democratization: A Theoretical and Conceptual Analysis," *Am. J. Comp. L.* 44 (Fall 1996): 605–26.

41. An Indonesian judge once responded to these questions with the comment that the judiciary should be independent from law. Entry of July 8, 1999.

42. See, e.g., Geyh, 161. ("The critical inquiry thus becomes, how much of each? Where should independence end and accountability begin?").

43. See, e.g., "President Bush Outlines Iraqi Threat," Cincinnati, Ohio (Oct. 7, 2002) at http://www.whitehouse.gov/news/releases/2002/10/20021007-8.html ("We cannot wait for the final proof—the smoking gun—that could come in the form of a cloud. . . . There is no easy or risk-free course of action.").

44. See, e.g., Daniel A. Farber, "Probabilities Behaving Badly: Complexity Theory and Environmental Uncertainty," *U.C. Davis L. Rev.* 37 (2003), 145–73.

45. See, e.g., Michael D. Greenberg, "Information, Paternalism, and Rational Decision-Making: The Balance of FDA New Drug Approval," *Albany L. J. Sci. & Tech.* 13 (2003): 663–80.

46. Where other strategies are unavailable in addressing dilemmas, similar value choices must be made. If pressed to choose between two (here presumably) incompatible strategies, reformers may justifiably favor the pursuit of incremental over systemic approaches, an emphasis on gradual over sudden change, the cultivation of understanding and action from the bottom-up over top-down, and rely ultimately on local over foreign expertise. This set of choices could be easily justified by taking full stock of powerful emergent properties that make profound, quick, executive, foreign interventions unlikely to succeed. Others may disagree, even persuade reformers in different contexts of other value choices, but it is only through a process of expressing these value choices that they can be challenged. This process of explication will further deepen the methodological understanding of alternative approaches to reform.

47. See Warren Weaver, "A Quarter Century in the Natural Sciences," in *The Rockefeller Foundation Annual Report* (1958), chap. 1 (distinguishing systems of disorganized from organized complexity, the character of which latter systems depends on the interactions of individual elements).

48. See Peter H. Schuck, *The Limits of Law: Essays on Democratic Governance* (Boulder, Colo.: Westview Press, 2000), 445 (noting the tendency of lawmakers to ignore the competing forces of social norms and markets: "Lawmakers are drawn to top-down forms

of law such as command-and-control rules, which seem authoritative, clear, rigorous, and relatively easy to enforce.").

49. Donald P. Green and Ian Shapiro, "Social Dilemmas and Free-Riding" in *Pathologies of Rational Choice Theory: A Critique of Applications in Political Science* (New Haven: Yale University Press, 1994), 88–93 (on experimental evidence).

50. See Duncan R. Luce and Howard Raiffa, *Games and Decisions: Introduction and Critical Survey* (New York: Wiley, 1957), 95 ("two suspects are taken into custody and separated") (emphasis supplied).

51. See John Henry Merryman, "Comparative Law and Social Change: On the Origins, Style, Decline and Revival of the Law and Development Movement," *Am. J. Comp. L.* 25 (1977): 457, 481.

52. As the result of such collaborative studies in Egypt, new legislation requires suits against the government to be mediated by retired judges. See Law No. 7/2000, Concerning The Establishment Of Conciliation Committees In Certain Litigations To Which The Ministries And Juridical Persons Are Parties (Egypt), and in India, see CPC, Section 89 (directing court to utilize dispute resolution mechanisms, Settlement of Disputes Outside the Court). This aforementioned law went into effect on July 1, 2002.

53. As Hayek admonished in his Nobel lecture: "To act on the belief that we possess the knowledge and the power which enable us to shape the processes of society entirely to our liking, knowledge which in fact we do not possess, is likely to make us do much harm." Friedrich August von Hayek, "The Pretense of Knowledge", *Am. Econ. Rev.* 79, no. 6 (Dec. 1989) (Nobel Memorial Lecture delivered on Dec. 11, 1974) 3–7, 7.

54. See Schuck, *The Limits of Law*, 446 (noting that "[a]lthough some of these political, bureaucratic, informational, legal, fiscal, motivational, cultural, and other barriers would elude even the most diligent, prescient lawmaker, many are readily predictable.").

NOTES TO CHAPTER 7

1. See chapter 3. A. 2. (providing a comparative framework for addressing a wide range of cross-border conflicts).

2. John Henry Merryman, "Comparative Law and Scientific Explanation," 104 (avoiding the question as beyond the scope of the article and as of secondary importance to "describe a way of going about comparative law" (quoting Harry Kalven, Jr., "The Quest for the Middle Range: Empirical Inquiry and Legal Policy," in *Law in a Changing America*, ed. Geoffrey C. Hazard, Jr. (Englewood Cliffs, N.J.: Prentice Hall, 1968)).

3. The foregoing analysis attempted to address and mitigate these risks by looking at a wide variety of concrete legal and nonlegal examples. It attempted to be mindful of the need to turn the critique inward. Finally, the discussion attempted to take a small step forward toward methodology when the impulse to leap was great.

4. See Charles Tilly, *Big Structures, Large Processes, Huge Comparisons* (New York: Russell Sage Foundation, 1984), 80 ("We must make sure that the classical logic of comparison, . . . fits our aims like a sweatshirt and not like a straightjacket. It should make the exercise more effective, rather than making it impossible.").

5. See, e.g., Andrew Huxley, "Golden Yoke, Silken Text," *Yale L. J.* 106 (1997): 1923, 1927–33. Huxley is content with the goal of discourse:

[R]egard the comparative method as a useful tool for generating new understandings of disparate cultures. Twenty years ago this would have been a truism. Now it has to be defended against the postmodern proposition that cultures can be so different as to be incommensurable. I shall argue for an alternative, postmodern approach that sees comparison as an area of conversation, a discourse, rather than a discipline. (Ibid.)

6. See Ugo Mattei, "An Opportunity Not to Be Missed," 718 ("While neither methodological awareness nor interdisciplinary efforts will naturally follow globalization, they represent the only chance for survival as well as the key for success of comparative law in the United States."). See also Reimann, "The End of Comparative Law," 62–65 (making the case for the decentralization and integration of comparative studies in the "non-comparative" U.S. law courses).

7. See also Hiram E. Chodosh, "Globalizing the U.S. Law Curriculum: The Saja Paradigm," *U.C. Davis L. Rev.* 37 (2004): 843–68.

8. See Geertz, 234 ("The turning of local forms of legal sensibility into reciprocal commentaries, mutually deepening may become impossible. But however that may be, there is . . . no choice.").

Bibliography

Abel, Richard L. "A Comparative Theory of Dispute Institutions in Society." *L. & Soc'y Rev.* 8 (1973): 217–347.

Abraham, Henry. Foreword. In *Comparative Judicial Systems: Challenging Frontiers in Conceptual and Empirical Analysis,* edited by John R. Schmidhauser. Boston: Butterworths, 1987.

Agrawala, Kumari. "History of Courts and Legislatures." In *The Indian Legal System,* edited by Joseph Minattur, 103–132. Dobbs Ferry, N.Y.: Oceana, 1978.

Alabama G. S. R. v Carroll, 97 Ala. 126; 11 So 803 (Ala 1892).

Alford, William P. "Making the World Safe for What? Intellectual Property Rights, Human Rights and Foreign Economic Policy in the Post-European Cold War World." *N.Y.U. J. Int'l L. & Pol.* 29 (1996/1997): 135–152.

Alford, William P. "On the Limits of 'Grand Theory' in Comparative Law." *Wash. L. Rev.* 61 (1986): 945–956.

Ali, Budiardjo, Nugroho, and Reksodiputro. *Diagnostic Assessment of Legal Development in Indonesia.* 5 vols. Jakarta, Indonesia: Cyberconsult, 1997.

Allen, Ronald J. "Idealization and Caricature in Comparative Scholarship." *Nw. U. L. Rev.* 82 (1988): 785–807.

Allen, Ronald J., et al. "The German Advantage in Civil Procedure: A Plea for More Details and Fewer Generalities in Comparative Scholarship." *Nw. U. L. Rev.* 82 (1988): 705–762.

Alvarez, Jose E. "Why Nations Behave." *Mich. J. Int'l L.* 19 (1998): 303–317.

Alvarez, Jose E. "Promoting the 'Rule of Law' in Latin America: Problems and Prospects." *Geo. Wash. J. Int'l L. & Econ.* 25 (1991): 281–331.

American Association of Law Schools. Law School Rankings May Be Hazardous to Your Health: A Message to Applicants from Law School Deans. 1998.

American Bar Association. An Independent Judiciary: Report of the ABA Commission on Separation of Powers and Judicial Independence. Washington, D.C.: American Bar Association, 1997.

American Law Institute. *Restatement of the Law, Second, Conflict of Laws.* St. Paul, Minn., 1971.

American Law Institute. *Restatement of the Law, Third, Foreign Relations Law of the United States.* St. Paul, Minn., 1987.

Amnesty International. *Campaign Launch Report: Take a Step to Stamp Out Torture.* New York: Amnesty, 2000. Available online at http://www.stoptorture.org/report/index .htm.

Angola. Constitution. Reprinted in Blaustein and Flanz.

Aristotle. *Categories and De Interpretatione.* Translated by J. L. Ackrill, edited by J. L. Hudson. Oxford: Clarendon Press, 1963.

Aristotle. *Metaphysics*. Translated by John Warrington. London: Dent, 1956.

Armer, Michael, and Allen D. Grimshaw, eds. *Comparative Social Research: Methodological Problems and Strategies*. New York: Wiley, 1973.

Asin, Stefanie. "Yeltsin Loves the Free Market." *Houston Chronicle,* Sept. 17, 1989, A1.

Atchison, Amy B., Lawrence Tobe Liebert, and Denise K. Russell. "Judicial Independence and Judicial Accountability: A Selected Bibliography." *S. Cal. L. Rev.* 72 (1999): 723–810.

Babcock v Jackson, 12 N.Y.2d 473; 191 NE2d 279 (NY Ct App 1963).

Barkun, Michael, ed. *Law and the Social System.* New York: Lieber-Atherton, 1973.

Barnes, David W., and Lynn A. Stout. *The Economic Analysis of Tort Law.* Belmont, Calif.: West/Wadsworth, 1992.

Barton, John H., et al. *Law in Radically Different Cultures.* St. Paul, Minn.: West Publishing Co., 1983.

Baum, Julian. "No Worries." *Far E. Econ. Rev.,* Oct. 30, 1997, 28.

Baxter, William. "Choice of Law and the Federal System." *Stan. L. Rev.* 16 (1963): 1–42.

"Bayelsa CJ Wants National Judicial Council Scrapped." Africa News Service, May 14, 2001.

Becker, Theodore L. *Comparative Judicial Politics: The Political Functioning of Courts.* Chicago: Rand McNally, 1970.

Beeson, Ian, and Chris Davis. "Emergence and Accomplishment in Organizational Change." *J. Orgn'l Change Mgmt.* 13 (2000): 178–189.

Berman, Harold J. Review of *Courts and the Comparative Historical Method. Yale L. J.* 91 (1981): 383–390.

Berman, Harold J. "World Law." *Fordham Int' L. J.* 18 (1995): 1617–1622.

Bernhard v Harrah's Club, 546 P2d 719 (Cal 1976).

Bickel, Alexander M. *The Least Dangerous Branch: The Supreme Court at the Bar of Politics.* 2d ed. New Haven: Yale University Press, 1986.

Binder, Guyora. "Institutions and Linguistic Conventions: The Pragmatism of Lieber's Legal Hermeneutics." *Cardozo L. Rev.* 16 (1995): 2169–2189.

Blair, Tony. *The Third Way: New Politics for the New Century.* London: Fabian Society, 1998.

Blair, Tony, et al., eds. *Third Way . . . Where To?* Nottingham, U.K.: Spokesman Press, 2001.

Blaug, Mark. *The Methodology of Economics: Or, How Economists Explain.* Cambridge: Cambridge University Press, 1980.

Blaustein, Albert P., and Gisbert H. Flanz, eds. *Constitutions of the Countries of the World.* Dobbs Ferry, N.Y.: Oceana, 1971–.

Blondel, Jean. *Comparative Legislatures.* Englewood Cliffs, N.J.: Prentice Hall, 1973.

Bohannan, Paul J. "The Differing Realms of the Law." In *The Ethnography of Law,* edited by Laura Nader, *Am. Anthropologist* (Special Publication) 67, no. 6, part 2 (1965): 33–42.

Bohannan, Paul J. *Justice and Judgment among the Tiv of Nigeria.* London: Oxford University Press, 1957.

Bohannan, Paul J., ed. *Law and Warfare: Studies in the Anthropology of Conflict.* New York: Natural History Press, 1967.

Bradley, Curtis A., and Jack L. Goldsmith. "The Current Illegitimacy of International Human Rights Litigation." *Fordham L. Rev.* 66 (1997): 319–370.

Bradley, Curtis A., and Jack L. Goldsmith. "Customary International Law as Federal Common Law: A Critique of the Modern Position." *Harv. L. Rev.* 110 (1997): 815–876.

Brietzke, Paul H., and Teresa L. Kline, "The Law and Economics of the Native American Casinos." *Neb. L. Rev.* 78 (1999): 263–347.

"Britain's Antiquated Courts." *Economist,* Sept. 16, 1995, 20.

Buddha's First Sermon. Translated by Sanderson Beck. Available at http://www.san.beck
.org/Buddha.html (accessed Feb. 20, 2002).

Bulletin of the European Communities. See "Commission Opinion."

Burley, Anne Marie. "Law among Liberal States: Liberal Internationalism and the Act of
State Doctrine." *Colum. L. Rev.* 92 (1992): 1907–1996.

Buscaglia Jr., Edgardo. *Judicial Corruption in Developing Countries: Its Causes and Economic Consequences.* Essays in Public Policy, no. 95. Stanford, Calif.: Hoover Institution Press, 1999.

Buscaglia Jr., Edgardo, Maria Dakolias, and William Ratcliff. *Judicial Reform in Latin
America: A Framework for National Development.* Essays in Public Policy, no. 65. Stanford, Calif.: Hoover Institution Press, 1995.

Caldwell, Bruce J. *Beyond Positivism: Economic Methodology in the Twentieth Century.*
London: George Allen & Unwin, 1982.

Camazin, Scott, et al., eds. *Self Organization in Biological Systems.* Princeton: Princeton
University Press, 2001.

Cappalli, Richard B. "Comparative South American Civil Procedure: A Chilean Perspective." *U. Miami Inter-Am. L. Rev.* 21 (1990): 240–310.

Cappelletti, Mauro. "Fundamental Guarantees of the Parties in Civil Litigation: Comparative Constitutional, International and Social Trends." *Stan. L. Rev.* 25 (1973): 651–715.

Cappelletti, Mauro. *The Judicial Process in Comparative Perspective.* Oxford: Clarendon
Press, 1989.

Cappelletti, Mauro. "Who Watches the Watchmen? A Comparative Study on Judicial Responsibility." *Am. J. Comp. L.* 31 (1983): 1–62.

Cappelletti, Mauro, et al. "Integration through Law: Europe and the American Federal Experience: A General Introduction." In *Methods, Tools, and Institutions.* Vol. 1 of *Integration through Law,* edited by Mauro Cappelletti, Monica Seccombe, and Joseph H.
Weiler, 3–68. Berlin: DeGruyter, 1986.

Capuano v. Italy, 13 Eur. Hum. Rts. Rep. 271 (1991).

Carl, Beverly M. "Peanuts, Law Professors and Third World Lawyers." *Third World Legal
Stud.* (1986) 1–13.

Carothers, Thomas. *Aiding Democracy Abroad: The Learning Curve.* Washington, D.C.:
Carnegie Endowment for International Peace, 1999.

Chandarachud, Dhananyaya Y. Note on Dimensions and Causes of Delay in the Courts in
the City of Bombay and in the State of Maharashtra. 1992. Unpublished and on file
with the author.

Chase, Oscar G. "Civil Litigation Delay in Italy and the United States." *Am. J. Comp. L.*
36 (1988): 41–87.

Chase, Oscar G. "Legal Processes and National Culture." *Cardozo J. Int'l & Comp. L.* 5
(1997): 1–24.

"China Defends Corruption Claims." CNN, Mar. 9, 2002. Available online at
http://www.cnn.com.

Chodosh, Hiram E. "Comparing Comparisons: In Search of Methodology." *Iowa L. Rev.*
84 (1999): 1025–1131.

Chodosh, Hiram E. "Emergence from the Dilemmas of Justice Reform." *Tex. J. Int'l L.* 38
(2003): 587–620.

Chodosh, Hiram E. "Globalizing the U.S. Law Curriculum: The Saja Paradigm." *U.C.
Davis L. Rev.* 37 (2004): 843–868.

Chodosh, Hiram E. "Indonesia." In *Legal Systems of the World: A Political, Social, and
Cultural Encyclopedia,* edited by Herbert Kritzer, vol. 2, 705–709. Santa Barbara,
Calif.: ABC-Clio, 2002.

Chodosh, Hiram E. Indonesia Notes. 1999–2003 (on file with author).

Chodosh, Hiram E. "An Interpretive Theory: The Distinction between Treaty and Customary International Law." *Vand. J. Transnat'l L.* 28 (1995): 973–1068.

Chodosh, Hiram E. "Judicial Mediation and Legal Culture." *Issues of Democracy* 4 (3) (1999): 6–12.

Chodosh, Hiram E. "Local Mediation in Advance of Armed Conflict." *Ohio St. J. on Disp. Resol.* 19 (2003): 213–227.

Chodosh, Hiram E. "Reflections on Reform: Considering Legal Foundations for Peace and Prosperity in the Middle East." *Case W. Res. J. Int'l L.* 31 (1999): 427–453.

Chodosh, Hiram E. "Reforming Judicial Reform Inspired by U.S. Models." *DePaul L. Rev.* 52 (2002): 351–381.

Chodosh, Hiram E., Niranjan Bhatt, and Firdosh Kassam. *Mediation in India: A Toolkit.* New Delhi: United States Education Foundation in India, 2004.

Chodosh, Hiram E., and Stephen A. Mayo. Combating *Judicial Corruption in Tanzania.* San Francisco: Institute for the Study and Development of Legal Systems, 2001.

Chodosh, Hiram E., and Stephen A. Mayo. "The Palestinian Legal Study: Consensus and Assessment of the New Palestinian Legal System." *Harv. Int'l L. J.* 38 (1997): 375–440.

Chodosh, Hiram E., et al. "Egyptian Civil Justice Process Modernization: A Functional and Systemic Approach." *Mich. J. Int'l L.* 17 (1996): 865–917.

Chodosh, Hiram E., et al. "Indian Civil Justice System Reform: Limitation and Preservation of the Adversarial Process." *N.Y.U. J. Int'l L. & Pol.* 30 (1998): 1–76.

Chua, Amy. *World on Fire: How Exporting Free Market Democracy Breeds Ethnic Hatred and Global Instability.* New York: Doubleday, 2003.

Clark, David S. "The Idea of the Civil Law Tradition." In *Comparative and Private International Law,* edited by David S. Clark, 11–23. Berlin: Duncker and Humblot, 1990.

Clark, David S. "Judicial Protection of the Constitution in Latin America." *Hastings Const. L. Q.* 2 (1975): 405–442.

Clark, David S. "The Selection and Accountability of Judges in West Germany: Implementation of a Rechtsstaat." *S. Calif. L. Rev.* 61 (1988): 1795–1847.

Clarke, Donald C. "Dispute Resolution in China." *J. Chinese L.* 5 (1991): 245–296.

Coffey, Ronald. Interventions in Securities Decisionmaking: Methodology and Analytics. 1992. Unpublished manuscript.

Cohn, Bernard C. "Some Notes on Law and Change in North India." *Econ. Dev. & Cultural Change* 8 (1959): 79–93.

Coleman, James S. "Metatheory: Explanations in Social Science." In *Foundations of Social Theory,* 1–26. Cambridge: Belknap Press of Harvard University Press, 1990.

"Commission Opinion on Hungary's Application for Membership of the European Union." *Bulletin of the European Union* (Supplement 6/97), 1997.

"Commission Opinion on the Czech Republic's Application for Membership of the European Union." *Bulletin of the European Union* (Supplement 14/97), 1997.

Connaughton, Anne Q. "Exporting to Special Destinations: Terrorist-Supporting and Embargoed Countries." In *Coping with U.S. Export Controls 1997,* 317–363. New York: Practicing Law Institute, 1997.

Conroy, John. *Unspeakable Acts, Ordinary People: The Dynamics of Torture.* New York: Knopf, 2001.

Cook, Walter Wheeler. "'Substance' and 'Procedure' in the Conflict of Laws." *Yale L. J.* 42 (1933): 333–358.

Council of Europe. "European Convention for the Protection of Human Rights." 20 March 1952, entered into force 18 May 1954, Eur. Treaty Ser., No. 9.

Crichton, Michael. *Prey.* New York: HarperCollins, 2002.

Cuban Liberty and Democratic Solidarity (Libertad) Act. *U.S. Code,* vol. 22, secs. 6021–6091 (2000).

Curran, Vivian Grosswald. "Cultural Immersion, Difference and Categories in U.S. Comparative Law." *Am. J. Comp. L.* 46 (1998): 43–92.

Curran, Vivian Grosswald. "Dealing in Difference: Comparative Law's Potential for Broadening Legal Perspectives." *Am. J. Comp. L.* 46 (1998): 657–668.

Curran, Vivian Grosswald. "Romantic Common Law, Enlightened Civil Law: Legal Uniformity and the Homogenization of the European Union." *Colum. J. Eur. L.* 7 (2001): 63–125.

Currie, Brainerd. *Selected Essays on the Conflict of Laws.* Durham, N.C.: Duke University Press, 1963.

CyberConsult et al. "Law Reform in Indonesia." 1997.

Dagan, Hanokh. *Unjust Enrichment: A Study of Private Law and Public Values.* New York: Cambridge University Press, 1997.

Dakolias, Maria. *Court Performance around the World: A Comparative Perspective.* Washington, D.C.: World Bank, 1999.

Dakolias, Maria. *The Judicial Sector in Latin America and the Caribbean: Elements of Reform.* World Bank Technical Paper no. 319. Washington, D.C.: World Bank, 1996.

Dakolias, Maria, and Javier Said. The World Bank, Judicial Reform: A Process of Change through Pilot Courts. 1999. Available online at http://www4.worldbank.org/legal/publications/JudicialReform-72.pdf.

Dakolias, Maria, and Kim Thachuk. "Attacking Corruption in the Judiciary: A Critical Process in Judicial Reform." *Wis. Int'l L. J.* 18 (2000): 353–406.

Daley, Suzanne. "French Judge Investigating Chirac Quits Bench." *New York Times,* Jan. 15, 2002, A6.

Damaska, Mirjan R. *The Faces of Justice and State Authority: A Comparative Approach to the Legal Process.* New Haven: Yale University Press, 1986.

D'Amato, Anthony. *The Concept of Custom in International Law.* Ithaca: Cornell University Press, 1971.

David, René. *Les Grands Systèmes de Droit Contemporains.* 3d ed. Paris: Dalloz, 1969.

David, René, and John E. C. Brierley. *Major Legal Systems in the World Today: An Introduction to the Comparative Study of Law.* 3d ed. New York: Free Press, 1985.

de Soto, Hernando. "The Mystery of Legal Failure." In *The Mystery of Capital: Why Capitalism Triumphs in the West and Fails Everywhere Else,* 153–206. New York: Basic Books, 2000.

Derma, Joseph J. "Dispute Resolution and China." Chapter 1311 in *Corporate Counsel's Guide to International Alternative Dispute Resolution,* edited by William A. Hancock. Chesterland, Ohio: Business Laws, 1997.

Deshpande, V. S. "Civil Procedure." In *The Indian Legal System,* edited by Joseph Minattur, 177–209. Dobbs Ferry, N.Y.: Oceana, 1978.

Dezalay, Yves, and Bryant Garth. *Dealing in Virtue: International Commercial Arbitration and the Construction of a Transnational Legal Order.* Chicago: University of Chicago Press, 1996.

Diamond, Arthur Sigismund. *The Comparative Study of Primitive Law.* University of London: Athlone Press, 1965.

Diamond, Arthur Sigismund. *The Evolution of Law and Order.* Westport, Conn.: Greenwood Press, 1973.

Diamond, Arthur Sigismund. *Primitive Law.* London and New York: Longmans, Green, and Co., 1935.

Diamond, Larry. Introduction to *The Self-Restraining State: Power and Accountability in*

New Democracies, edited by Andreas Schedler, Larry Diamond, and Mark F. Plattner, 1–12. Boulder, Colo.: Lynne Rienner, 1999.

Djankov, Simeon, et al. Courts: The Lex Mundi Project. Working Paper No. w8890. Cambridge, Mass.: National Bureau of Economic Research, 2002.

Domingo, Pilar. "Judicial Independence and Judicial Reform in Latin America." In *The Self-Restraining State: Power and Accountability in New Democracies,* edited by Andreas Schedler et al., 151–176. Boulder, Colo.: Lynne Rienner, 1999.

Drobnig, Ulrich, and Sjef van Erp, eds. *The Use of Comparative Law by Courts.* The Hague; London: Kluwer Law International, 1999.

Durham, W. Cole, Jr. "Foreword: Comparative Law in the Late Twentieth Century." *BYU L. Rev.* (1987): 325–333.

Durie, Mark, and Malcolm Ross, eds. *The Comparative Method Reviewed: Regularity and Irregularity in Language Change.* Oxford: Oxford University Press, 1996.

Durkheim, Emile. *De la Division du Travail Social.* Translated by George Simpson. New York: Free Press, 1947.

E. E. O. C. v Arabian Am. Oil Co., 499 US 244 (1991).

Edwards, Sebastian. "Capital Mobility, Capital Controls, and Globalization in the Twenty-First Century." *Annals* 579 (2002): 261–270.

Eggan, Frederick. "Some Reflections on Comparative Method in Anthropology." In *Context and Meaning in Cultural Anthropology,* edited by Melford E. Spiro, 357–372. New York: Free Press, 1965.

Egypt. Law No. 7/2000, Concerning the Establishment Of Conciliation Committees in Certain Litigations to which the Ministries and Juridical Persons are Parties.

Ehrmann, Henry. *Comparative Legal Cultures.* Englewood Cliffs, N.J.: Prentice Hall, 1976.

Elliot, Kimberly Ann, ed. *Corruption and the Global Economy.* Washington, D.C.: Institute for International Economics, 1996.

Ely, John H. "The Irrepressible Myth of Erie." *Harv. L. Rev.* 87 (1974): 693–740.

Emergence [journal]. Available at http://emergence.org/.

Engle, Karen. "Comparative Law as Exposing the Foreign System's Internal Critique: An Introduction." *Utah L. Rev.* (1997): 359–369.

Etzioni, Amitai, and Fredric L. Dubow. *Comparative Perspectives: Theories and Methods.* Boston: Little, Brown, 1970.

"Europe Moves to Ban All Exports of Hazardous Waste to Third World." *World Env't Rep.,* Jan. 17, 1996, 22.

European Community. "Treaty Establishing the European Economic Community." 25 March 1957, 298 *U.N. Treaty Ser* 11. Renamed "Treaty Establishing the European Community" by the Maastricht Treaty of 1992.

Ewald, William. "Comparative Jurisprudence: What Was It Like to Try a Rat?" *U. Pa. L. Rev.* 143 (1995): 1889–2149.

Ewald, William. "The Jurisprudential Approach to Comparative Law: A Field Guide to 'Rats.'" *Am. J. Comp. L.* 46 (1998): 701–707.

Fabian, John D. "The Paradox of Elected Judges: Tension in the American Judicial System." *Geo. J. Legal Ethics* 15 (2001): 155–176.

"The Fading of Fidel." *Economist,* Jan. 17, 1998, 13.

Farber, Daniel A. "Probabilities Behaving Badly: Complexity Theory and Environmental Uncertainty." *U.C. Davis L. Rev.* 37 (2003): 145–173.

Fauvarque-Cosson, Benedicte. "Comparative Law and Conflict of Laws . . ." *Am. J. Comp. L.* 49 (2002): 407–427.

Federal Rules of Civil Procedure (U.S.).

Felstiner, William L. F. "Influences of Social Organization on Dispute Processing." *L. & Soc'y Rev.* 9 (1974): 63–94.

Ferrarese, Maria Rosaria. "Civil Justice and Judicial Role in Italy." *Just. Sys. J.* 13 (1988–1989): 168–185.

Feyerabend, Paul K. *Against Method: Outline of an Anarchistic Theory of Knowledge.* Atlantic Highlands, N.J.: Humanities Press, 1975.

Fineman, Martha A. "Contexts and Comparisons." *U. Chi. L. Rev.* 55 (1988): 1431–1444.

Fisher, Roger, and William Ury. *Getting to Yes.* New York: Penguin Books, 1983.

Fiss, Owen M. "Against Settlement." *Yale L. J.* 93 (1984): 1073–1090.

Fiss, Owen M. "Out of Eden." *Yale L. J.* 94 (1985): 1669–1673.

Fletcher, George P. "The Universal and the Particular in Legal Discourse." *BYU L. Rev.* (1987): 335–351.

Foster v Leggett, 484 SW2d. 827 (Ky Ct App 1972).

Franck, Thomas M. *Fairness in International Law and Institutions.* Oxford: Clarendon Press, 1995.

Franck, Thomas M. "The New Development: Can American Law and Legal Institutions Help Developing Countries?" *Wis. L. Rev.* (1972): 767–801.

Franck, Thomas M. *The Power of Legitimacy among Nations.* New York: Oxford University Press, 1990.

Frankenberg, Gunter. "Critical Comparisons: Re-Thinking Comparative Law." *Harv. Int'l L. J.* 26 (1985): 411–455.

Frase, Richard S. "Comparative Criminal Justice as a Guide to American Law Reform: How the French Do It, How Can We Find Out, and Why Should We Care?" *Cal. L. Rev.* 78 (1990): 539–683.

Freyer, Tony A., and Paul M. Pruitt, Jr. "Reaction and Reform: Transforming the Judiciary under Alabama's Constitution, 1901–1975." *Ala. L. Rev.* 53 (2001): 77–133.

Fried, Robert C. *Comparative Political Institutions.* New York: Macmillan, 1966.

Friedman, Lawrence M. "Some Thoughts on Comparative Legal Culture." In *Comparative and Private International Law: Essays in Honor of John Henry Merryman on his Seventieth Birthday,* edited by John Henry Merryman and David S. Clark, 49–55. Berlin: Duncker and Humblot, 1990.

Friedman, Lawrence M., and Harry N. Scheiber, eds. *Legal Culture and the Legal Profession.* Boulder, Colo.: Westview Press, 1996.

Gardner, James A. *Legal Imperialism: American Lawyers and Foreign Aid in Latin America.* Madison: University of Wisconsin Press, 1980.

Gazzaniga, Michael S., ed. *The Cognitive Neurosciences.* Cambridge: MIT Press, 1995.

Gazzaniga, Michael S. *Nature's Mind: The Biological Roots of Thinking, Emotions, Sexuality, Language, and Intelligence.* New York: Basic Books, 1992.

Geertz, Clifford, *Local Knowledge: Further Essays in Interpretive Anthropology.* New York: Basic Books, 1983.

Gerber, David J. "Centennial World Congress on Comparative Law: Globalization and Legal Knowledge; Implications for Comparative Law." *Tul. L. Rev.* 75 (2001): 949–975.

Gerber, David J. "Extraterritorial Discovery and the Conflict of Procedural Systems: Germany and the United States." *Am. J. Comp. L.* 34 (1986): 745–788.

Gessner, Volkmar, Armin Höland, and Csaba Varga, eds. *European Legal Cultures.* Aldershot, U.K.: Dartmouth, 1996.

Geyh, Charles Gardner. "Customary Independence." In *Judicial Independence at the Crossroads: An Interdisciplinary Approach,* edited by Stephen B. Burbank and Barry Friedman, 160–190. Thousand Oaks, Calif.: Sage Publications, 2002.

Gladwell, Malcolm. "The Law of the Few: Connectors, Mavens, and Salesmen." In *The Tipping Point: How Little Things Can Make a Big Difference,* 15–29. Boston: Little, Brown, 2000.

Gledhill, Alan. "Laws Relating to Contract: The Indian Contract Act." In *The Republic of India: The Development of its Laws and Constitution,* 237–253. Westport, Conn.: Greenwood Press, 1970.

Glendon, Mary Ann. *Abortion and Divorce in Western Law.* Cambridge: Harvard University Press, 1987.

Glendon, Mary Ann, et al. *Comparative Legal Traditions in a Nutshell.* 2d ed. St. Paul, Minn.: West Group, 1999.

Glenn, H. Patrick. "Centennial World Congress on Comparative Law: Comparative Law and Legal Practice: On Removing the Borders." *Tul. L. Rev.* 75 (2001): 977–1002.

Gluckman, Max, ed. *Ideas and Procedures in African Customary Law: Studies Presented and Discussed at the Eighth International African Seminar at the Haile Selassie I University, Addis Ababa, Jan. 1966.* London: Oxford University Press, 1969.

Gluckman, Max. *The Ideas in Barotse Jurisprudence.* Manchester, U.K.: Manchester University Press, 1965.

Gluckman, Max. Introduction to *The Craft of Social Anthropology,* edited by A. L. Epstein. London: Tavistock Publications, 1967.

Gluckman, Max. *The Judicial Process among the Barotse of Northern Rhodesia* [Zambia]. 2d ed. Manchester, U.K.: Manchester University Press, 1967.

Gluckman, Max. *Politics, Law and Ritual in Tribal Society.* Chicago: Aldine, 1965.

Goldstein, Abraham. "Reflections on Two Models: Inquisitorial Themes in American Criminal Procedure." *Stan. L. Rev.* 26 (1974): 1009–1025.

Gordon, Deborah M., and Alan Kulig. "The Effect of Neighbours on the Mortality of Harvester Ant Colonies." *J. Animal Ecology* 67 (1998): 141–148.

Green, Donald P., and Ian Shapiro. "Social Dilemmas and Free-Riding." In *Pathologies of Rational Choice Theory: A Critique of Applications in Political Science,* 72–97. New Haven: Yale University Press, 1994.

Greenberg, David F. "Law and Development in Light of Dependency Theory." *Res. L. & Soc.* 3 (1980): 129–159.

Greenberg, Michael D. "Information, Paternalism, and Rational Decision-Making: The Balance of FDA New Drug Approval." *Alb. L. J. Sci. & Tech.* 13 (2003): 663–680.

Greenhouse, Linda. "Blank Check; Ethics in Government: The Price of Good Intentions." *New York Times,* Feb. 1, 1998, Sec. 4, p. 1.

Greenspan v. Slate, 12 NJ 426; 97 A2d 390 (1953).

Griggs v Riley, 489 SW2d. 469 (Mo Ct App 1972).

Gross, Samuel R. "The American Advantage: The Value of Inefficient Litigation." *Mich. L. Rev.* 85 (1987): 734–757.

Gulliver, P. H. "Dispute Settlement Without Courts: The Ndendeuli of Southern Tanzania." In *Law in Culture and Society,* edited by Laura Nader, 24–68. Chicago: Aldine, 1969.

Gulliver, P. H. *Social Control in an African Society: A Study of the Arisha. Agricultural Masai of Northern Tanganyika.* London: Routledge and Kegan Paul, 1963.

Gutteridge, H. C. *Comparative Law.* Cambridge: Cambridge University Press, 1946.

Häberle, Peter. "Grundrechtsgeltung und Grundrechtsinterpretation im Verfassungsstaat— Zugleich zur Rechstvergleichung als Funfter Auslegungsmethode." *Juristen Zeitung* 44 (1989): 913–919.

Hall, Gridley, and Burton Fretz, "Legal Services in the Third World." *Clearinghouse Rev.* 24 (Dec. 1990): 783–796.

Halverson, Karen. "Resolving Economic Disputes in Russia's Market Economy." *Mich. J. Int'l L.* 18 (1996): 59–112.

Hammergren, Linn Ann. Do Judicial Councils Further Judicial Reform? Lessons from Latin America, Working Paper No. 28. Washington, D.C.: Carnegie Endowment for International Peace, 2002. Available online at http://www.ceip.org/files/pdf/wp28.pdf.

Hammergren, Linn Ann. *The Politics of Justice and Justice Reform in Latin America: The Peruvian Case in Comparative Perspective.* Boulder, Colo.: Westview Press, 1998.

Hancock, William A., ed. *Corporate Counsel's Guide to International Alternative Dispute Resolution.* Chesterland, Ohio: Business Laws, 1997.

Hansen, Chad. "Chinese Language, Chinese Philosophy, and 'Truth.'" *J. Asian Stud.* 44 (1985): 491–519.

Hart, H. L. A. *The Concept of Law.* Oxford: Oxford University Press, 1961.

Hartford Fire Ins. Co. v California, 509 US 764 (1993).

Hasan, Manzoor. "Corruption in Bangladesh Surveys: An Overview." Available online at http://www.ti-bangladesh.org/docs/survey/overview.htm.

Helms, Ann Doss, and Laurie Lucas. "Preparing for the Unthinkable." *Press-Enterprise* (Riverside, Calif.), Jan. 11, 1998, D1.

Helms-Burton Act. See Cuban Liberty and Democratic Solidarity (Libertad) Act.

Henderson, Dan Fenno. "The Japanese Law in English: Some Thoughts on Scope and Method." *Vand. J. Transnat'l L.* 16 (1983): 601–620.

Henkin, Louis. *How Nations Behave: Law and Foreign Policy.* 2d ed. New York: Columbia University Press, 1979.

Hernandez-Esparza, (LIC.) Patricia. "Accounting Services for the 21st Century." *U.S.-Mexico L. J.* 8 (Spring 2000): 11–20.

Hittner, David, and Kathleen Weisz Osman, "Federal Civil Trial Delays: A Constitutional Dilemma?" *S. Tex. L. Rev.* 31 (1990): 341–360.

Hoebel, E. Adamson. *The Law of Primitive Man: A Study in Comparative Legal Dynamics.* Cambridge: Harvard University Press, 1954.

Hofstadter, Douglas R. *Gödel, Escher, Bach: An Eternal Golden Braid.* New York: Basic Books, 1979.

Holland, John H. *Emergence: From Chaos to Order.* Reading, Mass.: Addison-Wesley, 1998.

Holleman, J. F. "Law and Anthropology: A Necessary Partnership for the Study of Legal Change in Plural Systems." *J. Afr. L.* 23 (1979): 117–130.

Holy, Ladislav, ed. *Comparative Anthropology.* Oxford: Blackwell, 1987.

Horowitz, Donald L. "Constitutional Design and the Problem of Adoption: Proposals versus Processes." Ch. 1 in *The Architecture of Democracy: Constitutional Design, Conflict Management, and Democracy,* edited by Andrew Reynolds. Oxford; New York: Oxford University Press, 2002.

Horowitz, Donald L. "Foreword: Compared to What?" *Duke J. Comp. & Int'l L.* 13 (2003): 1–9.

Huanwen, Zhang. Excerpts of Address before the Third Session of the Eight Provincial People's Congress. In *Liaoning Ribao,* Mar. 7, 1995, at 3. Translated and reprinted in Liaoning Provincial Higher People's Court Work Report (BBC Summary of World Broadcasts, June 30, 1995).

Human Rights Violations Through Judicial Corruption. Available online at http://www.thinkcentre.org/article.cfm?ArticleID=739 (May 13, 2001).

Huxley, Andrew. "Golden Yoke, Silken Text." *Yale L. J.* 106 (1997): 1885–1950.

India. Arbitration and Conciliation Act, 1996. *Gazette of India,* New Delhi, the 16th Jan. 1996/Pausa 26, 1917 (Saka), Part III, Section 73.

India. Code of Civil Procedure.

"India Sets Changes to Tackle Mounting Court Cases." Reuters, Oct. 6, 1995. Available online in LEXIS, News Library, Wires File.

"India's Economy: Work in Progress; India's Economy Survey." *Economist*, Feb. 22, 1997, 3, 4.

Indonesia. Draft Law Regarding Amendment of Law Number 14 Year 1970 Regarding Basic Provisions on Judicial Authority.

Indonesia. Law No. 35/1999.

Indonesia. Law No. 14 of 1985 on the Supreme Court.

Indonesia. Law No. 14 of 1970 Concerning Basic Principles of Judicial Power.

Indonesia. Third Amendment to the 1945 Constitution of the Republic of Indonesia.

Intergovernmental Panel on Climate Change. *Methodological and Technological Issues in Technology Transfer*, edited by Bert Metz et al. Cambridge; New York: Cambridge University Press, 2001. Available online at http://www.grida.no/climate/ipcc/tectran/.

International Legal Assistance Consortium. "Report from an ILAC Mission to Iraq." 2003.

Jacobs, Jane. *The Death and Life of Great American Cities*. New York: Vintage Books, 1992.

Jain, S. N. "Judicial System and Legal Remedies." In *The Indian Legal System*, edited by Joseph Minattur, 133–147. Dobbs Ferry, N.Y.: Oceana, 1978.

Janis, Mark W. *Introduction to International Law*. 2d ed. Boston: Little, Brown, 1995.

Jarquín, Edmundo, and Fernando Carillo, eds. *Justice Delayed: Judicial Reform in Latin America*. Washington, D.C.: Inter-American Development Bank, 1998.

Johnson, Steven. *Emergence: The Connected Lives of Ants, Brains, Cities, and Software*. New York: Scribner, 2001.

Jones, Owen D. "Evolutionary Analysis in Law: An Introduction and Application to Child Abuse." *N.C. L. Rev.* 75 (1997): 1117–1242.

Juenger, Friedrich K. "American Jurisdiction: A Story of Comparative Neglect." *U. Colo. L. Rev.* 65 (1993): 1–23.

Juenger, Friedrich K. "The Need for a Comparative Approach to Choice-of-Law Problems." *Tul. L. Rev.* 73 (1999): 1309–1335.

Kahn-Freund, Otto. "Comparative Law as an Academic Subject." *L. Q. Rev.* 82 (1966): 40–61.

Kahn-Freund, Otto. "On Uses and Misuses of Comparative Law." *Mod. L. Rev.* 37 (1974): 1–27.

Kakalik, James S., et al. "Discovery Management: Further Analysis of the Civil Justice Reform Act Evaluation Data." *B.C. L. Rev.* 39 (1998): 613–682.

Kakalik, James S., et al. "Just, Speedy, and Inexpensive? An Evaluation of Judicial Case Management under the Civil Justice Reform Act." RAND Institute for Civil Justice, 1996. *Judicature* 80 (Jan./Feb. 1997): 184–189.

Kakouris, C. N. "Use of the Comparative Method by the Court of Justice of the European Communities." *Pace Int'l L. Rev.* 6 (1994): 267–283.

Katz, Lewis R., Lawrence Litwin, and Richard Bamberger. *Justice Is the Crime: Pretrial Delay in Felony Cases*. Cleveland: Press of Case Western Reserve University, 1972.

Kauffman, Stuart. *At Home in the Universe: The Search for Laws of Self-Organization and Complexity*. New York; Oxford: Oxford University Press, 1995.

Keller, Evelyn Fox, and Lee A. Segel, "Conflict between Positive and Negative Feedback as an Explanation for the Initiation of Aggregation in Slime Mold Amoebae." *Nature* 227 (1970): 1365–1366.

Keller, Evelyn Fox, and Lee A. Segel, "Initiation of Slime Mold Aggregation Viewed as an Instability." *J Theoretical Biology* 26 (1970): 399–415.

Keller, Evelyn Fox, and Lee A. Segel, "On the Aggregation of Acrasiales." *Biophysical Soc'y: Abstracts of the Annual Meeting* 13 (1969): A-69.

Kennedy, David. "New Approaches to Comparative Law: Comparativism and International Governance." *Utah L. Rev.* 1997: 545–637.

Kidder, Robert L. "Courts and Conflict in an Indian City: A Study in Legal Impact." *J. Commonwealth Pol. Stud.* 11 (1973): 121–139.

Kiikeri, Markku, ed. *Comparative Legal Reasoning and European Law.* Dordrecht; Boston: Kluwer Academic Publishers, 2001.

King, Gary, Robert O. Keohane, and Sidney Verba. *Designing Social Inquiry: Scientific Inference in Qualitative Research.* Princeton: Princeton University Press, 1984.

King, Henry T., and Theodore C. Theofrastous. "From Nuremberg to Rome: A Step Backward for U.S. Foreign Policy." *Case W. Res. J. Int'l L.* 31 (1999): 47–106.

Kline, Stephan O. "Judicial Independence: Rebuffing Congressional Attacks on the Third Branch." *Ky. L. J.* 87 (1999): 679–791.

Klitgaard, Robert E. *Controlling Corruption.* Berkeley: University of California Press, 1988.

Klitgaard, Robert E. "International Cooperation against Corruption." *Fin. & Dev.*, March 1998, 3–6.

Knott, Jack H., and Gary J. Miller. *Reforming Bureaucracy: The Politics of Institutional Choice.* Englewood Cliffs, N.J.: Prentice Hall, 1987.

Koh, Harold Hongju. "Is International Law Really State Law?" *Harv. L. Rev.* 111 (1998): 1824–1861.

Koh, Harold Hongju. "Transnational Legal Process." *Neb. L. Rev.* 75 (1996): 181–207.

Koh, Harold Hongju. "Why Do Nations Obey International Law?" *Yale L. J.* 106 (1997): 2599–2659.

Koh, Harold Hongju. *Why Nations Behave: A Theory of Compliance with International Law* (forthcoming).

Kohn, Melvin L., ed. *Cross-National Research in Sociology.* Newbury Park, Calif.: Sage Publications, 1989.

Kojima, Takeshi. Civil Procedure Reform in Japan, *Mich. J. Int'l L.* 11 (1990): 1218–1234.

Komesar, Neil K. *Imperfect Alternatives: Choosing Institutions in Law, Economics and Public Policy.* Chicago: University of Chicago Press, 1994.

Könz, Peider (Rapporteur). Introduction and Summary. In World Association of Judges & International Legal Center, *Court Congestion: Some Remedial Approaches: Conciliation, Pretrial, Training, Use of Auxiliaries and Electronic Devices . . . ,* 1–19. Buffalo: William S. Hein, 1971.

Kozyris, P. John. "Comparative Law for the Twenty-First Century: New Horizons and New Technologies." *Tul. L. Rev.* 69 (1994): 165–178.

Langbein, John H. "Cultural Chauvinism in Comparative Law." *Cardozo J. Int'l & Comp. L.* 5 (1997): 41–49.

Langbein, John H. "The German Advantage in Civil Procedure." *U. Chi. L. Rev.* 52 (1985): 823–866.

Langbein, John H. "The Influence of Comparative Procedure in the United States." *Am. J. Comp. L.* 43 (1995): 545–554.

Langbein, John H. "Trashing the German Advantage." *Nw. U. L. Rev.* 82 (1988): 763–784.

Larkins, Christopher M. "Judicial Independence and Democratization: A Theoretical and Conceptual Analysis." *Am. J. Comp. L.* 44 (1996): 605–626.

Lasser, Mitchel de S.-O.-l'E. "Comparative Law and Comparative Literature: A Project in Progress." *Utah L. Rev.* (1997): 471–524.

Lasser, Mitchel de S.-O.-l'E. "Judicial (Self-)Portraits: Judicial Discourse in the French Legal System." *Yale L. J.* 104 (1995): 1325–1410.

Lasser, Mitchel de S.-O.-l'E. "'Lit. Theory' Put to the Test: A Comparative Literary Analysis of American Judicial Tests and French Judicial Discourse." *Harv. L. Rev.* 111 (1998): 689–770.

Lauritzen v Larson, 345 US 571 (1953).

Lauterpacht, Elihu. *Aspects of the Administration of International Justice.* Cambridge, U.K.: Grotius, 1991.

Law Commission of India. Consultation Paper on ADR and Mediation Rules. 2003.

Law Commission of India. Consultation Paper on Case Management. 2003.

Law Commission of India. "One Hundred Twenty-Fourth Report on the High Court Arrears—A Fresh Look." 1988.

Law Commission of India. "Seventy-Ninth Report on Delay and Arrears in High Courts and Other Appellate Courts." 1979.

Law Commission of India. "Seventy-Seventh Report on Delay and Arrears in Trial Courts." 1978.

"Law Methodology, FYI." *US News & World Report: 1998 Annual Guide, Best Graduate Schools,* Mar. 2, 1998, 48.

Lawson, F. H. *Selected Essays.* New York: North Holland, 1977.

Leflar, Robert A. "Conflicts Law: More on Choice Influencing Considerations." *Cal. L. Rev.* 54 (1966): 1586–1598.

Legrand, Pierre. "How to Compare Now." *Legal Studies* 16 (1996): 232–242.

Lepaulle, Pierre. "The Function of Comparative Law with a Critique of Social Jurisprudence." *Harv. L. Rev.* 35 (1922): 838–858.

Lev, Daniel S. "Between State and Society: Professional Lawyers and Reform in Indonesia." In *Indonesia: Law and Society,* edited by Timothy Lindsey, 227–246. Sydney: Federation, 1999.

Lev, Daniel S. "Judicial Institutions and Legal Culture in Indonesia." In *Culture and Politics in Indonesia,* edited by Claire Holt, 246–318. Ithaca: Cornell University Press, 1972.

Lev, Daniel S. *Legal Evolution and Political Authority in Indonesia: Selected Essays.* London-Leiden Series on Law, Administration and Development, vol. 4. The Hague: Kluwer Law International, 2000.

Levine, David I. "Northern District of California Adopts Early Neutral Evaluation to Expedite Dispute Resolution." *Judicature* 72 (1989): 235–238.

Levy-Ullmann, Henri. "Observations générales sur les communications relative au droit privé dans les pays étrangers." In *Les transformations du droit dans les principaux pays depuis cinquante ans, 1869–1919,* 31–108. Paris: Librairie Générale de Droit et de Jurisprudence, 1923.

Lewis, Oscar. "Comparisons in Cultural Anthropology." In *Readings in Cross-Cultural Methodology,* edited by Frank. W. Moore, 50–88. New Haven, Conn.: HRAF Press, 1961.

Lijphart, Arend. "Comparative Politics and the Comparative Method." *Am. Pol. Sci. Rev.* 65 (1971): 682–693.

Lindsey, Timothy, ed. *Indonesia: Law and Society.* Leichardt, New South Wales: Federation, 1999.

Lipinski, Tomas A. "The Developing Legal Infrastructure and the Globalization of Information: Constructing a Framework for Critical Choice in the New Millennium—Character, Content and Confusion." *Richmond J. L. & Tech.* 6 (1999): 19 (Internet).

Lubman, Stanley. "Bird in a Cage: Chinese Law Reform after Twenty Years." *Nw. J. Int'l L. & Bus.* 20 (2000): 383–423.

Luce, Duncan R., and Howard Raiffa. *Games and Decisions: Introduction and Critical Survey.* New York: Wiley, 1957.

Luckham, Robin. "The Political Economy of Legal Professions: Towards a Framework for Comparison." In *Lawyers in the Third World: Comparative and Developmental Perspectives,* edited by C. J. Dias et al., 287–335. Uppsala and New York: Scandinavian Institute of African Studies, 1998.

MacIntyre, Alasdair. "Incommensurability, Truth, and the Conversation between Confucians and Aristotelians about the Virtues." In *Culture and Modernity: East-West Philosophic Perspectives,* edited by Eliot Deutsche, 104–122. Honolulu: University of Hawaii Press, 1991.

Maine, H. S. *Ancient Law: Its Connection with the Early History of Society and Its Relation to Modern Ideas.* London: John Murray, 1861.

Malavet, Pedro A. "Counsel for the Situation: The Latin Notary, A Historical and Comparative Model." *Hastings Int'l & Comp. L. Rev.* 19 (1996): 389–488.

Malimath, V. S., P. D. Desai, and A. S. Anand. "Report of the Arrears Committee 1989–1990." India: Law Commission, 1990.

Mankad, R. C. Report on Legal Systems & Court Management: Note on Case Management in Indian Courts. Unpublished.

Manning, Chris, and Peter Van Dierman, eds. *Indonesia in Transition: Social Aspects of Reformasi and Crisis.* Singapore: Zed Books, 2000.

Marcuse, Herbert. *One-Dimensional Man: Studies in the Ideology of Advanced Industrial Society.* Boston: Beacon Press, 1964.

Markesinis, Basil S. *Always on the Same Path: Essays on Foreign Law and Comparative Methodology.* Vol. 2. Oxford; Portland, Ore.: Hart Publishing, 2001.

Markesinis, Basil S. *Foreign Law and Comparative Methodology: A Subject and a Thesis.* Oxford; Portland, Ore.: Hart Publishing, 1997.

Markman, Ellen. "Constraints Children Place on Word Meanings." *Cognitive Sci.* 14 (1990): 57–77.

Markovits, Inga. "Hedgehogs or Foxes? A Review of Westen's and Schleider's *Zivilrecht im Systemvergleich.*" *Am. J. Comp. L.* 34 (1986): 113–135.

Martin, James. "Constitutional Limitations on Choice of Law." *Cornell L. Rev.* 61 (1976): 185–230.

Martínez Paz, Enrique. *Introducción al estudio del derecho civil comparado.* Buenos Aires: Abeledo-Perrot. 1960.

Massa v. Italy, 18 Eur Hum Rts Rep 266 (1994).

Masson, Paul. Globalization: Facts and Figures. Policy Discussion Paper No. 4. Washington, D.C.: International Monetary Fund, 2001.

Mattei, Ugo. *Comparative Law and Economics.* Ann Arbor: University of Michigan Press, 1997.

Mattei, Ugo. "An Opportunity Not to Be Missed: The Future of Comparative Law in the United States." *Am. J. Comp. L.* 46 (1998): 709–718.

Mattei, Ugo. "Three Patterns of Law: Taxonomy and Change in the World's Legal Systems." *Am. J. Comp. L.* 45 (1997): 5–44.

Mattei, Ugo. "Why the Wind Changed: Intellectual Leadership in Western Law." *Am. J. Comp. L.* 42 (1994): 195–218.

McCloskey, Deirdre N. *The Rhetoric of Economics*. Madison: University of Wisconsin Press, 1988.

McDougal, Myres S. "The Comparative Study of Law for Policy Purposes: Value Clarification as an Instrument of Democratic World Order." *Am. J. Comp. L.* 1 (1952): 24–57.

McGarvie, Richard E. "Judicial Responsibility for the Operation of the Court System." *Austl. L. J.* 63 (1989): 79–97.

McThenia, Andrew W., and Thomas L. Shaffer. "For Reconciliation." *Yale L. J.* 94 (1985): 1660–1668.

Medawar, Peter. *Pluto's Republic*. New York: Oxford University Press, 1984.

Mendelsohn, Oliver. "The Pathology of the Indian Legal System." *Mod. Asian Stud.* 15 (1981): 823–863.

Mendez, Juan E., Guillermo O'Donnell, and Paulo Sergio Pinheiro, eds. *The (Un)rule of Law and the Underprivileged in Latin America,* Part 3, Institutional Reform, Including Access to Justice, 227–337. Notre Dame: University of Notre Dame Press, 1999.

Menkel-Meadow, Carrie. "For and against Settlement: Uses and Abuses of the Mandatory Settlement Conference." *UCLA L. Rev.* 33 (1985): 485–514.

Menkel-Meadow, Carrie. "The Trouble with the Adversary System in a Postmodern, Multicultural World." *Wm. & Mary L. Rev.* 38 (1996): 5–44.

Merryman, John Henry. "Comparative Law and Scientific Explanation." In *Law in the United States of America in Social and Technological Revolution,* edited by John N. Hazard and Wenceslas J. Wagner, 81–104. Brussels: Emile Bruylant, 1974.

Merryman, John Henry. "Comparative Law and Social Change: On the Origins, Style, Decline and Revival of the Law and Development Movement." *Am. J. Comp. L.* 25 (1977): 457–491.

Merryman, John Henry. "How Others Do It: The French and German Judiciaries." *S. Cal. L. Rev.* 61 (1988): 1865–1876.

Merryman, John Henry. "On the Convergence (and Divergence) of the Civil Law and the Common Law." *Stan. J. Int'l L.* 17 (1981): 357–388.

Merryman, John Henry, David S. Clark, and John O. Haley. *The Civil Law Tradition: Europe, Latin America, East Asia*. 2d ed. Charlottesville, Va.: Mitchie, 1994.

Miedel, Florian. "Is West Germany's 1975 Abortion Decision a Solution to the American Abortion Debate? A Critique of Mary Ann Glendon and Donald Kommers." *N.Y.U. Rev. L. & Soc. Change* 20 (1994): 471–515.

Millar, Robert Winess. *Civil Procedure of the Trial Court in Historical Perspective*. New York: Law Center of NYU, 1952.

Miller, Jeffrey J. "Plea Bargaining and Its Analogues under the New Italian Criminal Procedure Code and in the United States: Towards a New Understanding of Comparative Criminal Procedure." *N.Y.U. J. Int'l L. & Pol.* 22 (1990): 215–251.

Montesquieu, Baron de. *The Spirit of the Laws*. Translated by Thomas Nugent. Cincinnati: Clarke, 1873.

Moog, Robert. "Delays in the Indian Courts: Why the Judges Don't Take Control." *Just. Sys. J.* 16 (1992): 19–36.

Moore, Sally Falk. "Law and Anthropology." *Biennial Rev. Anthropology* 6 (1969): 252–300.

Moore, Sally Falk. *Law as Process: An Anthropological Approach*. London: Routledge and Kegan Paul, 1978.

Moore, Sally Falk. "Legal Systems of the World: An Introductory Guide to Classifications, Typological Interpretations, and Bibliographical Resources." In *Law and the Social Sci-*

ences, edited by Leon Lipson and Stanton Wheeler, 11–62. New York: Russell Sage Foundation, 1986.

Moore, Sally Falk. "Treating Law as Knowledge: Telling Colonial Officers What to Say to Africans about Running 'Their Own' Native Courts." *L. & Soc'y Rev.* 26 (1992): 11–45.

Moore, W. E. "Global Sociology: The World as a Singular System." *Am. J. Soc.* 71 (1966): 475–482.

Morgenthau, Hans J. *Politics among Nations: The Struggle for Power and Peace.* 4th ed. New York: Knopf, 1967.

Morowitz, Harold. "Emergence and the Law." *Complexity* (Mar./Apr. 2000): 11, 12.

Morton, F. L., "Judicial Review in France: A Comparative Analysis." *Am. J. Comp. L.* 36 (1988): 89–110.

Myers, Steven Lee. "Whether to Bomb Is the Easy Part." *New York Times,* Feb. 1, 1998, A4.

Nader, Laura. "A Comparative Perspective on Legal Evolution, Revolution, and Devolution." *Mich. L. Rev.* 81 (1983): 993–1005.

Nader, Laura, ed. *The Ethnography of Law. Am. Anthropologist* (Special Publication) 67 (1965): 141–212.

Nader, Laura, ed. *Law in Culture and Society.* Chicago: Aldine, 1969.

Nader, Laura, and Barbara Yngvesson, "On Studying the Ethnography of Law and Its Consequences." In *Handbook of Social and Cultural Anthropology,* edited by John J. Honigmann, 883–921. Chicago: Rand McNally, 1973.

Nakagaki, Toshiyuki, Hiroyasu Yamada, and Ágota Tóth, "Maze-Solving by an Amoeboid Organism." *Nature* 407 (2000): 470.

Nardin, Terry. "Ethical Traditions in International Affairs." In *Traditions of International Ethics,* edited by Terry Nardin and David R. Mapel, 1–22. Cambridge: Cambridge University Press, 1993.

Needham, Rodney. *Counterpoints.* Berkeley: University of California Press, 1987.

Needham, Rodney. "Polythetic Classification: Convergence and Consequences." *Man* 10 (1975): 349–369.

Nelken, David, and Johannes Feest, eds. *Adapting Legal Cultures.* Oxford; Portland, Ore.: Hart Publishing, 2001.

"Neurobiology, Human Behavior, and the Law." Address at the Squaw Valley Conference of the Gruter Institute for Law and Behavioral Research, June 17–20, 1998.

Noonan, Jr., John T. *Bribes: An Intellectual History of a Moral Idea.* Collingdale, Pa.: Diane Publishing Co., 1984.

North, Douglass C. *Institutions, Institutional Change and Economic Performance.* Cambridge: Cambridge University Press, 1991.

Obiora, L. Amede. "Toward an Auspicious Reconciliation of International and Comparative Analyses." *Am. J. Comp. L.* 46 (1998): 671–682.

Office of Democracy and Governance. *Guidance for Promoting Judicial Independence and Impartiality.* Washington, D.C.: U.S. Agency for International Development, 2002.

Ogden, Charles K. *Opposition: A Linguistic and Psychological Analysis.* Bloomington: Indiana University Press, 1967.

Ogletree, Jr., Charles J. "From Mandela to Mthwana: Providing Counsel to the Unrepresented Accused in South Africa." *B.U. L. Rev.* 75 (1995): 1–56.

Øyen, Else. "The Imperfection of Comparisons." In *Comparative Methodology: Theory and Practice in International Social Research,* 8–18. Newbury Park, Calif.: Sage, 1990.

Paccione v. Italy, 20 Eur Hum Rts Rep 396 (1995).

Pace, Kimberly. "Recalibrating the Scales of Justice through National Punitive Damages Reform." *Am. U. L. Rev.* 46 (1997): 1573–1638.

"Pakistan Top Court backs Musharraf." CNN, Apr. 27, 2002. Available online at http://www.cnn.com/2002/WORLD/asiapcf/south/04/27/pakistan.supreme/index.html.

Palmer, George E. *The Law of Restitution.* Boston: Little, Brown, 1978.

Paulsen, Monrad G., and Michael I. Sovern. "'Public Policy' in the Conflict of Laws." *Colum. L. Rev.* 56 (1956): 969–1016.

Pinker, Steven. *How the Mind Works: The Surprising Science of Human Thought.* New York: W. W. Norton, 1997.

Pinker, Steven, and Paul Bloom. "Natural Language and Natural Selection." In *The Adapted Mind: Evolutionary Psychology and the Generation of Culture,* edited by Jerome H. Barkow, Leda Cosmides, and John Tooby, 451–494. New York: Oxford University Press, 1992.

Pizzi, William T. "Essay: Soccer, Football and Trial Systems." *Colum. J. Eur. L.* 1 (1995): 369–376.

Podgórecki, Adam. "Social Systems and Legal Systems—Criteria for Classification." In *Legal Systems and Social Systems,* edited by Adam Podgórecki et al., 1–24. Dover, N.H.: Croom Helm, 1985.

Pospisil, Leopold. *Anthropology of Law: A Comparative Theory.* 2d ed. New York: Harper and Row, 1992.

Pound, Roscoe. "Comparative Law in Space and Time." *Am. J. Comp. L.* 4 (1955): 70–84.

Pound, Roscoe. "What May We Expect from Comparative Law?" *A.B.A. J.* 22 (1936): 56–60.

Priest, George. "Private Litigants and the Court Congestion Problem." *B.U. L. Rev.* 69 (1989): 527–559.

Prillaman, William C. *The Judiciary and Democratic Decay in Latin America: Declining Confidence in the Rule of Law.* Westport, Conn.: Praeger, 2000.

"President Bush Outlines Iraqi Threat," Cincinnati, Oct. 7, 2002, at http://www.whitehouse.gov/news/releases/2002/10/20021007-8.html.

Przeworksi, Adam, and Henry Teune. *The Logic of Comparative Social Inquiry.* Malabar, Fla.: Robert E. Krieger Publishing Company, 1982.

Radbruch, Gustav. *Einfuhrung in die Rechtswissenschaft.* Stuttgart: K. F. Koehler, 1969.

Ragin, Charles C. *The Comparative Method: Moving Beyond Qualitative and Quantitative Strategies.* Berkeley: University of California Press, 1987.

Reimann, Mathias. "The End of Comparative Law as an Autonomous Subject." *Tul. Eur. & Civ. L. F.* 11 (1996): 49–72.

Reimann, Mathias. "The Progress and Failure of Comparative Law in the Second Half of the Twentieth Century." *Am. J. Comp. L.* 50 (2002): 671–700.

Reimann, Mathias, and Alain Levasseur. "Comparative Law and Legal History in the United States." *Am. J. Comp. L.* 46 (1998): 1–15.

Reisman, W. Michael. "Law from the Policy Perspective." In *International Law Essays: A Supplement to International Law in Contemporary Perspective, edited by Myres S. McDougal and W. Michael Reisman,* 1–14. Mineola, N.Y.: Foundation Press, 1981.

Reitz, John C. "How to Do Comparative Law?" *Am. J. Comp. L.* 46 (1998): 617–636.

Reitz, John C. "Why We Probably Cannot Adopt the German Advantage in Civil Procedure." *Iowa L. Rev.* 75 (1990): 987–1009.

Report by the Commission for Examining the Structure of a Case Management Department. Jerusalem: 1999.

Resnick, Mitchel, and Brian Silverman. Exploring Emergence [website]. Available at http://el.www.media.mit.edu/groups/el/projects/emergence/ (visited May 7, 2000).

Resnik, Judith. "Many Doors? Closing Doors? Alternative Dispute Resolution and Adjudication." *Ohio St. J. on Disp. Resol.* 10 (1995): 211–265.

Rheinstein, Max. "Comparative Law—Its Functions, Methods, and Usages." *Ark. L. Rev.* 22 (1968): 415–425.

Rheinstein, Max. *Einfuhrung in die Rechtsvergleichung.* 2d ed. Munich: Beck, 1987.

Rhode, Deborah L. "Procedural Pathologies and Prescriptions." In *In the Interests of Justice: Reforming the Legal Profession,* 82–96. Oxford: Oxford University Press, 2000.

Rhode, Deborah L. *Professional Responsibility: Ethics by the Pervasive Method.* 2d ed. Boston: Little, Brown, 1998.

Riles, Annelise, ed. *Rethinking the Masters of Comparative Law.* Oxford; Portland, Ore.: Hart Publishing, 2001.

Rinaldi, Sergio, et al. "Corruption Dynamics in Democratic Societies." *Complexity* 3 (5) (May/June 1998), 53–61

Robinson, Mark, ed. *Corruption and Development.* Portland, Ore.: Frank Cass and Co., 1998.

Rogers. Catherine A. "Gulliver's Troubled Travels, or the Conundrum of Comparative Law." *Geo. Wash. L. Rev.* 67 (1998): 149–189.

Romer, Thomas, and Barry R. Weingast. "Political Foundations of the Thrift Debacle." Ch. 6 in *Politics and Economics in the Eighties,* edited by Alberto Alesina and Geoffrey Carliner, 175–214. Chicago: University of Chicago Press, 1991.

Rose-Ackerman, Susan. "American Administrative Law under Siege: Is Germany a Model?" *Harv. L. Rev.* 107 (1994): 1297–1302.

Rose-Ackerman, Susan. *Corruption and Government: Causes, Consequences and Reform.* New York: Cambridge University Press, 1999.

Rose-Ackerman, Susan. "Redesigning the State to Fight Corruption: Transparency, Competition, and Privatization." *Public Policy for the Private Sector,* Note No. 75, April 1996. Available online at http://www.worldbank.org/html/fpd/notes/75/75ackerm.pdf.

Rowling, J. K. *Harry Potter and the Goblet of Fire.* London: Bloomsbury, 2000.

Rosenberg, Joshua D., and H. Jay Folberg. "Alternative Dispute Resolution: An Empirical Analysis." *Stan. L. Rev.* 46 (1994): 1487–1557.

Ruhl, J. B. "Complexity Theory as a Paradigm for the Dynamical Law-and-Society System: A Wake-Up Call for Legal Reductionism and the Modern Administrative State." *Duke L. J.* 45 (1996): 849–928.

Russian Federation. Constitution. Reprinted in Blaustein and Flanz.

Sacco, Rodolfo. "Legal Formants: A Dynamic Approach to Comparative Law (Installment 1)." *Am. J. Comp. L.* 39 (1991): 1–34.

Sacco, Rodolfo. "Legal Formants: A Dynamic Approach to Comparative Law (Installment 2)." *Am. J. Comp. L.* 39 (1991): 343–401.

Sachs, Jeffrey D. "Globalization and the Rule of Law." *Yale Law School Occasional Papers,* 2d ser., no. 4, 1998.

Saidov, A. "O Sravnimosti Sovremennykh Raznotipnykh Provovykh Sistem." 54 *Sov. Gos I Pravo* (Jan. 1984): 126–130.

Saikia, K. N. Report on Modernisation, Court Management and Alternative Dispute Resolution in Civil Judicial Process. 1996. Unpublished.

Salem Advocate Bar Ass'n v. Union of India, 35 S.C.R. 146–52 (2002).

Sampson v Channell, 110 F2d 754 (1st Cir 1940).

Santilli v. Italy, 14 Eur Hum Rts Rep 421 (1992).

Sarkar, Sudipto, V. R. Manohar, et al. *Sarkar Code of Civil Procedure.* 10th ed. Nagpur, India: Wadhwa and Company, 2004.

Sauser-Hall, Georges. *Fonction et Methode du Droit Compare.* Genève: Imp. A. Kündig, 1913.

Schlesinger, Rudolf B. Review of *Comparative Law and Social Theory. Cornell L. Q.* 50 (1965): 570–571.

Schlesinger, Rudolf B., et al. *Comparative Law: Cases, Text, Materials.* 6th ed. New York: Foundation, 1998.

Schlesinger, Rudolf B., et al. *Formation of Contracts: A Study of the Common Core of Legal Systems.* Dobbs Ferry, N.Y.: Oceana, 1968.

Schmidhauser, John R. "Alternative Conceptual Frameworks in Comparative Cross-National Legal and Judicial Research." In *Comparative Judicial Systems: Challenging Frontiers in Conceptual and Empirical Analysis,* edited by John R. Schmidhauser, 34–58. Boston: Butterworths, 1987.

Schmidhauser, John R., ed. *Comparative Judicial Systems: Challenging Frontiers in Conceptual and Empirical Analysis.* Boston: Butterworths, 1987.

Schmidhauser, John R. "Weberian Conceptual Framework for Comparative Judicial Research." Presentation at the Annual Meeting of the Southern Political Science Association, Atlanta, Georgia, 1978.

Schuck, Peter H. *The Limits of Law: Essays on Democratic Governance.* Boulder, Colo.: Westview Press, 2000.

Schwartz, Richard D., and James C. Miller. "Legal Evolution and Social Complexity." *Am. J. of Soc.* 70 (1964): 159–169.

"Schweiz: Neuer Anlauf fur die Verfassungsreform," *Neue Zuericher Zeitung,* May 5, 1995.

Sen, Amartya. *Development as Freedom.* Oxford: Oxford University Press, 1999.

Sethi, Justice R. P. *Code of Civil Procedure.* New Delhi, India: Professional Book Publishers, 2002.

Shapiro, Martin. "Courts." In *Handbook of Political Science: Governmental Institutions and Processes.* Vol. 5, edited by Fred I. Greenstein and Nelson W. Polsby, 321–371. Reading, Mass.: Addison-Wesley, 1975.

Shapiro, Martin. *Courts: A Comparative and Political Analysis.* Chicago: University of Chicago Press, 1981.

Sherman, Mark Andrew. Review of *Transfer of Prisoners under International Instruments and Domestic Legislation: A Comparative Study. Geo. Wash. J. Int'l L. & Econ.* 28 (1995): 495–548.

Shihata, Ibrahim F. I. Judicial Reform in Developing Countries and the Role of the World Bank. Paper submitted to the Seminar of Justice in Latin America and the Caribbean in the 1990s. San Jose, Costa Rica: Inter-American Development Bank, Feb. 1993.

Simmons, Beth A. "The Legalization of International Monetary Affairs." In *Legalization and World Politics,* edited by Judith Goldstein et al., 189–218. Cambridge: MIT Press, 2001.

Singer, Joseph W. "The Player and the Cards: Nihilism and Legal Theory." *Yale L. J.* 94 (1984): 1–70.

Singhania, D. C. "INDIA—Courts: Their Jurisdiction and Procedures." In World *Reports 1989–1996, Lex Mundi Doing Business Guides,* vol. IX, at 1447. Houston: Lex Mundi, 1997.

Sinha, Sh. S. B., "Alternative Dispute Resolution with Special Reference to Civil Procedure (Amendment) Act, 1999." *Nyaya Kiran,* 7–9. Delhi Legal Services Authority, 2003.

Smikle, Patrick. "Caribbean-U.S.: Immigrant Bashing Raises Concern." Inter Press Service, Apr. 29, 1997. Available on Westlaw electronic database at 1997 WL 7075076.

Societe Nationale v United States Dist. Ct. S. D. Iowa, 482 US 522 (1987).

Solomon, Jr., Peter H., and Todd S. Foglesong. "The Administration of Justice: Simplification and Efficiency." In *Courts and Transition in Russia: The Challenge of Judicial Reform,* 114–141. Boulder, Colo.: Westview Press, 2000.

Soubbotina, Tatyana P., and Katherine A. Sheram. *Beyond Economic Growth: Meeting the Challenges of Global Development.* New York: World Bank, 2000.

South Africa. Constitution. Reprinted in Blaustein and Flanz.

Spiethoff, Arthur. "Die Allgemeine Volkswirtschaftslehre als Geschictliche Theorie: die Wirtschaftsstile." In *Festgabe für Werner Sombart zur Siebenzigsten Wiederkehr Seines Geburtstages,* edited by Arthur Spiethoff, 51–84. Munich: Duncker & Humblot, 1933.

State v. Kargar, 679 A2d 81 (Me 1996).

"Statement Showing the Main Cases Instituted and Disposed of by Bombay High Court for the Period Ending July 30, 1996." Sept. 23, 1996. On file with author.

Steele, Stacey. "The New Law on Bankruptcy in Indonesia: Towards a Modern Corporate Bankruptcy Regime." *Melb. U. L. Rev.* 23 (1999): 144–160.

Stein, Eric. "Uses, Misuses—And Nonuses of Comparative Law." *Nw. U. L. Rev.* 72 (1977): 198–216.

Stewart, Martha. *The Martha Stewart Cookbook: Collected Recipes for Every Day.* New York: Clarkson Potter, 1995.

Stiefel, Ernst C., and James R. Maxeiner. "Civil Justice Reform in the United States—Opportunity for Learning from 'Civilized' European Procedure Instead of Continued Isolation." *Am. J. Comp. L.* 42 (1994): 147–162.

Storey, Reed K., and Silvia Storey. *The Framework of Financial Accounting Concepts and Standards.* Financial Accounting Series 181-C. Norwalk, Conn.: Financial Accounting Standards Board, 1998.

Stotsky, Irwin P., ed. *Transition to Democracy in Latin America: The Role of the Judiciary.* Boulder, Colo.: Westview Press, 1993.

Supreme Court Advocates on Record Association v. Union of India (1993), A.I.R. 1994 S.C. 268.

Supreme Court of Indonesia. "Academic Draft and Bill on Judicial Commission." 2003.

Supreme Court of Indonesia. "Court's Financial Management Reform." 2003.

Supreme Court of Indonesia. "Judicial Personnel Management Reform." 2003.

Supreme Court of Indonesia. "The Judicial System in Indonesia (General View)." Jakarta: The Supreme Court of Indonesia, May 10, 1993.

Supreme Court of Indonesia. "Permanent Judicial Education System Reform." 2003.

Swarns, Rachel L. "The World; An Election, Yes. But Free and Fair?" *Week in Review,* Mar. 17, 2002, sec. 4, p. 6.

Switzerland. Civil Code, 10 December 1907.

Tamanaha, Brian Z. *Bibliography on Law and Developing Countries.* New York: Kluwer Law International, 1995.

Tamanaha, Brian Z., and Richard Bilder. Review of *Law and Development. Am. J. Int'l L.* 89 (1995): 470–486.

Tanzania. Presidential Commission of Inquiry Against Corruption. *Report on the Commission of Corruption.* Vol. 1. 1996.

Tate, C. N., et al. "Judicial Institutions in Cross-National Perspective: Toward Integrating Courts into the Comparative Study of Politics." In *Comparative Judicial Systems: Challenging Frontiers in Conceptual and Empirical Analysis,* edited by John R. Schmidhauser, 7–33. Boston: Butterworths, 1987.

Thomas, David. "All in the Game: Driven by Riven to Superlatives." *Denver Post*, Oct. 31, 1997, A3.

Thurow, Lester C. "Globalization: The Product of a Knowledge-Based Economy." *Annals* 570 (2000): 19–31.

Tilly, Charles. *Big Structures, Large Processes, Huge Comparisons.* New York: Russell Sage Foundation, 1984.

Trachtman, Joel P. "Introduction: Toward Comparative Analysis of Institutions for International Economic Integration." *Nw. J. Int'l L. & Bus.* 17 (1996–1997): 351–353.

Transparency International. "Transparency International Releases New Bribe Payers Index (BPI) 2002." Available online at http://www.transparency.org/pressreleases_archive/ 2002/2002.05.14.bpi.en.html.

Trubek, David M., and Marc Galanter. "Scholars in Self-Estrangement: Some Reflections on the Crisis in Law and Development Studies in the United States." *Wis. L. Rev.* 4 (1974): 1062–1104.

Tumanov, Vladimir Aleksandrovich. "On Comparing Various Types of Legal Systems." In *Comparative Law and Legal Systems: Historical and Socio-Legal Perspectives,* edited by W. E. Butler and V. N. Kudriavtsev, 69–78. Dobbs Ferry, N.Y.: Oceana, 1985.

Ungar, Mark. "Independent Judicial Functioning." In *Elusive Reform: Democracy and the Rule of Law in Latin America,* 119–168. Boulder, Colo.: Lynne Rienner, 2002.

United Nations. "Basel Convention on the Control of Transboundary Movements of Hazardous Wastes and Their Disposal." 22 March 1989, 28 *Int'l Legal Matters* 649.

United Nations. "Charter of the United Nations." 26 June 1945, *U.S. Statutes at Large* 59 (1945): 1031; Treaty Series no. 993. Entered into force 24 Oct. 1945.

United Nations. "Convention on the Law of the Sea." U.N. Doc. A/CONF. 62/122, 21 *Int'l Legal Matters* 1261 (1982).

United Nations. "International Covenant on Civil and Political Rights." 16 December 1966, 999 *U.N. Treaty Ser.* 171.

United Nations. "Statute of the International Court of Justice." *U.S. Statutes at Large* 59 (1945): 1060; Treaty Series no. 993.

United Nations. "Universal Declaration of Human Rights." 10 December 1948, General Assembly Resolution no. 217A(III), U.N. Doc. A/3.

United Nations Conference on Trade and Development. FDI Inflows in Millions of Dollars. Available online at http://www.unctad.org/.

"U.S. Businessmen Enthused by Legal System in India." Reuters, Dec. 8, 1995.

U.S. Census Bureau. "Goods and Services Deficit Increases in May 2002." July 19, 2002. Available online at http://www.census.gov/indicator/www/ustrade.html.

U.S. Census Bureau. "Popular Table: Estimated Components of State Population Change: April 1, 2000 to July 1, 2001." Available online at http://eire.census.gov/popest/data/ states/tables/ST-EST2002-07.php.

U.S. Dep't of Justice. *1999 Statistical Yearbook of the Immigration and Naturalization Service.* Washington, D.C.: U.S. Government Printing Office, 2002. Available online at http://www.ins.usdoj.gov/graphics/aboutins/statistics/FY99Yearbook.pdf.

Vemlatesan, V. "Judiciary and Social Justice." *Frontline,* Oct. 11–17, 2000.

Venter, Francois. *Constitutional Comparison: Japan, Germany, Canada and South Africa as Constitutional States.* Cambridge, Mass.: Kluwer Law International, 2000.

Verma, Sonali. Reuters, New Delhi, July 1, 1997.

Voermans, Wim. *Councils for the Judiciary in EU Countries,* European Commission/TAIEX, Tilburg University Schoordijk Institute, 1999. Available at http:// cadmos.carlbro.be/Library/Councils/Councils.html#_toc4592267097.

Volcansek, Mary L., Maria Elisabetta de Franciscis, and Jacqueline Lucienne Lafon, *Judi-*

cial Misconduct: A Cross-national Comparison. Gainesville: University Press of Florida, 1996.

Volcansek, Mary L., and Jacqueline Lucienne Lafon. *Judicial Selection: The Cross-Evolution of French and American Practices.* Westport, Conn.: Greenwood Press, 1988.

von Hayek, Friedrich August. "The Pretense of Knowledge." Dec. 11, 1974 (lecture). *Am. Econ. Rev.* 79 (6) (Dec. 1989): 3–7.

Wagner, W. J. Review of *Comparative Law and Social Theory.* *Colum. L. Rev.* 64 (1964): 985–993.

Waldman, Peter. "Jurists' Prudence: India's Supreme Court Makes the Rule of Law a Way of Governing." *Wall Street Journal,* May 6, 1996, A1.

Wallace, J. Clifford. "Resolving Judicial Corruption While Preserving Judicial Independence: Comparative Perspectives." *Cal. W. Int'l L. J.* 28 (1998): 341–351.

Warwick, Donald P., and Samuel Osherson. "Comparative Analysis in the Social Sciences." In *Comparative Research Methods,* by D. P. Warwick and Samuel Osherson, 3–41. Englewood Cliffs, N.J.: Prentice Hall, 1973.

Watson, Alan. "The Cause of the Reception of Roman Law." In *The Evolution of Law,* 66–97. Baltimore: Johns Hopkins University Press, 1985.

Watson, Alan. *Legal Transplants: An Approach to Comparative Law.* 2d ed. Athens: University of Georgia Press, 1993.

Weaver, R. Kent, and Bert A. Rockman, eds. *Do Institutions Matter? Government Capabilities in the United States and Abroad.* Washington, D.C.: Brookings Institution, 1993.

Weaver, Warren. "A Quarter Century in the Natural Sciences." Chapter 1 in *The Rockefeller Foundation Annual Report,* 1958.

Webster's Collegiate Dictionary. 11th ed.

Weiler, J. H. H., and Joel P. Trachtman. "European Constitutionalism and Its Discontents." *Nw. J. Int'l L. & Bus.* 17 (1996–1997): 354–397.

Wexler, Leila Sadat. "The Proposed Permanent International Criminal Court: An Appraisal." *Cornell Int'l L. J.* 29 (1997): 665–726.

Whelan, Christopher J. "Labor Law and Comparative Law." *Tex. L. Rev.* 63 (1985): 1425–1454.

Widner, Jennifer. "Comparative Politics and Comparative Law." *Am. J. Comp. L.* 46 (1998): 739–749.

Wieacker, Franz. "Foundations of European Legal Culture." *Am. J. Comp. L.* 38 (1990): 1–29.

Wigmore, John Henry. *A Panorama of the World's Legal Systems.* Vol. 3. St. Paul, Minn.: West Publishing Co., 1928.

Winterton, George. "Comparative Law Teaching." *Am. J. Comp. L.* 23 (1975): 69–118.

Wolfke, Karol. *Custom in Present International Law.* Boston: M. Nijhoff, 1993.

Wong v Tenneco Inc., 39 Cal. 3d 126; 702 P2d 570 (Cal 1985).

Woolf, Lord Harry. *Access to Justice.* London: Law Society, 1997.

World Bank. "Reforming Courts: The Role of Empirical Research." *PREMNotes* 65. Washington, D.C.: World Bank, 2002. Available online at http://www1.worldbank.org/publicsector/legal/PREMnote65.pdf.

World Forum on Democracy. "List of Electoral Democracies." Available online at http://www.fordemocracy.net/electoral.shtm.

World Trade Organization. "General Agreement on Tariffs and Trade 1994." 15 April 1994, *33 Int'l Legal Matters* 1125.

World Trade Organization. *International Trade Statistics 2001.* Geneva: World Trade Organization, 2001.

Wright, Robin, and Shaul Bakhash. "The U.S. and Iran: An Offer They Can't Refuse?" *Foreign Policy,* no. 108 (Fall 1997): 124–137.

Young, Chun-Chi. "The Legal System of India." In *Modern Legal Systems Cyclopedia,* edited by Kenneth R. Redden, 9.80.5–9.80.42. Buffalo: William S. Hein, 1990.

Zekoll, Joachim. "Kant and Comparative Law: Some Reflections on a Reform Effort." *Tul. L. Rev.* 70 (1996): 2719–2749.

Zuckerman, Adrian A. S. "Justice in Crisis: Comparative Dimensions of Civil Procedure." In *Civil Justice in Crisis: Comparative Perspectives of Civil Procedure,* edited by Adrian A. S. Zuckerman, 3–52. Oxford; New York: Oxford University Press, 1999.

Zuckerman, Adrian A. S. "Reforming Civil Justice Systems: Trends in Industrial Countries." *PREMNotes* 46 (Oct. 2000). Available online at http://www1.worldbank.org/publicsector/legal/PREMnote_46.pdf (last visited, December 17, 2002).

Zuckerman, Mathew. "Squashing These Comparisons Like Squashing a Beatle." *Asahi Shimbun/Asahi Evening News,* Feb. 12, 1998, 1.

Zweigert, Konrad, and Hein Kötz. *An Introduction to Comparative Law.* 3d ed. Translated by Tony Weir. New York: Clarendon Press, 1998.

Zweigert, Konrad, and Hein Kötz. *An Introduction to Comparative Law.* Vol. 1. Translated by Tony Weir. New York: Clarendon Press, 1977.

Index